Double Lyric

Divisiveness and Communal Creativity in Recent English Poetry

DOUBLE LYRIC

Divisiveness and Communal Creativity
in
Recent English Poetry

MERLE E. BROWN

New York
COLUMBIA UNIVERSITY PRESS
1980

LIBRARY OF CONGRESS CATALOGING IN PUBLICATION DATA

BROWN, MERLE ELLIOTT, 1925–1978
DOUBLE LYRIC.

INCLUDES BIBLIOGRAPHICAL REFERENCES AND INDEX.
1. ENGLISH POETRY—20TH CENTURY—HISTORY AND CRITI-
CISM.   I. TITLE.
PR611.B7   821'.91409   80-11578
ISBN 0-231-05032-1

COLUMBIA UNIVERSITY PRESS
NEW YORK

Contents

Foreword

"Opposition is true Friendship." Blake's aphorism, I think, might serve as a motto for this book. Merle Brown has heard in recent British poetry an uneasy and often fierce self-divisiveness, a doubleness of speech that leads toward the discovery of community. In exploring that doubleness he has also composed a quietly polemical meditation on the nature of criticism. The critical methods most in favor during recent decades assume that the single mind can suspend itself before a poetic "object," master it in knowledge, build some consistent meaning from the clues and gaps in a "text," or trace there the ramifications of a linguistic system that denies the very presence of mind. In opposition to such methods, *Double Lyric* speaks for the dialogue that constitutes the life of both poetry and criticism.

Shaping the work of Geoffrey Hill, and to some extent that of Thom Gunn, Jon Silkin, and Charles Tomlinson, is a tensely judgmental inner dialogue that often seems to have generated two opposed but mutually inclusive centers of speaking and listening in the same poem. In other situations, of course, inner dialogue may lead to something quite different. Wallace Stevens' poems tend toward what Brown has called pluricentric worlds. Those of W. S. Merwin, Frank O'Hara, and John Ashbery often seek endless departures and transformations. Even within *Double Lyric* the chapter on Philip Larkin explores a poetic procedure antithetical to Hill's: an attempt to evade our inherent doubleness and attain a dismissive oneness with the reader—in effect, a perversion of the communal creativity celebrated elsewhere in this book. But in every situation, some inner dialogue must shape a live poem, which is no mere "object" or "text" but the verbal mediation of an expressive, heuristic, and critical act. Through such acts, in whatever medium, we constitute the "self-worlds" or "persons" that we are. And only as we attend to our inner divisions and encourage dialogue among them can we hear those "others" who seem to be, but never are, simply outside ourselves. Inner dialogue is a precondition of inter-personal community.

It follows that an encounter with a poem is an asymmetical dialogue between two communities of discourse. Only by speaking the poem can we hear it. By interrogating, opposing, qualifying, and further drawing out the implications of that speech, we hear with greater fidelity. And by listening carefully we can learn how the poem listens to itself. As acquaintance proceeds, our own community of discourse moves toward a deeper and more complex complementarity with that of the poem. For such reasons the double lyric assumes a potentially double reader. Indeed, its form will not appear, or will seem the figment of a critic's imagination, to a reader convinced that the only model of cognition is that of a single mind dominating an objective field.

The elucidation of recent British poetry in these terms no doubt requires a critic to be unusually alert to our usual mental divisions. As an American trained in the New Criticism, an admirer of the ethical but anti-philosophical criticism of F. R. Leavis, and an ex-positor of neo-idealistic aesthetics, Merle Brown had reason enough for such alertness. He was amply prepared to explore the tensions between English and American culture in the poetry of Silkin, Gunn, and Tomlinson. He could note in his own analytical acts the competing claims of British empiricism and Italian idealism. And he knew from often painful experience that a self-critical mind, born of opposition, must risk its present equilibrium in each new encounter. That is one reason why *Double Lyric* concludes by suggesting how Leavis moved toward a fuller awareness of the fact that creative collaboration needs a genuine dialogue of opposites. The tribute to Leavis' later criticism does not merely provide an analogue to the divisiveness and communal creativity traced in recent poetry; it also constitutes an indirect and modest *apologia*. In necessarily translating Leavis' awareness into a self-conscious form that he might have resisted, it expresses the position that Merle Brown had reached by way of a different but complementary journey.

Some differences from Leavis reflect the fact that *Double Lyric* speaks from within an American situation. Others appear in its allusions to Benedetto Croce—though it is important to note that Croce enters here as a limited thinker, who can adequately account for neither the ethical nor the self-critical aspects of poetry and can provide only one term in the opposition between "intuition" and "perception" in Tomlinson's best work. But perhaps the most pervasive differences result from three principles that Brown had long meditated: thought is "true" only as actual, only as a self-conscious thinking and not in its inert result; the act of thinking is in essence not only moral but dialectical; and its dialectic is inherently social. Those principles testify to the indirect and, I think, finally surmounted presence in *Double Lyric* of a philosopher who is never mentioned here. A retrieval of that omitted name may direct our attention to the agonistic thinking on which this book itself is founded.

In *Neo-Idealistic Aesthetics* (1966) Brown had expounded Giovanni Gentile's understanding of art as a "self-translation" that proceeds from immediate feeling to objective form by way of an interior but social dialectic. There is no ego or individual, Gentile had said in his *Genesis and Structure of Society*, "who does not have with*in* him (rather than just with him) an *alter* who is his essential *socius*, an object that is not a mere 'thing' opposed to him as a subject, but a subject like himself." Whenever a man speaks, "he hears himself speaking; hearer and speaker are the same man and yet not the same. They are two and they are one; a single personality doubles itself from within and is actually present and alive in the internal dialogue which constitutes the unique act of thought." That dialogue includes what the realist calls external things, "for in order to be *ours* the object must cease to be a thing and become another self." Grounded in this "transcendental society," life is for Gentile a movement of interpretation through the mediating of antitheses as each person widens his inner community. It follows that we genuinely understand the thought of another only as we re-enact and translate his thinking, and that a poem has its continuing life in such re-enactment and translation among its readers. Brown judged Gentile's aesthetics to be more cogent than either Croce's or R. G. Collingwood's; and, seeing the need to ground aesthetics in

practical criticism, he suggested that the most fruitful next step
might be to "integrate" it with "the criticism of a literature other
than Italian."

In *Wallace Stevens: The Poem as Act* (1970) he took that step.
Using a rather free version of Gentile's dialectic, he explored Stevens' poems as acts of "concrescence" that translate feeling into verbal form and subsume in their living dialectic a multitude of selves.
Such poems, he said, may be "the only truly social poetry. They are
not imitative of a large society composed of small people; they are
themselves, as poetic actions, small societies composed of large
people." A wry translation, surely, of Gentile's more sweeping pronouncement: "Instead of the community containing the individual,
it is the individual who contains—or rather establishes—the community, within his own act of self-consciousness." Nevertheless,
we may occasionally feel in the book on Stevens a gap between aesthetics and criticism that is filled by a rather hortatory impres-
sionism. A further maturing, I suspect, was needed: both a more
inward translation of Gentile's thought into critical procedure and a
shaking off (as *Double Lyric* would describe it occurring in Leavis'
career) of the unconscious tyranny exercised by the vestiges of a
non-dialogical model of experience.

During the next few years, as Brown founded and edited the
Iowa Review, that maturing occurred. A vigorous, astringent, and
pedagogically beneficent process it was, as I can testify from my
work with him on that quarterly and from our joint teaching in a
course on "Poetry and Dialogue." He first sketched the notion of a
"double lyric" in "Dodecaphonic Scales," a sprightly and admoni-
tory essay on ten young poets whose limited work evoked this retort from the muse: "Your poem of the act of the mind must accept
not just my body, but also my mind. I shall retain my independence
as you yours. . . . We shall be two in one or one in two, not just
two voices, but two centers of love and choice and feeling and gesture. I'll join you, but only in a double lyric, in which the cruelty of
poetry is at one with its generosity, its pain a humming of joy."
Brown had already stressed in "The Idea of Fiction as Fictive or Fictitious" the reciprocal judgment and co-creation that shapes at best
a novelist's relations to his characters and a critic's relation to a
poem. In "Francesco De Sanctis" he stated that the critic's task is to

show "that the very existence of the poem, to the extent that it is a genuine work of art, is nearly an impossibility." That "unlikelihood" results from the poem's being founded upon an inner *agon*. Then in "Gentile's *Filosofia dell'arte* and American Contextualism" Brown reformulated the "collaborative" aspect of Gentile's conception of criticism, taking it yet closer to the criticism of Leavis as it would be understood in *Double Lyric*. And in "Poetic Listening," an essay treating of Stevens, O'Hara, and Ashbery that Carolyn Brown tells me was written in the midst of the critic's own *agon* with Hill's poetry, he further sharpened his sense of that "listening" entailed by "what Giovanni Gentile calls a transcendental society of speaking and listening, of expressing and criticizing, of writing and reading."*

In *Double Lyric,* however, Gentile does not need to be mentioned—precisely because Brown had now freed himself from the notion of merely applying another man's aesthetic. Indeed, he knew well enough that the correlation of inner and interpersonal dialogue informs such various philosophical enterprises as Josiah Royce's absolute idealism, George Herbert Mead's naturalistic theory of socialization, and Maurice Merleau-Ponty's phenomenology of speaking—to say nothing of the work of Martin Buber, Louis Lavelle, and Gabriel Marcel. If Gentile's "actual idealism" has some pertinence to British poetry, it must be demonstrated through the critic's personal engagement. And surely that happens here— whether in the analyses of Hill's brilliantly dialectical poetry, where Brown has met his sternest challenge, or in the accounts of Silkin's inner stress, Gunn's discovery that the misanthropic individual is already a community, and Tomlinson's mediating of two poetic modes. Throughout, however, the aim is to let the poem judge the critic even as he judges it, and so to experience "the living pulse of human community." And such critical interplay, I think, has also taken Brown beyond Gentile's emphasis on society *in interiore homine*—an emphasis that so easily becomes an effective solipsism—

---

*"Dodecaphonic Scales," *Iowa Review* (Fall 1973), 113–26; "The Idea of Fiction as Fictive or Fictitious," *Bulletin of the MMLA* (Spring 1973), 62–73; "Francesco De Sanctis," *Journal of Aesthetics and Art Criticism* (Summer 1974), 447–92; "Gentile's *Filosofia dell'arte* and American Contextualism," *Enciclopedia '76–'77: Il Pensiero di Giovanni Gentile* (Istituto della Enciclopedia Italiana: Roma, 1977), 1:131–39; "Poetic Listening," *New Literary History* (Fall 1978), 125–39.

toward a sharper realization of that wounding and healing otherness to which we can only open ourselves.

That realization, which shapes the style of *Double Lyric* as it did not those of *Neo-Idealistic Aesthetics* and *Wallace Stevens*, sometimes becomes explicit—as when we are told of Gunn's movement toward an otherness "more painful and also more vital" than that merely within him, or of Leavis' sense that his encounter with Wittgenstein "exceeds any and all explanatory frameworks." (Gentile's system, along with others, has now dropped away: the critic's *agon* with the philosopher is over.) And in the last few pages of the book, when Brown describes Leavis' most mature criticism as being written no longer for the "representative" or "right" reader but for "an actual, living person with whom Leavis thinks through his thoughts in a collaborative way," that realization of necessary otherness becomes especially moving. The style of *Double Lyric* itself seems to owe much to just such a "special reader," a "hovering presence" whose "way of listening" gives to all its honest acerbities a tone of intimacy.

Merle Brown had already begun another manuscript, a study of contemporary American poetry that would no doubt have benefitted yet more from that presence, when he was stricken by cardiac arrest on December 15, 1978. But the double voice continues to speak in this book.

Thomas R. Whitaker
Yale University
June 1980

Acknowledgments

For permission to quote copyrighted material, grateful acknowledgment is made to the following publishers, agents, and authors:

W. H. Auden: from *Collected Shorter Poems 1927–1957*, copyright © 1966 by W. H. Auden. Reprinted by permission of Faber & Faber Ltd. and Random House, Inc.

Hart Crane: from *The Complete Poems and Selected Letters and Prose of Hart Crane*, edited by Brom Weber, Liveright Publishing Corporation, New York, N.Y. Copyright 1933, © 1958, 1966 by Liveright Publishing Corporation. Reprinted by permission of Liveright Publishing Corporation and Laurence Pollinger Ltd., London.

T. S. Eliot: from *Collected Poems 1909–1962* and *Murder in the Cathedral*. Copyright 1935, 1936 by Harcourt Brace Jovanovich, Inc.; copyright © 1963, 1964 by T. S. Eliot. Reprinted by permission of Harcourt Brace Jovanovich, Inc., and Faber & Faber Ltd.

William Empson: from *Collected Poems*, copyright 1949, 1977 by William Empson. Reprinted by permission of Chatto & Windus and Harcourt Brace Jovanovich, Inc.

Thom Gunn: from *The Sense of Movement*, © 1957 by Thom Gunn, from *Fighting Terms*, © 1962 by Thom Gunn, from *My Sad Captains*, © 1961 by Thom Gunn, from *Touch*, © 1967 by Thom Gunn, from *Moly*, © 1971 by Thom Gunn, and from *Jack Straw's Castle*, © 1976 by Thom Gunn. Reprinted by permission of Faber & Faber Ltd. From *To the Air* by Thom Gunn, copyright © 1974 by Thom Gunn. Reprinted by permission of David R. Godine, Publisher, Inc. Selections from *Moly* and *My Sad Captains* by Thom Gunn, copyright © 1961, 1971, 1973 by Thom Gunn, and from *Jack Straw's Castle and Other Poems* by Thom Gunn, copyright © 1971, 1973, 1974, 1975, 1976 by Thom Gunn. Reprinted by permission of Farrar, Straus & Giroux, Inc.

Thomas Hardy: from *Collected Poems*. Reprinted by permission of Macmillan Publishing Co., Inc.

Geoffrey Hill: from *For the Unfallen*, copyright © 1959 by Geoffrey Hill, from *King Log*, copyright © 1959, 1964, 1968 by Geoffrey Hill, from *Mercian*

William Carlos Williams: from *Paterson*, Book I, copyright 1946 by William Carlos Williams. Reprinted by permission of New Directions Publishing Corporation.

James Wright: from "A Blessing," copyright © 1961 by James Wright. Reprinted from *The Branch Will Not Break* by permission of Wesleyan University Press. "A Blessing" first appeared in *Poetry*.

W. B. Yeats: from *The Collected Poems of W. B. Yeats*, copyright 1940 by Georgie Yeats, renewed 1968 by Bertha Georgie Yeats, Michael Butler Yeats, and Anne Yeats. Reprinted by permission of A. P. Watt Ltd., London, Macmillan Publishing Co., Inc., New York, and Macmillan of Canada.

Permission to reprint previously published portions of this book has been generously granted by the editors of the following journals: *Agenda, boundary 2, Contemporary Literature, The Iowa Review, Journal of Aesthetics and Art Criticism, The Missouri Review,* and *The Southern Review.*

Gratitude is also due to the Guggenheim Foundation, the Department of English of the University of Iowa, and the Graduate College of the University of Iowa for their support.

Double Lyric

*Divisiveness and Communal Creativity in
Recent English Poetry*

CHAPTER ONE

Divisiveness in
Recent English Poetry

I t is tempting to explain away the difficulties an American reader has with recent English poetry by way of Donald Davie's claim that, in direct contrast to the barbarous energy of its American counterpart, English poetry, even at its best, is decadently subtle.[1] One could extend the division Davie makes into a basic opposition between an English conception of existence that is empirical and realist, based upon an acceptance of a historical and geographical scene or situation as unquestionably given, and an American conception that is idealist and activist, inherently questioning, active rather than scenic. The English poetry, moreover, that springs out of its world view would prove to be reflective rather than creative, a poetry of intelligent observation instead of intuitive insight. The danger, however, in drawing out such a division is that it will turn out to be applicable only to mediocre verse. Instead of responding to what is finest in his subject matter, one may be succumbing to that critical need for rendering his subject simple and manageable. For all authentic poetry, English as well as American, is both barbaric and refined, primitive and civilized, energetic and subtle. This is as true of the poetry of Thom Gunn, Geoffrey Hill, Philip Larkin, Jon Silkin, and Charles Tomlinson as it is of the poetry of T. S. Eliot.

Not a distinctive world view, or an existential stance, but a hesitancy to adopt one, to bring one's conflicts into resolution, is what is most striking in recent English poetry. Often, in my mind, this poetry rings in echo of William Empson's notion that poetry is most fully realized in the seventh type of ambiguity, where "the total effect is to show a fundamental division in the writer's mind."[2] What at first seems to be irresoluteness may turn out to be a divisiveness that results from the refusal to falsify by simplification.

Though less complex than the finest of modernist poems, like *The Waste Land* or perhaps Empson's own "Legal Fiction," these poems are more deeply divided, so much so, in fact, that I have been driven to call the best of them double lyrics. To think of them as having one "total effect" or as a "division in the writer's mind" would be to soften and blunt their deep divisiveness. They are simply not single in the modernistic sense of being an impersonal, contemplative act or artifice which reconciles opposite and discordant qualities. Nor, for that matter, are they single in the Marxist sense of reflecting society, "as it is," in such a way as to espouse the appropriate values. These poems cannot, moreover, be described adequately as unified by their intentionality according to any Neo-Kantian or phenomenological single investigator/field model of experience of which I am aware. Their deep divisiveness cannot even be touched by way of the notion of poems as "plural texts," endlessly playful verbal deferrals. They are anything but endless departures.

My conviction is that, at least in the strongest and most distinctively English poems of the past twenty years or so, two poetic modes, a poetry of empirically exact observation and poetry which is not only active, but which implicates and depends upon the act of its making—and each with its concomitant world-view—conflict contradictorily. Often these poems present quite overtly a dramatic antagonism between two persons or positions. But, just as important, the way that dramatic agon is treated is itself a dramatic agon. The poet strives to shape his subject objectively, so that the drama seems to be an illusion of reality, a conflict as it is, in and of itself. But knowing that that illusion is the product of his own effort, he tends to include within his dramatic presentation some sense of his own privileged and determining position as maker. Having gone that far, having disrupted the illusory objectivity of the dramatic conflict with the subjective thrust of his own making, having grounded illusion on truth, he may commit himself to something even more important and difficult. Having realized that he is the one shaping not only his own or the protagonist's position in the objective conflict, but also that of his antagonist, having recognized that every person's world view is, ultimately, created out of just such a privileged position, he may strive to evoke such a position for his antagonist as well as for himself. He may try to elicit a world like his own but expressive of his antagonist's sense of life, a world within which both the protagonist and he himself as self-conscious poetic shaper exist actively, just as the antagonist has been included as existing actively within his, the poet's world. Recent English poetry, when it works as poetry, has not renounced conflict, but depends on it.

Although numerous poems exhibit this divisiveness, I intend to focus on three poems, Jon Silkin's "Defence," Charles Tomlinson's "Prometheus," and Geoffrey Hill's "In Piam Memoriam," because, together, they represent the range of possibility and difficulty in recent English poetry. Because, moreover, the divisions that matter in this poetry are of a kind that manifest themselves only to a reader who lives through them imaginatively and thoughtfully, because they are permanently concealed from him who adopts an objective, empirical stance and tries to *see* them, it is imperative that one scrutinize a few poems rather than scanning a number of them.

The element of empirical observation is invariably there, in these poems, as a sort of leaden coating from which a reader is quite apt to turn away before the thing has a chance to catch fire. In the simplest of the poems that work, there will be, beyond the evoked illusion of reality, the poet's invisible act of awareness as that on which the illusion depends. In such a poem the poet has gone beyond mere pretence or make-believe, but he reserves the privileged position of self-aware maker to himself alone, so that the poem is apt to appear flagrantly tendentious. Because, however, the poet does not abandon his commitment to intelligent observation, his partisanship tends to be exposed as an indulgence; even though he may seem to have all the right reasons on his side, his advocacy rings with the hollowness of impotent rage. A poem like this succeeds as a poem by realizing imaginatively, critically, and judgmentally the poet's failure.

Of a number of aggressively assertive poems which Jon Silkin published in the mid-sixties, "Defence" is probably the most striking:

DEFENCE
(For Ann)

What 'one-in-five' can do
No man can quite do

> She arrived late, with this motto:
> 'Time used in reconnaissance
> Is not time lost'. Useful hint
> On how efficient our defences
> Would be. Sent from the *Home Office*
> On 'Work of some importance'.
> And 'The first thing' she said
> 'Is that there will be four minutes
> Of preparation before
> The thing is dropped. You should
> Instruct persons to stand
> In the centre of what room
> They like—for the blast,
> Unlike the bombs of the previous war,
> Will draw the walls out.
> There will be no crushing
> Of flesh. Instead
> On all sides walls will reveal
> The citizen unharmed.' Here a question,
> But 'No' she said 'we have
> From our *Intelligence*
> Absolute assurance
> Our capital is not targeted.'
> Total warfare, by arrangement.
> And she was sure, when pressed.
> 'But there will be devastation
> As we now suspect, in radius
> Of forty four miles.
> The water will be infected;
> The light from the thing, astonishing;
> Which though surprised by, we should
> Not look at; but shelter

Behind some object "to reduce
Damage to the tissue"
From radiation; or shelter
Under brown paper;
Or, if you can,—
Sheets soaked in urine.'

So women who crotchet, stop that;
Men labouring whose issue is
The two-handed house, set that aside.
Girls big and delicate
With child, turn on your side;
You will melt. The ravelling spider
And the scorpion whose prongs itch
Will fuse in a viscoid
Tar, black as a huge fly.
The whole of nature
Is a preying upon.
Let man, whose mind is large,
Legislate for
All passionate things,
All sensate things: the sensuous
Grass, whose speech is all
In its sharp, bending blade.
Leave not a leaf, a stone
That rested on the dead
To its own dissolution.

She left then,
As if she were with her feet
Turning an enormous,
If man-made, pearl
As means of locomotion.[3]

It seems the poem should have been written in any way but the
way it is. No matter how difficult it is to defend the poem, however, one remains certain of its excellence. If documentary in part,
as in the first stanza, which reminds one of Peter Porter's "Your
Attention, Please," then one wonders why it is not wholly so. If
personally expressive, like the epigraph and the second stanza,
which is a poetic translation of the import of the documentary

record in the first, then shouldn't the pretence of objectivity have been dropped? Or, if one is going to be fiercely personal and even ridicule the woman's posture as in the last stanza, if the focus is to be so sharp on the moral outrage of one's shaping act of response, then oughtn't the woman, or one of her more thoughtful superiors with a sense of the ironies of civil defence measures in an age of nuclear bombs, be given the chance to respond reasonably? As written, the poem seems based on dogmas which its method of development reveals to be insupportable. The dogma of a directly observable reality entails that what is directly heard and quoted be intelligible. Without relinquishing that dogma, the poet self-righteously affirms an opposite one—"What 'one-in-five' can do/ No man can quite do"—on the basis of which he reveals that what has been heard is immorally, unintelligibly insane. His own moral assurance is as blatantly absolute and unquestioning as the strategic assurance of the woman and of "our *Intelligence.*" The combination appears to be intolerable.

More disturbing, the poet violates the grounds of his self-righteousness from the start. The phrase "What 'one-in-five' can do/ No man can quite do" is egalitarian, affirming the equal value of every human being, and yet the style, with its pinched "quite" and its concision, is aristocratically prophetic. Moreover, after cunningly suggesting the whole poem in the first two and a half lines—the woman's excuse for being late is a baseless rationalization; the measures of defence she advocates have no value except to defend us against the knowledge of our defencelessness—the poet impatiently interrupts the woman and, with his "Useful hint/ On how efficient our defences/ Would be," sneers at her and uses her as a tool for his own purposes just as if she were not also one of those five the autonomous individuality of whom ought to be equally respected. And yet Silkin himself, in the introduction to *Flashpoint*, an anthology published two years before "Defence," in 1964, and including Porter's civil defence poem, berates Eliot for his failure to respect the autonomy of his characters:

> The difficulty in Eliot's poetry is that we increasingly experience a world whose creatures are denied their autonomy, let alone their existence. They are there as appurtenances of the poet's thought, at best as illustrations of what the poet is think-

ing . . . Such an attitude to human society is aristocratic. It may be 'spiritual', but it is still aristocratic. If this attitude could do away with the sense that it owned everything it saw, it would be more tolerable and fruitful. But it cannot. Its attitudes are those of appropriation. It is therefore difficult for the reader who genuinely feels inclusive attitudes, those which desire the inclusion of those members who will increase their own and society's fruitfulness, to assent to the aristocratic method. And this dissent, partial, or nearly total, will affect the reader's evaluation of that poetry, just as the artistocratic [sic] cluster of attitudes affects the poetry made.[4]

Perhaps by aggravating our sense of the contradictoriness of "Defence," this quotation can reveal just why the poem is powerful. The woman and the situation she represents have forced the poet to do more than express his moral outrage. They have forced him to do so in a morally outrageous way, even according to his own lights. The epigraph and the second stanza indicate that the poet remains committed to feeling "inclusive attitudes." As a poet he is identifying himself with "All passionate things,/ All sensate things," even with "the scorpion whose prongs itch." The moral crux of the poem lies hidden there. The woman's unnatural acceptance of a morally intolerable situation has forced the poet into a situation even more painfully intolerable because of the acuteness of his awareness of its nature. He and all that he loves, including women, men, and "Girls big and delicate/ With child," have been reduced to the condition of potentially helpless victims, of no more consequence than "a huge fly." As a result, he has been forced to become predatory himself, like the spider and the scorpion. The first stanza has been woven together so as to inflict a lethal sting. Because the woman had said "there will be four minutes/ Of preparation before/ The thing is dropped," one is forced to respond to her last suggestion with raucous, hateful laughter, envisioning, as the poet intends, all the citizens of the nation devoting the last moments of their lives to a hysterical effort to soak their sheets in urine. Because of his "inclusive attitudes," Silkin has been forced to rage in an intensely personal and exclusive way, in a manner so fierce as to remind one of the destructiveness of Swift's irony, as it is analyzed by Leavis in *The Common Pursuit*.

Silkin's argument against the anonymous woman from the

Home Office is not finally convincing. As an attack, it fails, logically, morally, and politically. But it is right poetically and ultimately. Silkin knows that one's humanity is manifested personally or not at all. He is denying the humanity of his antagonist by exhibiting that creature as simply not existing as a person. Silkin's culture, his very language, disallows any such accusation. It is out-of-bounds, simply not done, it is virtually obscene. As a result, the accusation can be made only in a totally personal and creative way. For it to be effective against the blank, inexorable, inertial power under attack, the author simply must expose himself as the vulnerable, personal creature he is. The only way to be invulnerable is to become anonymous, impersonal, and inhumanly ataraxic. The one way to reveal that another creature has allowed that to happen to him is to expose it in a personal way, in a way that exposes oneself as the "poor forked creature" he is. The excellence of the poem as a poem depends on his doing so.

The crucial questions forced upon the reader by a poem like "Defence" or like Charles Tomlinson's "Prometheus," the next poem to be considered, have to do not with the poet's realized intention, but with the way he is listening to himself in the poem. There is no question of how the woman from the Home Office is to be heard; the poet is in the poem as a protagonist intent on showing her up for the fool she is, worthy of our scorn and mockery. How the poet hears himself, however, is not so clear. An unsympathetic reader might well feel that he is so intent on exposing the folly of what he hears the woman say as to be deaf to the impotence and excess of his own voice. My response to that rests on the notion that, in these poems in which the poet is both poet and protagonist, one must be careful to allow for a critical attentiveness in the way the poet listens to himself which exceeds the limits of what he intends as a poet at one with himself as assertive protagonist. To my mind, Silkin has shaped the poem so that his hearing his rage against the woman as pathetically impotent is the enlivening silence which presses the poem into just the form it takes. The reader, I would say, who judges that the Silkin of this poem is out of control is simply hearing the poem the way Silkin himself hears it, but taking the credit for that hearing instead of bestowing it where it belongs, on the poet himself.

Tomlinson's "Prometheus" is more ambiguous in this regard. Tomlinson is clearly sharper, cooler, and more analytical than the poet of "Defence." And yet, putting himself into a poem as its protagonist is a new move for Tomlinson. In his first four volumes, he wrote mainly objective poems, poems as scenes, as illusions of reality that excluded any sense of the act of their making as implicated in their existence. *The Way of a World* (1969), the volume in which "Prometheus" appears, reveals a new awareness on Tomlinson's part that even truths of "a world" depend upon the constitutive act of the man who thinks that world observantly. This awareness, perhaps because of its novelty, seems, however, to falter at times, so that it is difficult to feel sure of the way Tomlinson is listening to the speaking forth of his words. He certainly intends, in "Prometheus," to be condemning Scriabin, the author of the tone poem "Prometheus," which he, Tomlinson, is listening to on the radio, on a stormy summer afternoon. He hears the aspirations of this music as apocalyptically extremist and he condemns Scriabin as ignorantly utopian, as promoting, in his desire for a new world, the violence of Lenin and even the tawdry mediocrity of the present-day welfare state in England. But how does he hear his denunciation of Scriabin and, along with him, Lenin, Trotsky, and Blok? Tomlinson has been criticized for being visually effective in his earlier poetry, but tone deaf.

PROMETHEUS

Summer thunder darkens, and its climbing
   Cumulae, disowning our scale in the zenith,
Electrify this music: the evening is falling apart.
   Castles-in-air; on earth: green, livid fire.
The radio simmers with static to the strains
   Of this mock last-day of nature and of art.

We have lived through apocalypse too long:
   Scriabin's dinosaurs! Trombones for the transformation
That arrived by train at the Finland Station,
   To bury its hatchet after thirty years in the brain

Of Trotsky. Alexander Nikolayevitch, the events
    Were less merciful than your mob of instruments.

Too many drowning voices cram this waveband.
    I set Lenin's face by yours—
Yours, the fanatic ego of eccentricity against
    The systematic son of a schools inspector
Tyutchev on desk—for the strong man reads
    Poets as the antisemite pleads: 'A Jew was my friend.'

Cymballed firesweeps. Prometheus came down
    In more than orchestral flame and Kérensky fled
Before it. The babel of continents gnaws now
    And tears at the silk of those harmonies that seemed
So dangerous once. You dreamed an end
    Where the rose of the world would go out like a close in music.

Population drags the partitions down
    And we are a single town of warring suburbs:
I cannot hear such music for its consequence:
    Each sense was to have been reborn
Out of a storm of perfumes and light
    To a white world, an in-the-beginning.

In the beginning, the strong man reigns:
    Trotsky, was it not then you brought yourself
To judgement and to execution, when you forgot
    Where terror rules, justice turns arbitrary?
Chromatic Prometheus, myth of fire,
    It is history topples you in the zenith.

Blok, too, wrote The Scythians
    Who should have known: he who howls
With the whirlwind, with the whirlwind goes down.
    In this, was Lenin guiltier than you
When, out of a merciless patience grew
    The daily prose such poetry prepares for?

Scriabin, Blok, men of extremes,
    History treads out the music of your dreams
Through blood, and cannot close like this
    In the perfection of anabasis. It stops. The trees
Continue raining though the rain has ceased
    In a cooled world of incessant codas:

Hard edges of the houses press
  On the after-music senses, and refuse to burn,
Where an ice-cream van circulates the estate
  Playing Greensleeves, and at the city's
Stale new frontier even ugliness
  Rules with the cruel mercy of solidities.[5]

    That Tomlinson places himself so precisely in the poem would indicate a clearer awareness on his part of what he is about than Silkin has in "Defence," in which the poet's position within the situation of the poem is left vague. Tomlinson's politics are unarguably clear. He thinks that the present conditions, represented by the ugly housing estate with its identical houses, including his own, and by the Renaissance love song being ground out for the purpose of selling ice cream, are the ridiculous and unforeseen result of the grandiose program implicit in Scriabin's dream. In the end, moreover, he accepts the conditions in which he lives as bearable, even if painfully ugly, because they are at least better than total destruction, the logical consequence of Scriabin's dream. As Donald Davie says, in praise of the poem: "Thus Tomlinson, when he thinks politically, lowers his sights and settles for second-best just as Larkin and Hardy do—but more impressively than either because so much more aware of, and pained by, the cost."[6]

    In a poem like "Prometheus," however, in which the poet is engaged himself in the poem as its protagonist, costs and awareness will be both political and poetic. Davie may be right about Tomlinson's political awareness; the way Tomlinson is hearing himself in the poem as a whole, however, is difficult to determine. How aware poetically Tomlinson is of the poetic cost of what he is doing in "Prometheus" is, finally, a question of tone and of the way he is listening to himself. And it is his poetic ear which is most in doubt in this poem. To my ear the voice is that of public address and even in places sounds hectoring. The situation, in contrast, is private: the non-public man, in his room, listening to the radio. Is Tomlinson aware of the contradiction between tone and situation? If so, the poem becomes ruthlessly self-condemnatory. The poet as protagonist is revealed to be a small man, self-important, self-righteous, condemning out of petty resentment the idealism of a man long dead, addressing him familiarly, with bravura, as though he, the little man, would not have been tongue-tied, or at least embattled—since there are clearly two sides to the issue—if it were the actual, living Scriabin he was condemning. Tomlinson sits in judgment of another; does the poem as a whole suggest that he also sits in silent judgment of himself? In private he denounces Trotsky directly: "Trotsky, was it not then you brought yourself/ To judgement and to execution, when you forgot/ Where terror rules, justice turns arbitrary?" Does the poet hear himself as having things awfully easy, denouncing where there is no danger of retort? When, moreover, he makes claims about the deterministic course of history, one worries as to whether he also hears the claims as a typical excuse little men make for doing nothing to alleviate their plight, which they blame on others. Does he sense the common, mean aspect of withdrawing into one's little nook, of making no effort to improve a situation, and of condemning any and all who do try, on the grounds that the results of their effort are inferior to the ends aimed at? The poet-protagonist's situation is small and secure, but the texture of the poem, its language, is grand. It is almost Promethean. Can Tomlinson be hearing the language as pretentious, or would attributing that judgment to him be a case of over-reading? Does he mean, by the way he listens to himself, by the shape of the poem, to suggest that the whole poem is like Greensleeves being used to sell ice cream, that he is using the language to pump himself, private man, up into the dimensions of a public poet-historian-judge, and of subjects as impressive as Scriabin, Blok, Lenin, and Trotsky, a frog puffing himself up to the size of an ox?

Probably if Tomlinson had been sensitive to the self-condemnatory implications of the poem, he would have felt obligated to revise it in such a way as to accentuate certain connections which, in the present condition of the poem, are so latent as to seem suppressed. Consider, for example, the following two passages and then the neglected connection between them. In the first passage, Tomlinson says:

> You dreamed an end
> Where the rose of the world would go out like a close in music.
> Population drags the partitions down
> And we are a single town of warring suburbs.

The linguistic quality of the second pair of lines in contrast to the first is superbly expressive. Scriabin dreamed there would be an end to beauty or value as remotely transcendent and that, after the revolution and in the new world, value would be immanent in every person so that each would be transparent to all. The actual consequence of the revolution, in contrast, is that we are all in contact with each other, but belligerently, each with a sense of his own value but denying that of the other. The poet-protagonist, of course, means to suggest that, though his dreams may have been pretty, Scriabin was a fool to imagine that a practical effort to implement it would lead to anything but its opposite.

In the second passage, the last stanza of the poem, Tomlinson expresses relief that "Hard edges of the houses . . . refuse to burn . . . and at the city's/ Stale new frontier even ugliness/ Rules with the cruel mercy of solidities." He is glad there are solid walls separating people from each other. The walls are so ugly that he wishes they would burn up (and hence the mercy of the solidities is cruel, for his taste is as refined as Scriabin's), but their being solid and fireproof is a mercy, because it does allow one his privacy and his sense of dignity and distinction.

The neglected connection between these two passages is as follows. The partitions are in truth down, as the first passage says, but perhaps they would not be down if they did not seem still to be up, as the second passage suggests, in the form of the hard edges and solid walls of the houses in "the estate." Placed within the walls of his own room, the poet-protagonist feels private and of distinctive worth. However, the mass media, including the radio, have invaded all such places. Although the protagonist's language may be elegant, his thoughts and his spiritual stance, the haughty moral condemnation by those without political power of any and all who have it or seek it, could not be more common, less private and distinctive than they are, for they are to be heard on the BBC and read in the *Times* and the *Guardian* every day. His feeling that he retains a personal distinctiveness is illusory.

If connections of this sort were accentuated, the silliness of the protagonist's hectoring tone, as adopted toward the dead, and of his historical determinism, as used to excuse his inaction, would come across as a judgment by the poem of itself. Without such revision, it seems that, in settling for second-best in politics, Tomlinson has also settled inadvertently for second-best in poetry, trying to be both a poet who is implicated within the poem as its protagonist and one who is not, who has remained outside the maelstrom of its activity. Although one may wish to remain indecisive as to whether "Prometheus" is great poetry, a failure, or just irritating verse, it cannot be all three, for, in contrast to politics, poetry allows for no compromises. While my uncertainties about the poem are meant to suggest that it is a failure, their primary purpose is to indicate the incredible difficulties and stresses, and the chance of disastrous failure or of magnificent success, to which a poet undertaking such a poem exposes himself.

Even though Geoffrey Hill's "In Piam Memoriam" is intensely immediate in its initial effect, repeated readings reveal that it is also folded back upon itself again and again so that, without dissipating its intensity and immediacy, it displays a dramatic mediation so intricate that the poem may be properly called a double lyric, with two originative centers instead of one, each at odds with and inclusive of the other. The poem was written as early as 1958 and printed in Hill's first volume, *For the Unfallen*, but its perfection is like that of the finest of his more recent poems, which have belatedly won him a wider respect in England than any other living poet. Anthony Thwaite, in the British Council *Poetry Today: 1960–1973*, says of Hill:

> His dense, formal, formidable poems have gradually established themselves, though he is still much less well known than he should be among ordinary readers of poetry: it is in the estimate of other poets that he stands particularly high—for example, in the answers to a 1972 questionnaire sent out by *The Review* to many poets and critics, the poet most often mentioned as a hopeful sign was Hill, specifically on the strength of his third and latest book, *Mercian Hymns* (1971).[7]

"In Piam Memoriam" lacks the manifest amplitude and scope of Hill's later poems, but its compacted, almost solipsistic infolding, though it may close the poem off as private from a hurried reading, includes for meditative rereadings a dramatic largeness.

IN PIAM MEMORIAM

I

Created purely from glass the saint stands,
Exposing his gifted quite empty hands
Like a conjurer about to begin,
A righteous man begging of righteous men.

II

In the sun lily-and-gold-coloured,
Filtering the cruder light, he has endured,
A feature for our regard; and will keep;
Of worldly purity the stained archetype.

III

The scummed pond twitches. The great holly-tree,
Emptied and shut, blows clear of wasting snow,
The common, puddled substance: beneath,
Like a revealed mineral, a new earth.[8]

On the surface, the poem is descriptive in method and argumentative in design. The glass saint of the first two stanzas represents a supra-temporal and supernatural abstractness, not unlike the instructions of Silkin's woman from the Home Office, and Scriabin's apocalyptic music (and perhaps echoing the poetic glass men of Valéry and Stevens). In the third stanza Hill presents a scene whose mode of existence is so clearly superior to that of the glass man that it renders him obsolete, of historical interest only, at best piously memorable. The natural vision may include purities like those of the saint as well as unfiltered crudities, but it is set forth argumentatively as excluding all artifice, all creating from glass rather than from the materials of nature.

The most obvious sign that either something more is going on than an argument in the form of a description, or else the poem is botched, is the striking contrast between message and style. The message puts natural emergence over the artificial creation of anything out of nothing. But the style of the poem seems quite unnatural and intricately wrought. There are gaps between the stanzas and the sentences are emphatic and clipped rather than supple and flowing. Indeed, down to the slightest details, the stanzas are in vivid contrast one to another: the "emptied and shut" of the holly-tree contrasts with the "gifted quite empty hands" of the saint; "the common, puddled substance" is opposed to the glass, "the scummed pond twitches" to the "sun lily-and-gold-coloured"; and so forth. It would seem, that is, that Hill is undermining his argument by his manner.

There is, however, just underneath the hammering of the syntax, an emotional impulsion which unites every part of the poem naturally and vigorously. The dominant feeling of the poem is revulsion. In the first two stanzas this revulsion develops from a fastidious contempt through disgust to the dismissive sarcasm of "A feature for our regard; and will keep." The movement of the stanzas, that is, is a turning away, a revulsion, from unnatural, abstract, ataraxic detachment. In a similar way, the movement of stanza III begins with a moment of revulsion, with the deliberately repulsive "The scummed pond twitches." In feeling, then, the natural movement of the third stanza from stagnancy to renewal is the same as the poet's movement in the poem as a whole from saintliness to naturalness. The way the two adjectives "stained" and "scummed" are slapped together confirms this similarity between the natural movement of the third stanza and the emotional movement of the entire poem. Thus, even though it is mediated, Hill's advocacy of nature over artifice is supported by the form as much as by the content. The verbal devices of the poem emerge out of its underlying emotion, out of a natural revulsion against the sterility of artifice.

Curiously, however, the end of the poem ("beneath,/ Like a revealed mineral, a new earth"), which ought to be a climactic release from the feeling of revulsion, is flat and empty, as though Hill has his reservations about natural as well as supernatural revelations. The tonal quality of that last line is very much like that of "A righteous man begging of righteous men," though its meaning is not suggestive of involution and sterility. Tonally, then, the poem ends as though Hill is discovering, with slow amazement, that the natural movement being affirmed in the third stanza is actually based on a model of spiritual transformation, on a process in which "the cruder light" is refined into lily and gold colors.

The entire poem has been an effort to put religious change in its place within a natural and temporal order. "Of worldly purity the stained archetype" means, beyond its literal sense, that the archetype has been weathered by the passage of time, that men have turned away from it and committed themselves to naturalness as they have discovered the immorality of inactive aloofness. Even to the end of the poem Hill remains opposed to such purity. Yet there is a counter thrust to the dominant impulsion of the poem, as though a second poem with a germinal center of its own were being written just out of sight, beneath the poem being read. According to this counter poem, that saintly magician with his empty but gifted hands, that beggar who takes without giving, is the ultimate source of natural transformation and rebirth. The feeling of revulsion, which is the pivot of Hill's movement from the artificial to the natural, is also the pivot of all religious development.

The poem ought not to be read as a New Critical contemplative resolution of opposite and discordant qualities—nor, for that matter, should the ambiguities of its words and phrases be ravelled out, in Empson's way, or its "lexia" be cut up into layers and dimensions, for such moves would destroy the powerful doubleness of the poem and turn it into a tame "plural text," a text mastered, that is, in the contemplative resolution of its scientific investigator, who has extracted what was the oneness and harmony of the New Critical poem as organism, reduced the poem to a stratified text, and then clothed himself in the serene harmony he has usurped. "In Piam Memoriam" is more like a propagandistic poem doubled upon itself than a unique organism or a plural text. Hill stands firmly for nature against artifice. The miracle of his poetic genius, however, is to create, out of the fount of his own, personal articulative center, a fount that is its opposite and double. The title of the poem must be read sarcastically if it is to be in harmony with Hill's insistence that nothing will come of nothing. According to the counter poem, however, the title should be read solemnly and awesomely, for it is from that very nothing that absolutely everything comes. Some dusky demon wrote that poem, not Hill. It exposes Hill to the same kind of ridicule which he exposes the saint to. For his natural effort to supersede religious miracle is shown to be no more than its derivative. Not that the exposure inactivates him or makes him waver in his commitment. Unless one is blind, all such belief and commitment exposes a person to ridicule. That is the elemental condition of genuine belief and the reason, as Eliot knew, that it is extremely rare. Such knowledge is what led Eliot to print overtly Marxist material in *The Criterion*, material exhibiting genuine belief, even though he was, as a devout Christian, deeply opposed to it.

The distinctive vitality of "In Piam Memoriam" depends on its disunity and incoherence. Its oppositional duality cannot be reduced even to an orderly unity of opposition. For the opposition itself is divided, taking one form in Hill's expression and another in that of his double. The meaning and expression of each is total and engulfs the other. "In Piam Memoriam," then, is two poems, or what I prefer to call a double lyric. It is not enough to call poetry like this dramatic, because there is no single scene within which its action takes place. Nor, to reverse matters, can it be called a conflict of scenes or worlds, taking place within a larger imaginative act, for each scene is presented as self-constituted and as including the other scene as constituted by a self that is other.

Whatever one's terms for such poetry, the emphasis must be on doubleness, duplicity, and divisiveness. The scene of the second stanza of "Defence" is so very different from the scene of the first stanza that one feels he is being forced behind both scenes, where, however, he fails to find a unifying authorial act of making, because he senses a source beyond the outraged poet in the light of which that poet is exposed as impotent. "Prometheus" has its spatial scene and its historical scene, but it cannot be read without one's feeling that the maker of those scenes is being called in question by those he condemns, those whose spatial place within the poem is strictly imaginary and whose historical reality seems to exceed the reach of the maker who would include it within his condemnation. The divisive nature of this poetic form seems to be betraying the poet, who in this case is too timid to take on what the form demands of him. Even as early as "In Piam Memoriam," Hill does face and meet those demands. Indeed, he can be said to create them. The radical duplicity, divisiveness, and otherness of Hill's finest poems have a double effect upon one's reading of other recent English poetry. They make one expectant that other poems equally fine but profoundly different can be created. They also give one a sense of excellence in relation to which it is possible to recognize another poem, like "Defence," as something lesser, and still another, like "Prometheus," as a failure.

Such poetry has the capacity to shake one free of any infatuation he may have with "poetics" or with "texts" and return him to a concern for poems as ardent as that which the poetry of Eliot elicited from Leavis fifty years ago. The relation between any genuine poem and an expert, imaginative reader is itself a divisiveness, as Leavis' best critical readings amply demonstrate. The vitality of that divisive relation, where the self-world of the poem touches that of the reader, goes dead if the poem is allowed to swallow up the reader or the reader the poem. The first often occurs among American New Critics; the second follows from a poem's being treated as "text" and deconstructed. Perhaps such deadening maneuvers can be blocked off by the best poems of Hill, Gunn, Larkin, and Silkin and Tomlinson—who have written better poems than "Defence" or "Prometheus"—for these poems are likely to keep the reader uneasy and alert in relation to them by that divisiveness which they manifest within themselves.

If one speculates as to why such peculiar and powerful poems are being written by English poets today, it is difficult not to think of them as intimately bound up with present-day English English, a language which had gradually come to be identical with the world on which the sun never sets, and, then, precipitously contracted into the language of but one small island. Perhaps creativity so powerful as to make poems with more than one self-originative center or self-world could only come out of an internationalism suddenly become also provincial, a deracinated language miraculously rooted anew, a sense of one's predicament as involving alienation but also a return home.

CHAPTER TWO

Flesh of Abnegation:
The Poems of Geoffrey Hill

Although Harold Bloom's claim that Geoffrey Hill is "the strongest British poet now alive" seems true to me, there is a complication in Hill's strength which Bloom surprisingly neglects in his introduction to *Somewhere Is Such A Kingdom*, a collection of Hill's three previously published volumes: *For the Unfallen* (1959), *King Log* (1968), and *Mercian Hymns* (1971). Unlike almost every other British poet now alive, Hill works very close to the poetry of T. S. Eliot, as though Eliot were what Bloom would, but does not, call Hill's Poetic Father. In the following comment. C. H. Sisson is pointing, I think, to this aspect of Hill's poetry, although Eliot's name is not mentioned:

> There is in Hill a touch of the fastidiousness of Crashaw, which is that of a mind in search of artifices to protect itself against its own passions. Hill is perhaps the only contemporary poet in English to feel such an impulse, and this is an indication of his potentialities.[1]

Eliot's peculiar fastidiousness towards non-crafted experience can be felt unmistakably in his pronouncement that "the more perfect the artist, the more completely separate in him will be the man who suffers and the mind which creates." Whereas most English poets turn away from Eliot in fastidious disgust at the sound of his aristocratic aloofness, Hill is too acute not to recognize the Eliotic aspect in his own revulsion from Eliot. In consequence, Hill holds Eliot close to himself, like Conte Ugolino the Arcivescovo Ruggieri, with a cruel, painful satisfaction.[2]

It is true that, like Eliot, Hill believes in a scrupulous separation of "the mind which creates" from "the man who suffers." Unlike Eliot, however, Hill focusses on the human suffering which accompanies "the mind in the act of finding/ What will suffice," the mind, that is, in its act of creating. Eliot tends to exempt "the mind which creates" from the scrutiny of his withering gaze. Most literary criticism, for instance, he finds to be far from any achieved excellence, but "the criticism employed by a trained and skilled writer on his own work," his own critical activity as a poet, that is, he is happy to call "the most vital, the highest kind of criticism."[3] The same kind of uncritical satisfaction informs Eliot's separating off, from all unreflected-upon experience which ends in "dung and death," that creative act of reviving past experience, not as it was, but in what he calls "its meaning," a restorative act which transforms the experience of a single life into that

> of many generations—not forgetting
> Something that is probably quite ineffable:
> The backward look behind the assurance
> Of recorded history, the backward half-look
> Over the shoulder, towards the primitive terror.[4]

Eliot's uncritical exemption of the restorative act from the primitive terror which it reveals in unreflected-upon experience, this is the soft spot into which Hill fixes his teeth with fierce delight. Hill's joy comes from exposing the unexamined terror in the examining experience, in the poetic act of resuscitating the past.

Bloom himself calls Hill's poems "a poetry turned against itself." If Eliot's assured presence is felt just beneath the troubled surface of Hill's poetry, then the following, explosive poem should prove characteristic of his fierce power:

History As Poetry

> Poetry as salutation; taste
> Of Pentecost's ashen feast. Blue wounds.
> The tongue's atrocities. Poetry
> Unearths from among the speechless dead
>
> Lazarus mystified, common man
> Of death. The lily rears its gouged face

> From the provided loam. Fortunate
> Auguries; whirrings; tarred golden dung:
>
> 'A resurgence' as they say. The old
> Laurels wagging with the new: Selah!
> Thus laudable the trodden bone thus
> Unanswerable the knack of tongues.[5]

Within Hill's poetry is a passion much like the innermost passion of Eliot's poetry: a terror of death, of death as emptiness, as meaninglessness, as existence separated from the ultimate Good, from that central sun of certain value. Thus, like Eliot, Hill feels the need to expose unexamined experience from the past to the sun of ultimate value by way of poetry. He would, that is, unearth "the trodden bone," the "common man/ Of death," by means of his own "knack of tongues," he would gild the dung, praise the bone. At the same time, he is uneasy about turning history into poetry. It is not at all certain that the Lazarus unearthed is really the same Lazarus as he who lay with the speechless dead. Unavoidably, poetry provides its own loam for whatever resurrected experience it contains; the unexamined experience it would expose may remain as it was, hidden within the earth where it was originally buried. There is a violent aspect to bringing something to light. The unearthing shovel often gouges the face of what it would expose. "Blue wounds" may sound more elegant than "dung and death," but the feast is ashen; atop the gilt dung is tar, Hill's uneasy sense that the trodden bone may, at bottom, be lauded so that the poetry, with its "knack of tongues," proves unanswerable. A poem which articulates such an exhumation, "History As Poetry" seems to be suggesting, can be at one with ultimate Goodness only if it excoriates itself for doing what it does. On behalf of "the speechless dead," who, though unearthed, remain speechless, the poet must answer back by calling in question the laudation of the dead by way of his own "knack of tongues." Hill, then, is Eliot turned against himself; he retains the value of what he does by doubting and criticizing it; Hill's poetry has its sun, but it is a black sun.

Much like Eliot's poetry, Hill's is so difficult to discuss because its uniqueness is not voiced, but only implicit in the critical way Hill listens to his words and rhythms. Ordinarily, the judgmental attentiveness of a poem is thought of as its universal aspect, whereas its individuality is felt to be in its voice or expressiveness. In Hill, in contrast, the touch of uniqueness inheres in the peculiar way he hears and criticizes and judges the voiced expression. The contempt and sarcasm of "History As Poetry" springs out of Hill's inward listening. Only after sharing what satisfied Hill in the way he listened to the poem, can one feel the full and exact ferocity of words like "ashen," "blue," "mystified," "provided," "wagging," and "laudable." The "resurgence" may make the trodden bone laudable, but the beneficiary is the surgeon, not the patient, as though psychoanalysis were finally, as Lacan waggishly insists, for the benefit of the psychiatrist. Undeniably, there is something morbid in Hill's unearthing the disease, the crumbly rot of the tar crusting the golden dung, of the poetic lauding of the trodden bone. "Til we be roten, kan we nat be rype." The great English poet now is the one who most vividly realizes the ripeness of seeing through the rottenness of one's saving himself by "saving" others.

Even as a word-man, or mainly because I am that,

> I am shadowed by the wise bird
> Of necessity, the lithe
> Paradigm Sleep-and-Kill.

These lines, placing as they do the word-man, the poet, in the position of the wordless mouse being shadowed by the predatory owl, conclude the first of Hill's "Three Baroque Meditations." The question of the poem is

> Do words make up the majesty
> Of man, and his justice
> Between the stones and the void?

So a poet might think, but Hill's doubts are demonic and mock at the pretentiousness of such a thought. Men exalt themselves by way of words in order to hide from the likelihood that the nature and value of their lives are no different from those of the wordless owl and mouse whose tryst in the sharp night acts out "the lithe/ Paradigm Sleep-and-Kill." By turning against words, by unearthing the ironic way men use words to sustain a mouse-like ignorance of their mouse-like existence, Hill does indeed attain a certain bitter majesty.

So regularly are Hill's poems lined with such a doubting, demonic self-mockery that Bloom's claim that "there are no bad poems in Hill's three books" does seem true, at least to the extent that every one of his poems manifests his distinctive strength. But that strength can be a liability. Some of Hill's poems fail because his mockery chokes words emerging out of remote regions of experience; cut off from the felt qualities of their experiential source, these mocked words make the mockery itself hollow. Such a claim is, of course, difficult to substantiate. Although I think, for instance, that the first Baroque meditation fails, that it does not manifest, along with Hill's mockery, the majesty which he is mocking—or manifests it not as felt experience, but only as an idea—it could be argued that I have not lived with the poem long enough to allow its depths to emerge, or it could be claimed that the force of the poem depends on its relation to the other two meditations.

Yet, if its object lacks any substance to resist it, the mockery does turn hollow. When this happens, the voice of the poem as it is listened to and criticized by Hill loses its characteristically rasping, grating tone and soars shrilly, on the verge of hysteria. I hear something like this in "An Order of Service," a little anti-Eliotic poem modelled on Stevens' "The Snow Man." Though meant to mock, the poem seems to me to spin emptily in exasperation with itself:

> He was the surveyor of his own ice-world,
> Meticulous at the chosen extreme,
> Though what he surveyed may have been nothing.
>
> Let a man sacrifice himself, concede
> His mortality and have done with it;
> There is no end to that sublime appeal.
>
> In such a light dismiss the unappealing
> Blank of his gaze, hopelessly vigilant,
> Dazzled by renunciation's glare.

So very arch. What can one say after that last line except "Ho, Ho, Ho," hollowly? Nothing awesome is allowed to appear in this Eliotic, ataraxic, anti-existential stance, whereas the quality of Stevens' snow man's non-being is realized so fully that even Bloom misses Stevens' own repudiation of that stance, perhaps because it is conveyed only by tone and rhythm and is full not just of revulsion and repudiation, but of fear at the power of the snow man's emptiness. Hill's poem does not even hint at the frightening power which renunciation can bestow on a man, a power exercisable not just in religion or in philosophy, but also in poetry, in science, in politics, and in literary criticism. Eliot's greatness always combines strength with weakness. Hill's weakness may be that he left Eliot's weakness to Larkin and has adopted only his strength.

When a poem of Hill's works as a poem, the felt quality of what is being mocked is experientially manifest. Even so, it is almost never unequivocally manifest as Hill's own experience. The words, the very voice, of the poem come to him from elsewhere, seeming to belong to another, so that Hill's poetic identity is felt to be purely critical, that of a demonic mocker, inaudibly auditing. This proves true even in what at first appears to be an autobiographical poem, the first of "Soliloquies":

THE STONE MAN
To Charles Causley

Recall, now, the omens of childhood:
The nettle-clump and rank elder-tree;
The stones waiting in the mason's yard:

Half-recognized kingdom of the dead:
A deeper landscape lit by distant
Flashings from their journey. At nightfall

My father scuffed clay into the house.
He set his boots on the bleak iron
Of the hearth; ate, drank, unbuckled, slept.

I leaned to the lamp; the pallid moths
Clipped its glass, made an autumnal sound.
Words clawed my mind as though they had smelt

Revelation's flesh . . . So, with an ease
That is dreadful, I summon all back.
The sun bellows over its parched swarms.

The adult who does the recalling and is appalled by his capacity to "summon all back" cannot be entirely dissociated from Hill himself. Hill at least half accepts Ransom's conviction that one cannot both be in love and write a love poem, so that he is not exempt from the judgment of the title, with its implication that the person who can summon the dead back with ease, the chosen poet, must be made of stone, can ride the winged horse of poetry only if he has faced the Medusan gaze and been permanently stunned, or "Dazzled by renunciation's glare." So far as one can tell, Hill is the adult who was the child who, sensing the mere mortality of his father, conceded his own mortality and had done with it, going at the lamp like "the pallid moths," sacrificing himself to Pentecostal poetry, which makes an "autumnal sound." But even if the adult and Hill are one, the split between the adult as talented poet (who can summon back and sum up his father's life with the four words, "ate, drank, unbuckled, slept") and the adult who contemns that talent (who knows there is something damnable about such word power) is decisive. Hill's own sense of identity and value comes down hard and heavy on the side of the mocker, so that the stone man is kept at a remove from Hill himself, is only equivocally Hill himself. Indeed, the last line of the poem, "The sun bellows over its parched swarms," in its lack of the stony clarity of the rest of the poem, seems to smear the poem with its flush of fury, as though Hill dismisses the adult with his stunned dread and ensures by his rage that he himself is not mistaken for stone. Although the aim of the poem may be the unmitigated truth about oneself as a chosen poet, the sharpness of the split between what is condemned and the condemning, even between the speaking and the listening—as though Hill must keep the self he condemns at a remove from himself even though it is himself—forces one to concede the partial accuracy of Sisson's claim that Hill's poetry is defensive in its fastidiousness.

The special sense in which Hill's poems are quintessentially "flesh of abnegation" may be most directly evident in "September Song," a miniature masterpiece in which the whole of Hill is set sharply against the whole of Eliot. The deep impulsion of the *Four Quartets* is a withdrawing from the flesh, the poetry mattering, but only as one says "the poetry does not matter." It is not a poem of withdrawal, because Eliot stays so close to the flesh, of experience and of language; it is the experience of withdrawing which Eliot sustains with exquisite tact throughout the poem. Its visual counterpoint is the greatest of Mannerist paintings, Pontormo's "Cena a Emau," in which the flesh and worldliness of the disciples, who occupy the foreground, is all turned in awe and wonder to the upper center, where Jesus, still seated at the table but with a sense of the ascension upon him, is disengaging from this world with the most anguishing pity and regret in his eyes and face and raised hand. Although the greatness of the *Quartets* as a poem depends on Eliot's vivid realization of the flesh of words, images, rhythms, and experiences from which he is withdrawing, the threat of the poem is undoubtedly toward a final disengagement from self and world, so that a fervent reader must find himself moved to commit himself to silence and solitude and sacrifice—or else, as happens in Leavis' last and most elaborate critique of the *Quartets*, in *The Living Principle*, to a committed, vigorous resistance to what the poem would move one to.

Unlike Leavis, Hill has accepted and lived through the Eliotic death to flesh, to self, and to world. As he manifests in "September Song," he could not himself survive, as a man of flesh and blood, the mass extermination of Jews during the Second World War. This elegy for a death camp victim is necessarily an elegy for himself: it shows how and why he died, it justifies that death and even bestows a certain majesty on it by insisting that it would have been monstrous not to have died. But "September Song" is not at all otherworldly. It is rather the worldliness of otherworldliness, the vital embodiment of death, or, in Hill's own explosive phrase, it is "flesh of abnegation."

SEPTEMBER SONG
born 19.6.32–deported 24.9.42

Undesirable you may have been, untouchable
you were not. Not forgotten
or passed over at the proper time.

As estimated, you died. Things marched,
sufficient, to that end.

Just so much Zyklon and leather, patented
terror, so many routine cries.

(I have made
an elegy for myself it
is true)

September fattens on vines. Roses
flake from the wall. The smoke
of harmless fires drifts to my eyes.

This is plenty. This is more than enough.

Eliot's conscience compels him to turn away from the flesh. Hill
will not allow himself the comfort of such withdrawn hiddenness;
out of the cloister he compels his craven spirit, his withdrawn de-
featedness, to expose itself. Thus, the characteristic movement of
Hill's poems is a withdrawal from and a return to the sensuous embodiment of poetry, a withdrawal from natural rhythms, from what
Hill calls "the inertial drag of speech" in his fine essay on rhythm,
"Redeeming the Time,"[6] and then, following upon a radical critique of those rhythms, a return to time embodied but redeemed,
natural process transformed into dramatic act.

It is important that the overt signs of this profound revulsion
turning upon itself not be isolated, and so trivialized, as devices of
the craft; and yet it is just as important that the depths of the poems
not be left as mere depths, that the surfacing, the objectifying, be
recognized as what makes the poems incontrovertibly shareable.
The turn, the crucial redemption of time, in "September Song,"
may be glimpsed in

Just so much Zyklon and leather, patented
terror, so many routine cries.

The power and anguish of the poem explodes out of the simple
elision of "just" before the second "so." One's first, the natural,
way of reading "so many routine cries" is to sense the elided "just"
as intended, so that what comes at one are "just so many routine
cries." The parenthetical stanza that follows—"(I have made/ an

elegy for myself it/ is true)"—is grounded and empowered by those two lines. The poet could not but die, hearing so many death cries which were being heard by others as "just so many routine cries." Within the parentheses, the "it" is put at the end of the second line for emphasis, so that "it/ is true" means that this elegy is a true elegy, that I did truly die when I heard so many cries and knew that human beings were treating those cries as "just so many routine cries." And yet, "it/ is true" also retains its concessive meaning; it is true that this elegy is for myself, not just or mainly for that Jew born in 1932 and deported in 1942. I was born in 1932 myself and like Margaret it is myself I am grieving for, I am *that* soft and self-indulgent and contemptible and certainly dismissable, my death negligible in comparison to the enormity of the death that compelled it by sympathetic shock.

A radical, rhythmical disjuncture occurs between the first two stanzas and the parenthetical third stanza of the poem. In the first two stanzas, there is a certain archness, a rasping sarcasm, a doubleness saying "What else would you expect?" and at the same time "It is unbelievable that such cruelty could become expected, routine, and a single human being survive it." In the third stanza, though the dismissive casualness is there as latent, the overt tone is solemn and funereal. From having been "in stride" (after all, the attitude of the first two stanzas must be a common way in which people have come to terms with the death camps), Hill in the third stanza breaks "out of stride." That shift of stride signifies a transformation of natural process into the "drama of reason," of a grammatical into a moral copula. As Hill himself says of the comparable shift in Wordsworth's "Intimations Ode," from "Heavy as frost, and deep almost as life!" to "O joy! that in our embers/ Is something that doth live," "the poet immediately breaks continuity, thrusts against the arrangement, the settlement, with a fresh time-signature" ("Redeeming the Time," p. 104).

The shift in time-signature is moral. Hill means by it to imply that the attitude, style, the expressed sarcasm, of the first two stanzas are a deadness. The cleverness of the antithesis between "undesirable" and "untouchable," the humor of "at the proper time," the understatement of "as estimated" and "marched,/ Sufficient," those are devices available only to dead men; no living man could use them. So Hill disowns and damns himself as a poet, taking his stand against abnegation by embodying it in a poetic flesh that is judged to be dead and rotting.

A new time-signature also governs the last four lines. The rasping and the solemnity are both gone. The lines float out numbly, remotely, as autumn experienced by a man settled into his death. "Fattens" and "flake" are rotten, over-ripe, the smoke does not flare against the smoke from the harmful fires of stanza two, as the smoke "From the heaps of couch-grass" does flare against the fires of war, in Hardy's "In Time of 'The Breaking of Nations.' " September experienced in this way is "more than enough" in the sense that it can be experienced by a human being aware of the death camps only if he is dead; the connection between these lines and the first three stanzas is numb, anaesthetized, a matter of mechanical bolting. The poem as a whole is self-repudiatory, its "flesh of abnegation" putrid and festering. Hill himself is alive in the way he listens to the song; it is the Hill and all England that sing the song, morally righteous, fat and somnolent, that are dead.

Hill's poems regularly fall somewhere between Croce's notion that, though poems may include judgments, the distinctively poetic quality of a poem is non-judgmental and Yvor Winters' conviction that poems are, in essence, judgmental statements. The uniqueness of Hill's poems inheres in those fiercely individual judgments which silently envelop the expressive line of the poem. The judgment which makes the "flesh of abnegation," the words "fattens" and "flake," fester is not explicit, but is recognized inferentially as incontrovertibly there.

Perhaps the crucial moral judgments in poems of achieved excellence are invariably silent. Hill's best known poem may show why this is so.

OVID IN THE THIRD REICH

non peccat, quaecumque potest peccasse negare,
solaque famosam culpa professa facit

(Amores, III, xiv)

I love my work and my children. God
Is distant, difficult. Things happen.
Too near the ancient troughs of blood
Innocence is no earthly weapon.

I have learned one thing: not to look down
So much upon the damned. They, in their sphere,
Harmonize strangely with the divine
Love. I, in mine, celebrate the love-choir.

The stated judgments of the poem all belong to the speaker. He, clearly enough, judges himself to be innocent, to live in that sphere, and the damned to be guilty, but even though innocent he does not look down on the damned "so much," because he has learned that he too would be damned if he had lived "Too near the ancient troughs of blood," if he had taken an active part in civil or military strife, because there evil, damnable weapons are necessary. The second, unspoken judgment of the poem is, of course, that the speaker is not bad enough to be received among the damned nor good enough to be with God, that his sphere is the *vestibolo d'Inferno*, among those who lived without infamy and without praise, among those whose blind life was so base, so contemptible, that "we will not talk of them, but look and pass on." The title, the epigraph (read in the light of the poem, its meaning changes to "He who denies that he sins commits the unpardonable sin"), and the first two lines indicate that this silent condemnation of the speaker is not just one's own, but first and foremost Hill's. "I love my work and my children" is heavy with "the inertial drag of speech." The person who says it "minds his own business," feels, anyway, that he cannot understand the why of things enough to take a stand against anything. Hill's denunciation of the speaker is indubitable, if only implicit.

What matters most, however, is that the judgment is made not just of the stance, but also of its own living self-justification. Ordinarily, one feels that in satire the person being satirized is being presented as formed in the light of the satiric judgment. As a result, one is suspicious of satire, doubting that what is being condemned was ever truly like what it seems to be as condemned, knowing that the person being judged had himself a very different judgment of himself from that of the satirist, and not trusting the satirist because he failed to give that counter judgment its full and just weight. After all, every person and act and argument can be judged and found wanting from some position or other. To judge another person only while allowing that person to exhibit his own self-judgment as fully as possible, that is the secret, silent, poetic alternative to the commandment, "Judge not, that ye be not judged." The poet judges another, but only in such a way as to include that other's judgment of himself, and, inferentially, of the critical poet who judges him.

Hill, for example, grants the speaker his full strength in the poem's last line, "Love. I, in mine, celebrate the love-choir." The line is full of bepuzzlement, of pauses on the verge of hesitant awe, its seven accents widening the line's space meditatively. "Strangely" in the line before prepares no doubt for this line so that it can be heard in its contemplative, detached fullness. As a result, Hill's own fierce condemnation of the speaker is put in its place as damnable, as based upon a very questionable assurance, a commitment no doubt at odds with ultimate Goodness. But the speaker will not look down so much on Hill. Hill's lack of genteel reciprocity makes him seem exposed and vulnerable.

One of Hill's poems—and for some it must be his finest—is an exception to most of what has been said thus far. In the second of the "Three Baroque Meditations," there is no pause or hesitation between the expressing and the listening, so that mouse and owl, victim and predator, apologist and condemner are at one supra-metaphorically, supra-socially, in a blinding flash of mystic self-hate and hate-of-self-hate:

> Anguish bloated by the replete scream.
> Flesh of abnegation: the poem
> Moves grudgingly to its extreme form,
>
> Vulnerable, to the lamp's fierce head
> Of well-trimmed light. In darkness outside,
> Foxes and rain-sleeked stones and the dead—
>
> Aliens of such a theme—endure
> Until I could cry 'Death! Death!' as though
> To exacerbate that suave power;
>
> But refrain. For I am circumspect,
> Lifting the spicy lid of my tact
> To sniff at the myrrh. It is perfect

In its impalpable bitterness,
Scent of a further country where worse
Furies promenade and bask their claws.

So fierce is Hill's critical awareness, so intense its light, that the body of the poem can hardly move. "Flesh of abnegation" is the anguish of the act of withdrawing from the fleshy self, but only when that anguish is turned against itself, forced back into an enfleshed form. The "replete scream" fuses the primal, bestial scream from which one would withdraw and the angelic hosannah to which one would withdraw, the real and the imagined, *Wahrheit und Dichtung*, crushed and compacted together as never before, as if these fifteen lines contained and condemned the whole of the *Four Quartets*. "Bloated" suggests that the "flesh of abnegation" is that of a drowned man and also on the point of bursting. The rhythm stalls and stalls, word by word, hardly making its way to the end of the sentence. The sentence that follows is a momentary escape into the poet's opposite, the changelessness in the outside dark, the peace of death which Hill will not allow himself. The sentence moves with a sleekness which itself reminds one of the momentum of the *Quartets*.

But refrain. For I am circumspect

Do I, Hill asks, refuse to abandon myself to the Eliotic dark, to its comforting balm, because I am afraid of it, fastidiously circumspect, not really going beyond Eliot, but actually stopping far short of him? That fear and doubt is what he smells as he turns back from the darkness and faces his own poem. Against the perfection of death, what alternative can he offer himself but an "impalpable bitterness," with its hint of living hells even more self-anguishing than the living hell of this poem. Choosing against the finally achieved serenity of an Eliotic death to self, Hill settles himself down into one of the lowest circles of the Inferno, along with Ugolino.

In that circle as transformed by Hill, however, the deepest anguish is radiant with the hard, clear light of unmitigated truth. Is there another poem in English that brings together with such a crack self-defeatedness and the pride of absolute mastery? After such a poem, could its author ever walk straight and direct and exposed again? To me it seems unavoidable that from this mystic miracle Hill would move on to the more indirect, ampler forms of "Funeral Music," "The Songbook of Sebastian Arrurruz," *Mercian Hymns,* and the more recent "Lachrimae." The indirectness of those sequences should be read with a sense of what it means for Hill to write with absolute directness and immediacy, as he did this once, in "Anguish bloated by the replete scream." Imagine the so fully exposed Hill of the extraordinary photograph on the back cover of *Somewhere Is Such A Kingdom* as just having emerged from this poem, and one's awe of Dante will soar. Steiner may have said our factories and death camps are modelled on Dante's Inferno (a reason we no longer believe in an otherworldly Hell), but Hill's poetry is where an idea not unlike that lives.

CHAPTER THREE

Geoffrey Hill's
"Funeral Music"

To note the indirectness of "Funeral Music" may be a step towards discovering the centrality to all of Hill's later sequences of the conviction, which he shares with Coleridge, that "meditation is central to practice."[1] This discovery will prove most profitable if it is also recognized that Hill is not referring to thoughtful preparation for action or to brooding over events after they have occurred, but to meditation which is simultaneous with action.

Complaints concerning Hill's indirectness, as though it were a poetic weakness, usually stem from a neglect of this commitment on his part to the oneness of thought and action. C. H. Sisson, for example, in reacting to the two-page essay Hill appended to the eight poems of "Funeral Music," says:

> I find these explanations curious, and perhaps see them as more significant than they are. They seem to imply a notion of the sequence as artifact, as something worked towards and built, which suggests a growing distance between the poetic impulse and the words which finally appear on the page—a gain in architectonics, perhaps, but at a price which is so often paid, by all but the greatest writers, in a loss of immediacy. This is no more than a suspicion of what—as I see it—would be an unfortunate direction.[2]

That is, however, the direction Sisson thinks Hill has moved in, for of *Mercian Hymns* (published in 1971, four years after "Funeral Music" first appeared, in Jon Silkin's *Stand*), he asks: "Is the choice of prose a mark of growing deliberation and a gap between the conception and the performance?" And Hill's more recent sequence, "Lachrimae" in *Tenebrae* (London: André Deutsch, 1978), Sisson refers to "as indicating another mode for this singularly direct mind which, none the less, seems impelled to seek indirect utterance." For Sisson, immediacy and directness go along with a sense of experience, including poetic experience, as a flowing process rather than a human action; even Hill's indirection and meditativeness are spoken of as something to which Hill is "impelled." Great poetry, for Sisson, is unclogged verbal flow, an unimpeded stream between impulse and performance. For poetry like Hill's, in which human making, like all practice, achieves excellence only if impeded, clogged, and disrupted by hard thinking, Sisson's notion of poetry as process cannot but be an obstruction which makes the immediacy of the mediation of "Funeral Music" seem indirect to his thought-free viewing.

It is a different sort of directness which Jon Silkin is missing when he says that Hill found a way "to incarcerate the reader, and perhaps the writer also, in an inescapable response," but his method fails "to release him from a pre-occupation where the event has been so internalised that there results more response than event itself." [3] The longer sequences require some "developed structure," Silkin grants, but Hill unfortunately "meets the problem without conceding to narrative a function it might usefully fulfil in his work," because, it would seem, he prefers "internal impulsions" to "dramatic action." Of "Funeral Music" itself, Silkin says:

> the battle of Towton, and its murderousness, it not encapsulated as dramatic action, but brooded on after the event, thereby allowing the external state of the field and the state of the mind experiencing and responding to it to meet. It is the self-questioning, the doubts, the beliefs half-held with a conviction of personal honesty, the motives and the state of the spirit, that interest Hill, rather than the shaping action of narrative. Nevertheless, these things too have their form of collision with other minds, and through action, alter and are altered. And they could also, I feel, build a narrative unity that Hill has only tentatively, if at all, used. [4]

With his modernistic bias, Sisson is impelled to regret the absence of a direct, psychic flow; Silkin, with his Marxist bias, misses a

direct, objective flow, a collision of forces within an established setting. For him, a poem is a strategy by means of which the poet im-
prisons or captivates the citizen, forcing him to respond in a determined way, and then releases him, purging him of preoccupations
and anxieties so that he can function properly and healthfully. Such
directness or immediacy, though it may require much thought of a
strategic nature prior to the experience of the poem itself, calls for
an absence of thought in that experience totally at odds with Hill's
sense not just of poetic experience, but also of human excellence,
whether in primarily active or primarily meditative behavior.

Hill's sequences, and especially "Funeral Music," on which I
intend to focus, succeed in the light of their own difficult conception. They should not be read as lyrical, as impulse bodied forth in
words, or as narrative, as an "accumulating and continuous action." They are double lyrics or dramatic lyrics and are more authentic, closer to the way thoughtful, engaged human beings actually behave, than anything of a self-expressive nature can be, or
anything that can be staged objectively or theatrically. It is not
enough, moreover, to think of "Funeral Music" as a meeting of subject and object, as Silkin does when he says that Hill has written the
poem so as to allow "the external state of the field and the state of
the mind experiencing and responding to it to meet." For that notion blanks out what is most striking about these poems, that they
are polycentric, including as part of them more than one originative
center. Beyond presenting a scene or any "illusion of reality," they,
first of all, implicate the act of their making by Hill himself. Furthermore, having recognized that this gives him as maker a special
privilege not possessed by any of his antagonists within the scene
or field of his making, Hill strives to double the poems, so that one
scene is always more than one, not only that constituted by him as
maker and including his antagonist, but also that which his antagonist constitutes and which includes him. The peculiar result of this
is that when a reader slides, as is apt to happen, into taking a line
in only one way, he feels the line being pulled away from him, or at
least blurring, doubling up, so that he must check his glasses or rest
his eyes. It is as though, as one viewed *Othello*, he also attended to
Othello's constituting a drama that encompasses Iago and Shakespeare as they have encompassed him in their dramas; as if Anna,

behind the words, is writing out a world which includes Levin and Tolstoy as she is included in their world; as though, as one reads *Women in Love*, he is also reading a second novel, *Men in Love*, written by Ursula-Frieda. Impulse and word, mind and field, these models simply do not touch the sharp-edged magnificence towards which Hill strives even in his finest short poems, but especially in his recent sequences.

Because these sequences are so dense, so multi-layered, so polyphonic, it is hard to say anything that is more than partly true of them. Even such a concession, moreover, is only partly true, for the uniqueness of these poems is beyond the reach of linguistic, structural analysis, by means of which intricacies can be shown, but not power, not explosiveness, not anguish, and not insight. These poems are genuine dramas, each line being vied for by opponents each of whom is a charged source of the line itself, so that it tends to double up disrelatedly, the linkage, the oneness so vividly and livingly unique as to exceed not just one's language but almost one's capacities for experiencing. I shall try to simplify without falsifying, beginning with the first poem of "Funeral Music," Hill's first major sequence:

> Processionals in the exemplary cave,
> Benediction of shadows. Pomfret. London.
> The voice fragrant with mannered humility,
> With an equable contempt for this World,
> 'In honorem Trinitatis'. Crash. The head
> Struck down into a meaty conduit of blood.
> So these dispose themselves to receive each
> Pentecostal blow from axe or seraph,
> Spattering block-straw with mortal residue.
> Psalteries whine through the empyrean. Fire
> Flares in the pit, ghosting upon stone
> Creatures of such rampant state, vacuous
> Ceremony of possession, restless
> Habitation, no man's dwelling-place.[5]

The poem may be recognized as setting forth quite objectively the nature of the lives and deaths of the three men in whose memory "Funeral Music" is written, Suffolk (beheaded 1450), Worcester (beheaded 1470), and Rivers (beheaded 1483). They were Christian Neo-Platonists, viewing this world as a cave, this life as a procession of shadows. It is a no-man's land, a place to leave, especially since the death of the body is the release of the soul into a life of beatific immortality, its flight accompanied by the sound of psalteries "through the empyrean."

But the poet-historian who observes also judges these soldier-martyrs, with a contempt the equal of their contempt for this world. The word "vacuous" brings his dismissive judgment to the forefront. For the soldier-martyrs themselves, the word has to do with the emptying of the worldly, bodily aspect of the ceremony as the soul is possessed by way of a seraph and escorted to heaven. For the poet the word means that the whole show is a monstrous sham. The dualism of these Christians is just an elaborate excuse for their being so brutal, for their killing and being killed in this violent way. Each line should be read not just within its Christian framework, but also within that of the poet-historian, who would pull these "creatures of such rampant state," rampant as beasts of prey, but also as souls ready to spring into heavenly ghostliness, back into the flesh shockingly, with such lines as "Struck down into a meaty conduit of blood" and "Spattering block-straw with mortal residue." Repulsive it is, and their doubling their sight, believing the blow delivered by seraph as well as by axe, softened what they saw and so encouraged both victim and persecutor to take part, equably, in what was not at all the masquerade they took it to be.

However, reading the poem with an ear for the poet's sarcasm (to be heard clearly at least from the word "mannered" in line three on), one senses a growing worry on Hill's part over the similarity between the way he is dismissing the dualistically conceived lives of the soldier-martyrs and the way they dismissed the worldly aspects of their lives. For instance, the string of dismissive phrases with which the poem ends rises away from that pit not just spatially, but also temporally, not just toward the empyrean, but also toward the present, toward that comfortable dwelling-place which is the poet-historian's study, where he remains above action, meditatively. Thus, the string of phrases meant to free the poet from the murderous tangle of his subjects (the freedom to be self-righteous which Silkin missed in the sequence) actually entangles the poet in the very mesh he was using to entangle those subjects. Experienced doubly, that is, the string of phrases reveals the poet as observer and judge to be observed and judged. He uses his professional distinction between himself as observer and his subjects as the observed to escape the truth about his predicament just as his subjects used their religious distinction between soul and body to make their escape. In the short poem "History as Poetry," also to be found in *King Log*, Hill articulates his sense that a poetry which resuscitates the dead can avoid moral condemnation only by subjecting itself to such self-questioning that its primary form becomes self-condemnatory. The first poem of "Funeral Music" exceeds the reach of that poem by bringing the dead back to life in such a way that they observe and judge the very poet-historian who has exhumed, observed, and judged them. Thus chastened, Hill earns a truly liberating release from that reprehensible predicament of staring at another person whose eyes are closed, the predicament next to unavoidable by not just historians, but almost all observers. Though he cannot live by the Christian prescription, "Judge not . . . ," Hill attains a comparable innocence by way of experience, creating a poem-world in which he is judged as he judges, seen as he sees.

Although "Processionals in the exemplary cave" allows for the reading just given, it may not by itself require it. What makes the reading necessary—and this sort of thing is true of the sequence as a whole and of Hill's other sequences—is the gap between that first poem and the poem which follows it, "For whom do we scrape our tribute of pain?" Hill's move from the "they" and the implicit "one" of the first poem to the "we" which colors the second pervasively is what makes one stall uncertainly in the inaudible, invisible gap between the poems. One will connect with the developmental impulse in that gap and, as a result, read the first poem as suggested above, so that he experiences even in it the transformation of "one" and "they" to "we" and thus feels the rightness of the "we" of the first line of the second poem, only, I think, as he recognizes that the basic drama of "Funeral Music" is a combat between two forms of history, two ways of relating oneself as contemporary poet-historian to the past. The unheard way, which works silently behind the poem the actuality of which one is following and which presses everywhere against that actuality, is T. S. Eliot's way.

Even though Eliot observed that the trouble with the *Cantos* is that Pound's hells are always "for the other people" he conceives of the past as occurring without understanding, as in need of the poet-historian, who redeems it by giving it a new form within his understanding. Event and understanding, action and thought, soul and intellect—and this even in the *Four Quartets*—are, for all but the martyr-saint and the poet-historian, essentially separate. The martyr-saint, like the poet-historian, is utterly objective, impersonal, at one with God as Truth, as intellect. He achieves impersonality, which is what Beckett, in *Murder in the Cathedral*, means by losing one's will in God, finding "freedom in submission to God." The saint, that is, like the historian, is free of the laws determining history as an object of study. When Beckett is insisting that the priests unbar the door so that the knights may murder him, he condemns them for arguing

> by results, as the world does,
> To settle if an act be good or bad.
> You defer to the fact. For every life and every act
> Consequence of good and evil can be shown.
> And as in time results of many deeds are blended
> So good and evil in the end become confounded.
> It is not in time that my death shall be known;
> It is out of time that my decision is taken
> [. . .]
> I give my life
> To the Law of God above the Law of Man.[6]

As objective poet-historian, as playwright, as a man who has given himself up to a perfect understanding of past events, Eliot is at one with the single point of awareness within the flux of the past which can be called supratemporal, that of the martyr-saint. As a result, Eliot has no interest in the facts of Beckett's worldly life, the "meagre records" with which he says Tennyson tampered "unscrupulously."[7] His soul as historian, like Beckett's as saint, has become impersonally objective, at one with Intellect as "absolute law," "sufficient grace." For them alone, belief and understanding, soul and intellect, are absolutely identical. The rest of us, in contrast, the priests, the knights, the audience of the play, who live by the Law of Man, are radically flawed.

The subject of *Murder in the Cathedral* is the martyr-saint as set against "you others," mainly the soldier-knights, who are used as our representatives. There is no such split in "Funeral Music." In his essay appended to the sequence, Hill emphasizes that of the three soldiers in whose memory the poem was written, two were soldier-poets and the third was "patron of humanist scholars" in addition to being "the Butcher of England." Although their behavior seems more remote from Hill's than Beckett's from Eliot's, and, as much as Hill strives to reach an Eliotic position outside the "murderousness" of their lives, he is forced, both in his mortality and in his evasiveness, to accept his oneness with them. Action and meditation are at one. He is no better than they are.

They are, moreover, as good as he is, from which inference the second poem of the sequence proceeds:

> For whom do we scrape our tribute of pain—
> For none but the ritual king? We meditate
> A rueful mystery; we are dying
> To satisfy fat Caritas, those
> Wiped jaws of stone. (Suppose all reconciled
> By silent music; imagine the future
> Flashed back at us, like steel against sun,
> Ultimate recompense.) Recall the cold
> Of Towton on Palm Sunday before dawn,
> Wakefield, Tewkesbury: fastidious trumpets
> Shrilling into the ruck; some trampled
> Acres, parched, sodden or blanched by sleet,
> Stuck with strange-postured dead. Recall the wind's
> Flurrying, darkness over the human mire.[8]

The soldier-poets are granted the meditativeness of the poet-historian as he is given an active involvement in their death and dying. The distinction between them as dead and him as living is erased so that the observations, the Neo-Platonic hopes, and the acidic doubts are all fused as part of the experience of the "us" of the poem. Because of the firm oneness of the poem, its doubleness is so delicate as to be almost inarticulable. Even in its unarticulated light, however, the crudeness which results from Eliot's splitting apart of action (that of the knights) and meditation (Beckett's and his own) is made harshly apparent. Nonetheless, the poem is double and needs to be read two ways at once. One way emphasizes the desperate desolation of the worldly battle, the worthlessness of all it involved, unless it was undergone with "an equable contempt," as is implicit in the phrase "fastidious trumpets/ Shrilling into the ruck," a phrase that points to that image of beatific redemption imagined in lines six and seven, "the future/ Flashed back at us, like steel against sun,/ Ultimate recompense." The way of reading that doubles this blames the desolation on the beatific image, and insists that the desolation, the trampled acres, are the only reality, and the paradisal image for which one sacrifices his worldly self destructively is truly a monstrous, illusory fancy, "fat Caritas, those/ Wiped jaws of stone." There is, furthermore, a sense of how much alike beatific atonement and the desolation of utter loss are. The last sentence, "Recall the wind's/ Flurrying, darkness over the human mire," which seems an awful judgment on the meaninglessness of the Battle of Towton and the lives and deaths it engulfed has an element of awesome mystery in its hushed silence which seems at one with the beatific "Suppose all reconciled/ By silent music." There is a touch of that peace that passes understanding in the way the poem ends, just as there is a touch of arbitrary destructiveness in the "reconciled/ By silent music," because it is preceded by the slightly frivolous "Suppose" and then followed by an appositive image which with its "Flashed" and "steel against sun" sounds harsh, aggressive, and militant, even if the "ultimate recompense." Curiously, the angelic, the heavenly, music is harsher ("fastidious trumpets") than its worldly counterpart, "the wind's/ Flurrying."

The movement of "Funeral Music" is, thus, linear, developmental, sequential. There is a momentous thrust forward between the first and second poems; the second bears the first with it and yet grows beyond it in the subtlety and delicacy of its onenesses and its divisivenesses. And yet, though the individual poems do not move as sonnets—in which sestet follows octet and yet must be experienced as simultaneous with it—the sequence as a whole does work in just that way. One reads the second poem as building on the first and going beyond it, but once one has done that, he cannot but return to the first poem and feel and respond to it as containing what he had discovered as the essential, silent combat of the gap, that between Hill and Eliot, and also the mysterious doubleness that pervades the communal oneness of the second poem.

Consider, for instance, the phrase "Psalteries whine through the empyrean," which read at this point will doubtless seem the very heart of the first poem. It is an unavoidable evasive movement toward heaven, following upon the anguishing repulsiveness of "Spattering block-straw with mortal residue," which one really does not want to contemplate at all. It echoes these two lines from "Little Gidding," which open the Dantesque "dead patrol" episode:

> After the dark dove with the flickering tongue
> Had passed below the horizon of his homing[9]

The movement of Eliot's lines is in accord with his form of history; it is a movement of disengagement from the worldly and temporal. The "dark dove" is a fighter bomber on the way to being the Holy Ghost, the one destructive in an earthly way, the other, though also snakelike with its "flickering tongue," destructive for salvation. Hill's lines are implicated in the same movement, from spattered block-straw to empyrean. But the word "whine" adds a movement, drags the fleeing ghost back into its flesh, which marks all the difference between Eliot and Hill. The ascent is a movement of craven self-pity, even though twanged out on psalteries. Moreover, especially with Eliot's "dark dove" fighter bomber evoked, one cannot but recall "The nasal whine of power whips a new universe" from "Cape Hatteras," and, with that recall, he will also recognize that Hill's judgment of this *poésie des departs* is not at all Eliot's (who felt that by way of it Baudelaire glimpsed beatitude), but is much the same as Crane's

> Seeing himself an atom in a shroud—
> Man hears himself an engine in a cloud![10]

Sensing his small empty worthlessness, man soars heavenward as an aeronaut. Crane has been scorned for lauding modern technology in its expansive conquest of space. Like Hill, he did, it is true, sympathize with that effort because he recognized the authenticity of the need behind it; but, also like Hill, Crane felt the emptiness of the effort (to be sensed even in the "engine in a cloud," which, because of the clanging rhyme with "shroud," is felt to be indistinguishable from the "atom in a shroud"), so that he insisted that the flight must be curved back earthward, or else it will turn back of its own accord in an uncontrollably destructive way.

"Funeral Music" is held together not by a narrative line or by recurrent imagery, but by problems in the relationship between the poet-historian and his subject, the soldier-poets. Even though it seems magnificent when read as both sequential and simultaneous, it is always edged with a problem in painful need of solution, so that it does not move like a broad and deep river, but twists and turns, swerves or shrinks. If, for instance, their oneness, their being a "we," is implicit in the "one" and "they" of the first poem, the unison of the "we" of the second is ruffled by a latent doubleness. The "we" of that poem is not an achieved oneness which is then sustained for the rest of the sequence. Indeed, it is immediately broken by the sarcasm with which the third poem opens: "They bespoke doomsday and they meant it by/ God." Even more striking that poem is made up of four quite discrete voices, ranging from a modern voice that dismisses the whole bloody mess with " 'Oh, that old northern business . . .' " to a voice spoken from the field itself, at the end of the battle: "Blindly the questing snail, vulnerable/ Mole emerge, blindly we lie down . . ."

In response to such disintegrative cacophony, the fourth poem is Hill's single, mortal combat with Averroes, who would put an end to conflict by collapsing all diversity into a single identity, that of the mind, the Intellect, as "absolute law," "sufficient grace." Speaking in his own, single voice, Hill refuses to reject the world as a "waste history" or "void rule"; arguing against any sort of Eliotic fusion of soul with intellect and against structuralist reductions of individual men to anonymous Language, he insists on his own identity, on the inviolability of his soul, and with his single voice he is arguing for us all. The gentle, isolate beauty of the fourth poem is drowned out at once, however, by the large, common "we" voice which speaks the whole of the fifth poem. This "we" begins by echoing the last line of the fourth poem, to show that it thinks of itself as in entire accord with Hill. At the start, at least all Christians are meant to be included in its "we"; but by the end it is clearly excluding from its "we" all its opponents, who of course are to be thought of as "the damned." Indeed, as the poem ends, it is affirming the unison of its "we" while enjoying the howls of those it is torturing to death,

> Those righteously-accused those vengeful
> Racked on articulate looms indulge us
> With lingering shows of pain, a flagrant
> Tenderness of the damned for their own flesh:

The colon with which the fifth poem ends and the way the sixth begins

> My little son, when you could command marvels
> Without mercy, outstare the wearisome
> Dragon of sleep, I rejoiced above all—
> A stranger well-received in your kingdom.

indicate that one of "the damned" is speaking the sixth poem (he addresses his own flesh tenderly with "My little son") and that he is no more or less partisan than the inflated "we" of the fifth poem, whom Hill pricked sharply with his use of "righteously-accused" in place of "rightly-accused."

Hill's closeness to the dying soldier-poet of the sixth poem is confirmed by the seventh poem, which is a duet between Hill and another soldier-poet, whose sense of himself is the same as that of the soldier-poet of the sixth poem. The voice in quotation marks is that of the soldier, who died in the Battle of Towton and who wins our admiration by judging himself, his life, and the murderous behavior of the armies, with both of which he identifies his existence, as damnable and abandoned to oblivion. The other voice is that of the impersonal, modern poet-historian, who by way of images presented objectively concurs harshly and objectionably with the judgment of the self-condemning soldier:

> Reddish ice tinged the reeds; dislodged, a few
> Feathers drifted across; carrion birds
> Strutted upon the armour of the dead.[11]

This conclusion to the poem fixes fearfully the sense that the men who fought at Towton are of no more consequence or value than carrion birds. When the armies met, at noon, "each mirrored the other;/ Neither was outshone." At the end, their armor mirrors the carrion birds, which strut as they strutted. The dislodged feathers may be from the helmets of the dead or from the carrion birds; it is a matter of indifference.

The eighth and last poem tends to evaporate vaguely unless it is read in close relation with the end of the seventh.

> Not as we are but as we must appear,
> Contractual ghosts of pity; not as we
> Desire life but as they would have us live,
> Set apart in timeless colloquy:
> So it is required; so we bear witness,
> Despite ourselves, to what is beyond us,
> Each distant sphere of harmony forever
> Poised, unanswerable. If it is without
> Consequence when we vaunt and suffer, or
> If it is not, all echoes are the same
> In such eternity. Then tell me, love,
> How that should comfort us—or anyone
> Dragged half-unnerved out of this worldly place,
> Crying to the end 'I have not finished'.[12]

Especially as it ends, the seventh poem has the narrowest and most fierce focus of the entire sequence. The very rhythm of its last line affects one like sharp blows on the chest. The eighth poem, in contrast, is like an escape of breath, a withdrawal, an evacuation. It is like a release of pressure, the mouth of a balloon untied and the air going out of it. Hill seems to have contrived the poem as an emergency exit from the torment, allowing for a touch of that "vital relaxation" which is the pride of Larkin's poetry. Who is "we"? Who is "they"? Is there any specifiable referent of "Each distant sphere of harmony" or for "such eternity"? The lines seem so ungraspable that one wouldn't feel it if they were being pulled away from him. It seems touched with a light or hollow heart, as if one were to chuckle mindlessly at Hill's finishing the sequence with the phrase, " 'I have not finished'."

No matter how the poem is read, it seems clear that evasiveness must be a crucial part of it. The evasiveness, however, is clearly judged to be just that within the poem. In consequence, by folding the poem back into relation with the rest of the sequence, one discovers that, even though evasive, the poem has a strength and significance equal to its concluding position.

Like the rest of the sequence, this eighth poem is two poems. In one poem, the "we" is the soldier-poets; in the other, the "we" is the modern poet-historian and his like. If the "we" is the soldier-poets, the "they" refers to modern poet-historians who set their subjects apart in an unending line of historical reconstructions of their lives. If, in contrast, the "we" is the modern poet-historian and his like, then the "they" is soldier-poets, whose past lives, dualistically split between the brutish and the spiritually evasive, have determined that the "we" must live, appear, and bear witness as it does. Hill encourages one to slip about with both of these readings by making "Set apart" modify ambiguously both "us" and "they." There is, moreover, an evasiveness about both poems which prevents their being dramatically at odds. At least in the first sentence, which covers the opening seven-and-a-half lines, the "we" seems to refer not just to the soldier-poets and not just to the modern poet-historian and his like, but to all men, indiscriminately. That "we must appear," as "Contractual ghosts of pity," echoes the first line of the entire sequence, suggesting that in "this worldly place," not one's being or reality is in question, but only one's appearance. As by contract, all men, who are really souls, are required to appear pitiably, in the flesh, as in chains. The "they" would then refer vaguely to non-human forces, to the gods of Olympus or the inexorable forces of nature, or, in any case, to whatever is, unspecifiably, "beyond us,/ Each distant sphere of harmony forever/ Poised, unanswerable." Those "spheres" cannot be pressed into definite meaning, because, however one takes them, they slip away as "beyond us" toward the unthinkably non-human. The effect of the first sentence is thus an evaporating away from the fearful definiteness of the end of the seventh poem. Each specific "we" is not just itself to the exclusion of the other, but also the vague, inauthentic, rhetorical "we" whose inflatedness dominated the fifth poem.

The second and third sentences of the poem pull divisively away from this doubling, tripling "we" of the first sentence and also from each other. With its "vaunt and suffer" and its stern resignation, the second sentence clearly belongs to the exemplary self-judging soldier-poets of poems six and seven. In contrast, the third and concluding sentence,

> Then tell me, love,
> How that should comfort us—or anyone
> Dragged half-unnerved out of this worldly place,
> Crying to the end 'I have not finished'.

belongs to the poet-historian, most particularly in the personal, isolate form he takes in the fourth poem, defending his soul against Averroes. As he is heard here, squirming evasively, fudging, self-deceiving, soft, and craven, one feels that Hill is bringing the whole sequence to bear upon himself in the form of a self-judgment as pitiless as that which the soldier-poet of the seventh poem made of himself. The language suggests that the speaker is adopting an unearned conviction (not unlike Milton's conviction in "How soon hath time") that there are superhuman creatures, perhaps seraphim, to do the dragging, that if this world is "this worldly place," then perhaps there is also an otherworldly place, and that, if one is only "half-unnerved," it is because the other half of him senses that his cry, 'I have not finished,' will be heard by him who has otherworldly tasks in store for him. The tone of this last sentence calls attention to itself as self-judged, especially because of the strength of the sentence just before it, where the very idea of "comfort" is unthinkable, and also in contrast with the calm, unruffled objectivity of the poet-historian at the end of the seventh poem, where his descriptive lines judge implicitly not himself, but another.

The most striking way, however, in which Hill brings to the forefront the self-condemnatory quality of this last sentence is in its echoing the end of "Dover Beach." "Then tell me, love" echoes

Ah, love, let us be true
To one another! for the world, which seems
To lie before us like a land of dreams,
So various, so beautiful, so new,
Hath really neither joy, nor love, nor light,
Nor certitude, nor peace, nor help for pain;
And we are here as on a darkling plain
Swept with confused alarms of struggle and flight,
Where ignorant armies clash by night.[13]

The innermost problem of "Dover Beach" is much like that of "Funeral Music": when "the Sea of Faith" has withdrawn "down the vast edges drear/ And naked shingles of the world," and yet armies continue to "clash by night," then they must be called "ignorant" because of the meaninglessness, the bestiality, of their behavior. What else can one do himself but withdraw in fearful comfort with his love, who materializes out of nowhere upon call, her presence unfelt and unprepared for until this last moment. Hill's phrase, "Then tell me, love" brings Arnold's poem to mind with a jolt not because the words or phrasing or even the subject are so much alike, but mainly because his "love" is so unexpected, and Arnold's poem is the classic case of such an arbitrary gesture of evasion. Hill's "love" has none, of course, of the romantic feeling of Arnold's; there is no "ah", no "let us be true." No, his "love" is a gutted word, it is the "love" spoken by shopkeeper to customer. Hill's commonness and softness as poet-historian is exposed, thus, by being pushed up against the commonness and softness of Arnold.

Unquestionably, Hill is crushed by the end of the sequence. But his being so comes through as extraordinary strength, comparable to that of the soldier-poets of poems six and seven. They expose and judge and accept themselves as abandoned. Finding such austere resignation unbearable, Hill makes his evasions, but exposing them and condemning them for what they are. He shares the need of Eliot to align himself as poet-historian with a superior position like that of the martyr-saint, but, unlike Eliot, at the very time he gives vent to that need, Hill exposes it to the withering light of truth. Against Eliot's tendency, even in *Four Quartets*, to withdraw into "a world of speculation," Hill binds the meditativeness of his poetry fiercely to ethical action in a worldly sense. Because of this, it must be sharply distinguished from that philosophical aspect of Eliot's poetry which has led Alessandro Serpieri, in his *T. S. Eliot: le strutture profonde* (Bologna, 1973), to treat Eliot as a precursor of all the main "deep structure" movements of the century, which begin close to experience, close to poetry, close to the pang of the flesh of language, but then light-headedly beat a quick retreat to the mountainous clouds of abstractive vacuousness. Hill himself underwent the movement, but did not succumb to the massiveness of its inertial drag. Instead he has wrestled himself away from it and bent himself back into a strange, dramatic oneness with men, both of the past, like Tiptoft, Rivers, and Suffolk, and the present, like T. S. Eliot, who are fundamentally different from him.

CHAPTER FOUR

Poetic Omissions in Geoffrey Hill's Most Recent Sequences

Breaks, gaps, disjunctures have been important in Geoffrey Hill's poetry almost from the start, but they are most striking in three recent sequences, "The Songbook of Sebastian Arrurruz" (which concludes *King Log*, 1968), *Mercian Hymns* (1971), and "Lachrimae" in *Tenebrae* (London: André Deutsch, 1978). The texts of these sequences are themselves so simple as to make one question momentarily whether the finest poet in England is not trying to imitate its most popular, Philip Larkin. But no, the difference is as extreme as ever. Hill achieves the simpleness of his text in a way that charges one's sense of it with concentrated depth and intensity; what he omits, that which goes unsaid, is evoked as part of one's experience of the text with as much precision as is given to what one sees and hears; the two are interdependent and each grows and grows as if the other were its necessary soil. The power of these sequences increases as one's awareness of exactly what Hill has omitted increases. They are a "hoard of destructions."

Larkin's simpleness is very different. He excludes complications before he begins. If a reader is at all aware of what is missing from the poems, it is with an awareness he himself brings to the poems. Larkin's simplicity is much the same as that which leads Richard Kuhns to treat Wittgenstein's *Tractatus* as a work of art which he likens to the poetry of Valéry. Wittgenstein decides from the start to leave out everything except what is the case, the facts, the world. God, self, the mystical are on principle out of bounds. So, Kuhns says,

> Somehow the writer, the producer of texts, must hide what he feels. And the very effort to hide that side of thought, so strenuously exhibited in the *Tractatus*, leads us to sense something beyond the text, as God and the self lie beyond the world of facts. All of the creative thinker's mystical reality lies outside the text, as the mystical lies outside the world. In both the unutterable is, in this sense, contained in what is uttered.[1]

A sharp, positivistic distinction between fact and fiction, what can and what cannot be said, is to be found in the *Tractatus*. But surely the refusal to give any attention to what does not fall within the limits of the facts is as close as Wittgenstein comes to containing the unutterable in what is uttered. In a similar sense, but only in this sense, the complications which Larkin excludes are contained in his poems.

Larkin, of course, is a poet, not a philosopher, but he and Hill differ in another way which associates him with a recent Oxonian derivation from Wittgenstein, the notion that poetry is an "imitation speech-act." On the evidence of the poems, Larkin starts out, like any good popular entertainer, with a clearly established notion of a single common audience in which he would evoke an identifiable response. This does not require that he know anything about "common people," if they exist, but only that he know the "common" side of people, the weary, slack, self-indulgent, self-satisfied, inattentive, unquestioning, no-nonsense side. Hill, in contrast (but unlike the modernist poets Larkin dislikes for concentrating on their material and technique to the utter neglect of any audience), writes always for the most fully alive, emotionally vibrant, and mentally alert audience of which he is capable. To do this, he need not know about "extraordinary people," only about the "extraordinary" side of people, those aspects brought into play when a person is most fully alive and attentive. Though he has been accused of it more than once, Hill is no more "academic" than Larkin; he exceeds the academy on one side as Larkin does on the other. The joy of Larkin's poetry comes in moments of "happiness," when one is ignorant and complacent; the joy of Hill's comes in moments when one's self and world have the largeness that frees one to be aware, painfully, of his ignorance and to seek to understand their more baffling aspects. The success of Larkin's poems depends on one's feeling no need to ponder what he leaves out. Hill's poems require that one recover what has been omitted. Of course, Hill's omissions, unlike Larkin's, are recoverable. That is what makes them poetic.

The first of the eleven poems of "The Songbook of Sebastian Arrurruz" should serve to show with what an extraordinary inner ear Hill is attending to his every word. Since at no time does Hill show a sappy, indulgent affection for the sound of his own voice—a notable thing in Larkin—it does not come as a surprise that he attributes the poems of the "Songbook" to a fictitious Spanish poet said to have lived from 1868 to 1922. Hill is, however, wholly, personally engaged in the poem, though his presence is felt as silent.

> Ten years without you. For so it happens.
> Days make their steady progress, a routine
> That is merciful and attracts nobody.
>
> Already, like a disciplined scholar,
> I piece fragments together, past conjecture
> Establishing true sequences of pain;
>
> For so it is proper to find value
> In a bleak skill, as in the thing restored:
> The long-lost words of choice and valediction.[2]

The first four words are a cry of pain, pure, unmitigated, unmediated. The second four exude the calm of disciplined, scholarly propriety. The unutterable, raw pain and calm resignation, this human passion-act is what is omitted from the "text" but evoked between the two halves of the first line. It is impossible that the poet could survive without his wife. The thought of being without her is a horror. And yet he has been without her for ten years and he has survived, just as anyone would expect, for that is just the way things go. The two halves of the experience behind the line are as common as could be. Their being held together is so close to being emotionally unbearable, even in the imagination, that one wants, like a good Wittgensteinian, to quote the master's "What we cannot speak about we must pass over in silence" and to deny that poetic omissions have a force and precision that make them entirely different from those of philosophy. But the almost obsessive power of an omission like the one with which the "Songbook" opens grows in relation to one's efforts to evade it, to break it down into comfortable fragments. What one needs in order to read this and the other recent sequences is what Hill refers to as "the capacity to go against one's own apparent drift."[3] That is the most noteworthy aspect of these poems, of Hill's language, of this character, Sebastian Arrurruz, with whom he is, in my judgment, more fully in harmony than with any other figure of his creation.

Not that the "Songbook" touches upon what might be called Hill's "private life," or is a veil for a disruption of his own marriage. The poem is personal in a different sense. Hill is asking, what if, instead of following the common, evasive practice of slamming the door on the anguish of one's wife's leaving him and busying oneself archaeologically with "the provenance of shards glazed and unglazed," what if one keeps all his acumen turned back on that anguish, all his acuteness on such harrowing loss? Or, in relation to Hill's ever-present secret sharer, what if Eliot had not turned away from anguishing personal experience into a life of impersonal, spiritual devotion; what if the Harry of *The Family Reunion* had not been allowed to make his escape by way of a spiritual beloved like Agatha from his emotional entanglement with his drowned wife? As Stendhal said, the English forgive because they forget; hence their emptiness. Latins never forgive because they are too passionate in their love and in their hate ever to forget. The fiction of the sequence as Spanish is personally meaningful in a way that is distinctly Hill's.

The "Songbook" is just eleven fragments pieced together with scholarly discipline, but they are not just fragments for they are "true sequences of pain," past moments of pain ordered painfully. In appearance, they are the result of "a bleak skill," a scholarly ordering of data; read as including the omitted, evocable experience, they have the value of "the thing restored," felt life brought back alive. What is omitted, for instance, is a syntactical link between "Ten years without you" and "Already" in line four. When that link is felt, when one realizes that the poet is surprised that in so short a time as ten years he could have achieved the self-control to have even a thought about his loss without breaking down, then the first four words of the poem cannot be mistaken for an elliptical statement of fact, but will have the immediacy of pure outcry.

The second poem of the sequence begins in such a way as to call attention to the true link of pain between one fragment and another. The first poem ends with the suggestion that the poet might restore in this songbook the words with which his wife and he chose to separate and said farewell. The first of the four fragments of the second poem goes:

'One cannot lose what one has not possessed'.
So much for that abrasive gem.
I can lose what I want. I want you.

I take the first line as something his wife actually said to him as she was leaving. For ten years that devastating remark has been grating against him and now, finally, he can retort, dismissively, with his "So much," as though it had not been very much, and cleverly, with the play on "want" as meaning both lack and desire. The amazement of the lines no doubt comes from the breakdown of temporal distance in the poet's experience. The ten-year span is felt as necessary for the poet to put these words down, but in putting them down he collapses into the moment ten years before, when the words were spoken, at which point he was so flooded with grief that the idea of calling those words—which, of course, declare that he never did possess her as his love so he should not think of himself as actually losing her—"that abrasive gem" (echoing the sarcasm of "What a gem!") exceeds imagining. Even imaginatively, even by himself ten years after the event, the poet's control is matched by the uncontrollability of his passions. Reason and passion, present and past, the imaginary and the real, their coming together as true sequences of pain is the unutterable, the unsayable, which one experiences from poem to poem of the sequence, so long as one does not read like a sieve, letting the words go through emptily, but rather exercises one's "capacity to go against one's own apparent drift" and attends to the way in which Hill is listening to what is set down.

Such meticulous precision embodying such agony, there has

probably been nothing quite like it since Petrarch. Of course, in contrast to the *Canzoniere*, the "Songbook" is limited to eleven brief poems. In contrast, however, to the slackness of the relations among Petrarch's poems, Hill's poems are bound with such fiery threads of omitted pain as to have the largeness of "true sequences of pain," in spite of their sparse and fragmentary character. The innermost felt meaning of two of the poems set next to each other is apt to come upon one slowly; each burns durably with a fire embedded deeply at its center. The real explosion, however, the experience of which frees one from his sense that human beings are now unavoidably small, without courage, without the capacity to love in pain, occurs when the central fires of the two poems touch in the gap between them. Consider, an instance of this, the following pair:

9 A Song From Armenia

Roughly-silvered leaves that are the snow
On Ararat seen through those leaves.
The sun lays down a foliage of shade.

A drinking-fountain pulses its head
Two or three inches from the troughed stone.
An old woman sucks there, gripping the rim.

Why do I have to relive, even now,
Your mouth, and your hand running over me
Deft as a lizard, like a sinew of water? [4]

On the other side of the Mediterranean, pursuing his archeological interests, the poet concentrates on the reverse of what matters to him, even now, ten years later. By shedding light the sun does, and only in this way, lay down a foliage of shade. The truth of this first stanza is its disturbing barb: it nestles securely in one's dormant imagination, asking softly if some deep emotional defeat is not necessarily the obverse side of every scholarly career. The second and third stanzas then provide the sunny and shady sides of a single, personal experience of the poet's. The effect of the second stanza issues out of its special omission, one's sense of the lonely, motionless, empty man making his minute observation. What then floods his mind, in the third stanza, is a question in part answered by the first: as shade to sun, so the necessity that whatever he views, however remote in appearance from anything to do with his wife, it will bring some aspect of her nature or behavior back to mind. What comes back to him this time, in those last two lines, is exceedingly sensuous and delicate. The slightest hint of the ungraspable, unpossessable, insubstantial quality of her beauty and attractiveness will probably not occur to one until the poem has settled for some time up against what follows:

10 To His Wife

You ventured occasionally—
As though this were another's house—
Not intimate but an acquaintance
Flaunting her modest claim; like one
Idly commiserated by new-mated
Lovers rampant in proper delight
When all their guests have gone.
[1921] [5]

The seeing double of this poem is a form of astigmatism; its two halves relate with an overlapping, blurring effect. The more obvious half, with its focus on the wife alone and on her strangeness, is wrenched out of focus by the odd suggestion of the last three lines that the wife, who as one of the guests of the lovers, or so it would seem, must have gone away, is nonetheless present enough to be "idly commiserated" by them. Out of this distortion must surely come the other half of the poem with its sense that the lovers are the husband and the wife, not in her strangeness, but in his sense of how he imagined her as sharing the delight he felt in their love-making. The delicate, endearing quality of "ventured occasionally" and "Flaunting her modest claim" suggests that he adored her so much as to feel that he and she were like "new-mated/ Lovers rampant in proper delight" just because of her strange aloofness, so that even for him, in the intensity of love-making, she was present both as the imagined one of the lovers and as the ghostly guest idly (because not exactly attended to) commiserated by the lovers, both actual and imagined. He loved her as if the delight were mutual, but only or mainly because it was not, because she was there to be commiserated, never having entered into the love-making with abandon.

But, then, his relation with her even when they were together and their love seemed fullest was, strictly speaking, the obverse side of his relation with her in the ninth poem, after they have been separated for many years. Nothing is so ungraspable as "a sinew of water," as if one truly loved another only after she was dead and become as insubstantial as a shadow. The poet may now have to renege on his earlier, petulant insistence that he can lose what he wants. His wife could never really have left him if her strangeness, her remoteness, her always being absent from him, is what he most loved in her. Perhaps he is no more than a self-wounded martyr; if he is mourning a lack, the very joy lost was based on a lack. There was no real touch between him and another. His entire life has been, as it is, self-enclosed. He has no grounds for grieving, then, for his grief is his joy.

By analogy, moreover, Hill must face the possibility that, having set this poem against the Eliotic tendency to slide evasively away from personal pain to ataraxic detachment, his own self-indulgent pleasure as a poet has to do with his always seeing double, always being double, never that is being able to love another wholly or even live a single event wholly, because he is always also thinking of something else, always also composing a line, being a poet as well as a husband. Say, however, that being whole requires being double, "A seeing and unseeing in the eye." But what a queer, self-torn wholeness. Say, even, Eliot was, perhaps, so great a poet because he was able to live a love relation with such single wholeness that it became a grief from which he had to withdraw evasively; so his poetry is impersonal because he had a personality from which to escape. Hill, in contrast, does not withdraw evasively, because evasive withdrawal is an essential part of even his most intensely emotional relationship, as though one were to say that a man could never truly die because there was so much deadness in his life. Hill's greatness, in the "Songbook" as elsewhere, spins unmistakably and awesomely out of that silent maelstrom of self-criticism, a greatness that makes one wish he could relax a little, after the manner of Larkin.

Hill's longest work, *Mercian Hymns*, a volume composed of thirty short prose poems, is like *The Waste Land*, if one can imagine it as written at the end of Eliot's career as a critique of all that he had done out of his sense of being Catholic, Royalist, and Classical. Whereas Larkin speaks openly of his dislike for Eliot and Pound and ignores them in his work, Hill's minimalist poems are not small because, instead of ignoring Eliot and Pound, he takes them on in an effort to supersede them. It is not his subject matter or his view of his subject so much as it is this intimate relation between his poetry and that of his immediate, great predecessors that makes Hill's work quintessentially historical.

Donald Davie, treating the making of poetry as determined by what precedes it historically, claimed that it is inevitable that Pound's disastrous career

> will rule out (has ruled out already, for serious writers) any idea that a poet can or should operate in the dimension of history, trying to make sense of the recorded past by redressing our historical perspectives. . . . the poet's vision of the centuries of recorded time has been invalidated by the *Cantos* in a way that invalidates also much writing by Pound's contemporaries. History, from now on, may be transcended in poetry, or it may be evaded there; but poetry is not the place where it may be understood.[6]

This statement sounds slightly foolish now, because of Hill's volume. Contemporary in the Crocean sense, like all serious history, *Mercian Hymns* sets forth Hill's sense of England's past in combative, critical relationship with a radically different sense of that past, a sense that itself had a strong influence on the way England took part in the Second World War, that war being, of course, crucial to the most recent part of Hill's sense of England's past. Although that past sense of the past is only latent in *Mercian Hymns*, it is nonetheless against it that the poem is composed, and it is delineated sharply, even if only implicitly, as inflated and false. It was T. S. Eliot's sense of the past and that of his main authority, Christopher Dawson, whose *The Making of Europe* shows England and Europe emerging as Catholic, Imperial, and Classical (at about the time of the death of Offa, King of Mercia and the main figure in *Mercian Hymns*). Hill's volume is poetry, but it is also quintessential history in the sense that it presents that felt tangle out of which a recent historian, like Christopher Brooke, in his *The Saxon and Norman Kings* (Macmillan, 1963) writes of the formative years of England in a way that is sharply at odds with Dawson's way, back in 1931. The conflict, it should be added, is not just academic, for Dawson's way was Eliot's way and it was the way that carried the Empire into and through the Second World War. If there is any single event in history a detestation of the sordid qualities of which centers Hill's life as man and poet, it is that war.

The matrix out of which *Mercian Hymns* germinates is not just a poetic and a historical motive, but also an ethical one. As Hill's recent essays indicate, he feels very close ethically to Simone Weil (for whose *The Need for Roots* Eliot wrote the preface). The crucial sequence of her thoughts out of which the *Hymns* grow is as follows:

> Four obstacles above all separate us from a form of civilization likely to be worth something: our false conception of greatness; the degradation of the sentiment of justice; our idolization of money; and our lack of religious inspiration . . . Our conception of greatness is the very one that has inspired Hitler's whole life.[7]

Offa as King of Mercia from 756 to 796 and also as what Hill takes him to be, "the presiding genius of the West Midlands, his dominion enduring from the middle of the eighth century until the middle of the twentieth (and possibly beyond)," has no "sentiment of justice," idolizes money, and is without a trace of religious inspiration. Weil, who of course makes no mention of Offa, adds that

> Each of us can at this very moment commence Hitler's punishment inside his own mind, by modifying the scope of the sentiment attaching to greatness. This is far from being an easy matter, for a social pressure as heavy and enveloping as the surrounding atmosphere stands opposed thereto. So as to be able to carry it out, one has to exclude oneself spiritually from the rest of society . . . [One should] make a pact with oneself to admire in history only those actions and lives through which shines the spirit of truth, justice, and love.[8]

The Offa figure of the *Hymns* is presented as "great" in the sense that he is powerful, dynamic, aggressive, combative, fearful, and fearsome, a maker of strategies in the line of "animal cunning." What he lacks, essentially, is "the spirit of truth, justice, and love."

If one follows out the page numbers of the references in the Notes appended to the *Mercian Hymns* (they are made to seem just fussy enough to remind one of the Notes appended to *The Waste Land*), he will find that, unlike Eliot, Hill is truly being helpful. He is pointing, mainly, to the important omission from the *Hymns*, that sense of English history against which he is struggling. For example, he begins by saying that his title comes from Sweet's *Anglo-Saxon Reader*, Oxford (Twelfth Edition, 1950), pp. 170–80. The inclusion of edition and page numbers at first amuses, but when one turns to them he finds a section entitled "Mercian Hymns," and six religious songs in a non-West-Saxon dialect, one of which is a translation of the Benedictus (Luke 1.68–79) and another of the Magnificat (Luke 1.46–55). Following up what Hill says next ("A less-immediate precedent is provided by the Latin prose-hymns or canticles of the early Christian Church. See Frederick Brittain, ed., *The Penguin Book of Latin Verse*, Harmondsworth [1962], pp. xvii, lv.), one finds, amid some commentary, the *Te Deum*. It is not, then, the omission from the *Mercian Hymns* of any hint of religious inspiration that is striking so much as the omission of religious magnificence, of the Christian worship of an omnipotent Father, the *Patrem immensae majestatis* of the *Te Deum*, the mighty monarch who arranged the Pax Augusta so that his religion could spread, the religiosity which goes along with the Roman Empire and with its intellectual glorification by way of classical thought, Vergil's, Augustine's, and Eliot's favorite, Dante, for whom Church and Empire were inseparable and interdependent.

Dawson's England-Europe originates out of a theocracy which he finds to be more thorough than its Byzantine counterpart, the Carolingian Empire, with Charlemagne's sense of his holiness as emperor bolstered by that Anglo-Saxon learned monk, Alcuin, who, one may guess, found Offa too uncouth (he must, indeed, have been illiterate) for his purposes. The locked knot of Church, State, and Culture is what Dawson as well as Eliot were defending in the thirties against the rising tide of barbarism (communist and, for Eliot at least, also fascist). In contrast to the magnificent tradition which Eliot was defending, Hill's *Hymns* are thorough prose, without poetic aura. Of course, they are constantly calling attention to what they lack, the resonance of a glorious, good, truthful, beautiful civilization, that civilization which Dawson presents as historically existent and of which Eliot dreamed himself to be a part. Dawson felt that the historical truth of the eighth and ninth centuries could be found only in or through the monasteries. The only written records were there, the only civilized life of the time took place in them. Outside there were no cities, scarcely even any markets, and life went on tribally, barbarically. Christopher Brooke, in contrast (and what Hill actually presents in the *Hymns* is in accord with Brooke's approach) rules out all written records from the monasteries as illegitimate, because, by ornamenting their subjects with their own religious culture, the monks falsified them. Limiting himself to archeological evidence, Brooke gives the impression that Dawson's "crowned knot of fire" was an illusion.

Hill's Offa is earthy, bestial, greedy, selfish, ignorant, and cunning. He comes at one as condemned by the omitted vision, a king like Charlemagne or like Alfred the Great. At the same time, with scruples about saying only what is the case, like Brooke, by sticking to prose and omitting the poetry, Hill is condemning the Eliot-Dawson State-Church-Culture knot as false and inflated. Thus, beyond what Simone Weil or any of his sources could have taught him, Hill is condemning the Hitler figure as he is and he is condemning the myths with which he has been grandly disguised. A man needs roots, Hill agrees with Simone Weil. One's own roots, one's West Midland roots, are ugly facts and glorious illusions to hide those facts. Having made a pact with himself "to admire in history only those actions and lives through which shines the spirit of truth, justice, and love," Hill is evidently finding nothing to admire. That he would admire, that he must find something worthy of admiration, this, however, is the deepest omission from the *Hymns*, that which gives its unsavory facts and grandiose illusions their peculiarly thud-like quality. If one attends only to what is given in the *Hymns*, as though they were small verse like Larkin's, the volume would not be so poignantly repulsive. Even the epigraph, however, to the English edition, a quotation from C. H. Sisson about the essential sameness of public and private life, calls attention to Hill's sense that what truly matters in both private and public life are men's ends, their objectives; and if there is anything obviously missing from the givenness of the *Hymns*, it is attention to ends in the sense of "What for, what ultimately for?"

The lack of any attention to ends and also Hill's sense that the ends dwelt upon and spread glossily over the past by the preceding generation were illusions are brought together vividly in the twenty-fourth and twenty-fifth hymns. Hill imagines, in the twenty-fourth, a master mason whose accurate sense of Offa's nature led him in his work to confuse "warrior with lion, dragon-coils, tendrils of the stony vine." How can one best view that artist's work?

> Where best to stand? Easter sunrays catch the oblique face
>   of Adam scrumping through leaves; pale spree of
>   evangelists and, there, a cross Christ mumming child
>   Adam out of Hell
>
> ('Et exspecto resurrectionem mortuorum' dust in the eyes,
>   on clawing wings, and lips)[9]

The best place to stand is where one can see the "dust in the eyes," see that the notion of the resurrection of the dead was just part of royal policy, an opiate for the masses. The master mason knew that and embodied it in his work, and Offa knew it too. He, for instance, could make nothing of "remorse" (see the tenth hymn). If a man was killed, his wergild, his value, had to be paid and that was an end of it, an adequate exculpation of the killer. The idea of remorse, of penance, of a penitentiary, of being imprisoned for a time in a monastery, as was the practice in Italy, the notion that man's life differed spiritually from that of badger and raven, Offa never took such an idea seriously.[10]

An "I," "brooding on the eightieth letter" of Ruskin's *Fors Clavigera*, says he speaks the twenty-fifth hymn "in memory of my grandmother, whose childhood and prime womanhood were spent in the nailer's darg." The two paragraphs which follow the first one (it is repeated as the fourth and final paragraph) go:

> The nailshop stood back of the cottage, by the fold. It
>   reeked stale mineral sweat. Sparks had furred its low

roof. In dawn-light the troughed water floated a damson-bloom of dust—

not to be shaken by posthumous clamour. It is one thing to celebrate the 'quick forge', another to cradle a face hare-lipped by the searing wire.[11]

That one's end is the glory of an empire like that of Rome (suggested by the chorus, *Henry V* v, 1–45, from which a note says the phrase 'quick forge' comes, though the line number of the phrase is not given so that one must skim the whole passage and catch a flash of such glory) and the immortal life of one's soul is fiercely repudiated here in sorrow over the way a life was wasted because of such illusions. The hymn is made personal by the way Hill takes on Eliot in the sentence: "In dawn-light the troughed water floated a damson-bloom of dust—// not to be shaken by posthumous clamour." This sentence recalls Eliot's

> My words echo
> Thus, in your mind.
> But to what purpose
> Disturbing the dust on a bowl of rose-leaves
> I do not know.[12]

The purpose, it will be remembered, is to recall the rose garden of one's first world, that image of perfection from childhood out of which Eliot's "religious inspiration" grows. The "damson-bloom of dust" floating on "the troughed water" in the nailshop where the "I"'s grandmother spent her childhood will not be shaken as was Eliot's "dust on a bowl of rose-leaves," because there was no hint of beauty in the childhood she was forced to expend for the glory of church and empire. The fragility of the voice of "Burnt Norton," its not being "clamorous," simply points to the delusion Eliot too was under. Living English poets, it seems, have difficulty keeping their memory of Eliot separate from that of Churchill.

Not, however, that Hill is being merely personal, grinding away against Eliot with animus. Probably the *Pisan Cantos*, especially as they are viewed by Donald Davie, are as important an antagonist in the *Mercian Hymns*, as the fourteenth hymn should manifest.

> Dismissing reports and men, he put pressure on the wax, blistered it to a crest. He threatened malefactors with ash from his noon cigar.

> When the sky cleared above Malvern, he lingered in his orchard; by the quiet hammer-pond. Trout-fry simmered there, translucent, as though forming the water's underskin. He had a care for natural minutiae. What his gaze touched was his tenderness. Woodlice sat pellet-like in the cracked bark and a snail sugared its new stone.

> At dinner, he relished the mockery of drinking his family's health. He did this whenever it suited him, which was not often.[13]

Davie is full of praise for Pound's "care for natural minutiae" in the *Pisan Cantos*, emphasizing the Brother Wasp passage of canto 83 and "the green midge half an ant-size" of canto 80. Davie claims:

> These perceptions are possible only in an attitude of humility about the place of the human in relation to the non-human creation. And it was the shock of Pound's appalling predicament in the American prison-camp of 1945, awaiting trial for treason, that restored to him this humility, after the steady crescendo of raucous arrogance through the Chinese History and American History cantos of the years before.[14]

Davie is convinced that "this capacity for sympathetic identification with inhuman forms of life" is an adequate basis for the ethical life, a point he pushes hard in reference to Charles Tomlinson's poetry in the well-known interview with Alvarez, "A New Aestheticism?" In the fourteenth hymn, Hill is lining up Offa's hatred of and violence against all makers of men (who by making men are malefactors because every new man is another personal threat to Offa) with his tender care for woodlice and snail (Davie, in praising Pound's care for "inhuman forms of life," lumps together wasp and ant, as though they were, for his purposes, indistinguishable). Offa's hatred of men and his tenderness for woodlice and snail are not at all incompatible: together they suggest that Offa himself did not belong to the human family and so they indicate why his drinking his family's health was a mockery he relished. His "care for natural minutiae" flatters his sense of his own capacity for tenderness and so releases him to be as brutal as possible, ordering mass murders by a flick of "ash from his noon cigar."

C. H. Sisson has said that *Mercian Hymns* is Hill's most accessible poetry. For me this is inaccurate. Most of Hill's poems look dense and difficult. The simple text of the *Hymns* is deceptive and misleading, for its real poetry is silent, on the other side of the prose. Perhaps, as the epigraph to the English edition would suggest, Sisson himself is so absorbed in the ends of human acts that he feels their omission from the *Hymns* with the immediate force with which other readers would feel the presence in the text of merely strategic, cunning, self-serving behavior. In any case, the innermost truth of the *Hymns* is Hill's need for and failure to find, either in the facts or the illusions of his history, its prose or its poetry, anything worthy of one's utmost admiration.

The "Lachrimae" is just the opposite of *Mercian Hymns*, for its poetry smacks one in the eye, even so soon as its subtitle, "or Seven tears figured in seven passionate Pavans," or seven rhyme-clanged (half aslant) sonnets or imitation sonnets. Its essential omission too is special to it, being not so much in opposition to Eliot as an effort to redo "Ash Wednesday," replacing its weakest aspect, its doctrinal stiffness, with that incompleteness, that groping, that holding back, which has won admiration for "The Hollow Men." [15]

The innermost reality of *Mercian Hymns* is the omission of anything worthy of wholehearted admiration. In the "Lachrimae" Hill accepts that reality and even exacerbates it: in all of history, even when presented most poetically and most selectively, there is nothing worthy of such admiration. Indeed, nothing articulated, nothing put in words, even in words most heavily resonant with centuries of valuing, can hold one's devotion. In the climactic sixth sonnet, Hill discovers, with a forcefulness not to be sensed anywhere before, that, however regrettable it may seem, an essential quality of that which one can admire wholeheartedly is its being withheld. Moreover—and the forcefulness of the sonnet comes from this—he realizes that the right counterposition for himself is that of withholding his admiration. The discovery that the absence of his wife had always been an essential part of her attractiveness to him resulted for Sebastian Arrurruz in a condition of "now almost meaningless despair." In the "Lachrimae" the poet has turned from his Laura to his Lord and, more important, to match the withheld quality of the object of his devotion he replaces frenzied adoration with a withheld, aloof hesitancy to commit himself. Like his Lord, he absents himself from the text of the "Lachrimae."

As in "Funeral Music," the "Lachrimae" builds from one poem to the next, and yet, once the sixth sonnet is reached, the others are pulled up into simultaneity with it, so that, what had seemed like hollowness during the experience of building is felt to be folded inside-out so as to manifest the withheld quality of fulfillment. The first sonnet, for example, is built in relation to one of Sisson's best known poems, "The Usk." That poem begins with these four lines in italics:

> *Christ is a language in which we speak to God*
> *And also God, so that we speak in truth;*
> *He in us, we in him, speaking*
> *To one another, to him, the City of God* [16]

and then he proceeds to show how far he, the poet, though devoutly religious, is from any such happy condition. In the sestet of "Lachrimae Verae," Hill echoes these lines in such a way as to put the whole sequence, which is stalling helplessly in the octet, in motion:

> I cannot turn away from what I do;
> you cannot turn away from what I am.
> You do not dwell in me nor I in you
>
> however much I pander to your name
> or answer to your lords of revenue,
> surrendering the joys that they condemn. [17]

The "poetic," sing-song, rocking motion which comes at one almost sassily indicates that the language of the City of God is not something the poet aspires to, as Sisson does, but something from which he withholds himself, as though it could be spoken only by one who was nodding his head somnolently, or else mockingly. The rhythm echoes that of the second stanza of a poem Hill admires extravagantly, Wordsworth's "Intimations Ode":

> The Rainbow comes and goes,
> And lovely is the Rose,
> The Moon doth with delight
> Look round her when the heavens are bare,
> Waters on a starry night
> Are beautiful and fair;
> The sunshine is a glorious birth;
> But yet I know, where'er I go,
> That there hath past away a glory from the earth.

The sing-song rhythm of the lines indicates that though the earth, these scenes, and the very language being used remain pretty, a glory has passed out of them which alone made them worthy of one's adoration. So the language of the "Lachrimae," the language of the City of God, has been emptied of God.

The Italian critic Gianfranco Contini said that great poetry has the capacity to elicit different sorts of admiration generation after generation, to each his own, and that what he admires most about Dante's *Commedia* are its memorable phrases! A comparable hollowness rumbles beneath a sentence Hill used, enigmatically, in a recent essay: "Failing a grammar of assent, syntax may serve."[18] Even in the first sonnet, such cynicism seems to shade into something like the "wistful attention" Simone Weil was said to have devoted to the Church to which she could never, finally, assent. Or, read "Ash Wednesday" in this way: the words of Christ are tolerable because the communal phrases are heard as coming from afar, as muffled, and the speaker (who hears those phrases) is still outside the Church, taking part in Ash Wednesday in its earliest form, when it was still a question whether the aspirant would be allowed to join the communion, so that his Ash Wednesday would become what it was not as yet, a part of the ritualized church calendar, the suffering and deprivation sown with the seeds of triumphalism, anguish sealed comfortably within providential assurance. The Hill of the "Lachrimae" is on the other side of that condition. Surrendering joys according to the season, he does not come in touch with his "Crucified Lord," but rather senses that his sacrifice is for His "lords of revenue," perhaps for the propertied clergy. As a result, his assent is withheld.

The line between the first and the sixth sonnet of the sequence is a fine one, but there is genuine development which can be summed up as follows. In the first, the poet withholds his assent from what nonetheless is his religion, because every aspect of its realization in this world is corrupted by worldliness. The spiritual achievement of the sixth sonnet coincides with Simone Weil's claim that "for religious feeling to emanate from the spirit of truth, one should be absolutely prepared to abandon one's religion . . . if it should turn out to be anything other than the truth."[19]

Lachrimae Antiquae Novae

Crucified Lord, so naked to the world,
you live unseen within that nakedness,
consigned by proxy to the judas-kiss
of our devotion, bowed beneath the gold,

with re-enactments, penances foretold:
scentings of love across a wilderness
of retrospection, wild and objectless
longings incarnate in the carnal child.

Beautiful for themselves, the icons fade;
the lions and the hermits disappear.
Triumphalism feasts on empty dread,

fulfilling triumphs of the festal year.
We find you wounded by the token spear.
Dominion is swallowed with your blood.[20]

What looms behind these words is that the poet's Lord, naked and yet unseen, is simply not an object to be worshipped and is in no sense contained even within the poet's words of address, "Crucified Lord." The poet's own counterposition is one of "objectless longings," based on the sense that to take part in communion is to turn the truth into a saleable object, to swallow his Lord's blood is to swallow dominion, lordship entailing ownership, a sliding from the Lord to his "lords of revenue."

A theologician elsewhere relied on by Hill, D. M. MacKinnon, has argued that "the most devastating intellectual and spiritual temptation [for the Gospelers] was that of presenting the catastrophic course of events"—leading up to and away from the Crucifixion— "as expressive of the working of a traceable providential order."[21] The triumphalism of *Acts* indicates a succumbing to that temptation, and, for MacKinnon, it is coarse when compared with Luke, where victory comes only after a "supremely searching temptation," so that the victory is a "muted" one. MacKinnon even goes so far as to claim that the seeds for an acceptance of the holocaust of the Jewish people were sown by an apologetics which found "the Pax Augusta the divinely ordered setting for the advance of the Gospel in spite of the fierce resistance of the Jewish authorities."[22] It is such triumphalism, in any case, which has caused Hill to withhold his assent to the religion of his church.

Simone Weil's suspicions of poetry are as fierce as her suspicions of religion. After condemning Ariosto for dedicating *Orlando Furioso* to his patron, the Duke of Este, she says:

> Virgil had far too deep a sense of the proprieties to publicly place on record a commercial transaction of this nature . . . Poetry is not something for sale. God would be unjust if the *Aeneid*, which was composed under these conditions, were worth as much as the *Iliad*.[23]

Hill withdraws his assent from all the objects of his religion, and he refuses himself to be one of its objects, a communicant. Similarly, however encrusted with historical values the words of these sonnets may be and however much they seem to have been reworked by Hill, they come at one touched with dismissiveness, they tend to fade before one's eyes. Instead, the words do not belong to Hill or to our time at all; they belong rather to the sources Hill lists at the end of the sequence, to John Dowland, Peter Philips, Quevedo, Lope de Vega, and an unknown author of "A Cristo Crucificado." True beauty is at one with truth, and one feels that it is withheld from Hill's words (for they are his not to sell, to dismiss) as his Lord is withheld from the church to which Hill cannot, finally, assent.

In this culminative sonnet, however, Hill's withholding himself is felt to be a genuine spiritual achievement, because it is at one with the withheld quality of his Lord, with His being naked and unseen. How much this achievement resembles that of Hill's mortal enemy, that characteristic movement of withdrawal in the Eliot of the *Four Quartets*. Such a moment of atonement must, however, since it occurs in a poem by Hill, be followed by a seventh and last sonnet, which suggests that the withheld condition of the sixth is really just an exalted form of perpetual procrastination, a justification for endlessly putting off the moment when one openly welcomes his Lord. As a result, the sequence ends with Hill jolted loose from his momentary joy, from any sense of the rightness of the self-contradictory nature of his life, as man and poet, with each poem experienced as a crucifixion in the sense that it breaks the unsayable by saying it but only thus keeps that unsayable, that ultimate Good, alive, as the unbreakable which is being broken. It all begins to sound too formulaic, another ponderous Heideggerian pronouncement.

Living with Hill's poetry for any length of time, one must feel heavy-laden, keeping up such a mass of dense and stunning, stringent and yet magnificent poetry. At the end of a poem, or especially of a sequence, however, it seems evident that Hill himself travels light. He leaves the poems behind, as detritus. If there is a man on the dump, one who settles down to beat out his belief on an "old tin can, lard pail," it will not be the excruciatingly self-critical poet, but his reader-critic. Even under such chastisement, it seems right to insist that, if the basic movement of the Lord is from Logos to flesh and then back by ascent to invisibility, the movement of this poet, in contrast to that of his Lord and of Eliot, is from flesh to spirit to flesh, brokenly. That movement is as important to "Genesis," the first poem in Hill's first volume, the climactic line of which is "There is no bloodless myth will hold," as it is to his most recent sequence.

CHAPTER FIVE

Larkin and His Audience

Readers of Philip Larkin's poetry keep writing about it, even though they recognize how simple and clear it is, because they also sense that its most distinctive aspect is indefinable, not just in criticism of the poetry, but in the poetry itself. Because this aspect of Larkin's poetry seems by its very nature to be inexpressible, it needs speaking of in as many ways as possible, if the very sense of it is not to lapse. It seems that only the obvious can be said of Larkin, and that everyone who has written on him has said it again and again, in one way or another, since it is as simple and clear as a glass of water. Yet, because it cannot be defined, doubts remain as to whether either his most sympathetic critics, like John Wain, David Timms, and Alan Brownjohn, or his more severe, like Colin Falck, Donald Davie, and Calvin Bedient are responding to what makes Larkin's poetry of distinctive value.

Of Larkin himself, however, there can be no doubt. His choice of "Absences" as his own favorite poem for the anthology, *Poet's Choice*, as early as 1962, indicates that even then he had a sure sense of the indefinable aspect of his poetry that gives it its value. For "Absences" comes closer than any other of Larkin's poems to being explicit about what is inexplicable.

> Rain patters on a sea that tilts and sighs.
> Fast-running floors, collapsing into hollows,
> Tower suddenly, spray-haired. Contrariwise,
> A wave drops like a wall: another follows,
> Wilting and scrambling, tirelessly at play

Where there are no ships and no shallows.

Above the sea, the yet more shoreless day,
Riddled by wind, trails lit-up galleries:
They shift to giant ribbing, sift away.

Such attics cleared of me! Such absences! [1]

John Press uses "Absences," in a recent article, as an instance of
those of Larkin's poems which "evoke a world transcending the
contingencies and imperfection of daily existence," a world "whose
nature can be hinted at by the medium of images drawn from the
inexhaustible realm of nature—sun, moon, water, sky, clouds, distance." [2] Donald Davie's unarguable point that Larkin buys "sympathy with the human, at the price of alienation from the non-
human" should insure that Press is not misheard as saying that
"Absences" is a nature poem, a poem sympathetic with the non-
human. [3] For Press says only that Larkin *uses* images from nature,
and it is clear that the phrase, "the inexhaustible realm," is the
critic's, not the poet's. Press is, however, wrong to attribute a transcending world to the poet. Larkin himself is more precise. He says
of the poem: "I fancy it sounds like a different, better poet rather
than myself. The last line, for instance, sounds like a slightly unconvincing translation from a French symbolist." [4]

If "Absences" does evoke a transcendent world, it is only in the
shape of an unconvincing translation. That is what Larkin likes
about the poem. What remains, in the place of that disbelieved, denied world, is the indefinable aspect of his poetry to which I have
been pointing. The poem is "cleared of me," the biographically
identifiable ego is absent from it. Yet it is no world, natural or supernatural. It is a very human attending and exclaiming; it is nothing, that unobjectifiable, un-delimitable act of observing, thinking,
and speaking. The act itself cannot be seen or heard; in truth, it
cannot even be thought, because to think it is to objectify it, to treat
it as a mental object or fact, whereas its essential nature, as an act
that arches over and assimilates both self and world, is to be irre-
ducible to that which is other than itself, to the posited, to the fac-
tual. There is, however, nothing superhuman, Teutonic, or metaphysical about it, even though it is no part of the world as it is

thought about in the *Tractatus*. By alliterating "absences" with "attics," Larkin calls attention to its humanness, even its commonness. It is awesome only in the sense that it is invulnerable, but it is available to any and all who will simply pull back from the existent world and live the invisible, inaudible, inarticulable attending aspect of their humanity along with whatever else they have to do and suffer in the real, existent human and non-human world. Larkin is very careful to help his audience hear the last line in just this, the proper way. The conspicuous alliteration in the last line of the first stanza insures that, as the absence of all human beings is being affirmed, their presence as the undefinable act of viewing the sea as free of all human beings is gently suggested. The sea is made to remind one of a funhouse, with its collapsing floors, its tiltings and drops, its playfulness. The indefinable aspect of the poem, the saving, indefinable aspect of humanity, to which even the vast images of the sea and the sky are inadequate, is safe and homey. It has nothing to do with the fearfulness of nihilism or existentialistic absurdity. It is that absolute security into which the poem leads one to retreat from the meaninglessness of existence, of everything objective, whether ideal or real.

It is not otherworldly, only non-worldly. The "yet more shoreless day" does, of course, have its shores, as does everything in the objective world, whatever its expanse. Even the final exclamation, "Such absences!" is pressed into a delimited shape by the verbal imagining of the undelimitable no-thing who does not give himself up even to the poem as object, offering it as a self-consuming artifact, to be broken down along with all selves as entities, and assimilated into the perfect freedom of being invisibly pleased. In such freedom, there is no respect for persons, there is no hierarchic stratification, one and all are anonymous. The most authentic statement Larkin has made outside his poetry is: "I think it's important not to feel crushed."[5] That is the essence of the inexplicable freedom that gives his poems their distinctive value. However silly Larkin is willing to make himself seem within his poems, he is never crushed, because he has his true life in that undelimitable, uncrushable act of attending, of imagining, of speaking. His poems make an appeal, it is true, as though Larkin were an entertainer, who would as a result be subject to anxieties concerning the ups and downs of audience response. If the appeal fails, however, the loss is the reader's, not Larkin's, for he is never fully engaged in any objective situation or encounter, whereby he might be hurt or crushed. The same sort of aloofness, indeed, is what he offers to all, not as a way of life, but as an aspect of whatever way of life one may be connected with. It is easy of access and priceless because invulnerable.

"Solar," a poem in Larkin's most recent volume, *High Windows*, is enough like "Absences" to indicate how steady his fidelity has been. It is quite clearly "a slightly unconvincing translation from a French symbolist."

> Suspended lion face
> Spilling at the centre
> Of an unfurnished sky
> How still you stand,
> And how unaided
> Single stalkless flower
> You pour unrecompensed.
>
> The eye sees you
> Simplified by distance
> Into an origin,
> Your petalled head of flames
> Continuously exploding.
> Heat is the echo of your
> Gold.
>
> Coined there among
> Lonely horizontals
> You exist openly.
> Our needs hourly
> Climb and return like angels.
> Unclosing like a hand,
> You give for ever.[6]

Actually, this poem is an unconvincing translation not of a French symbolist, but of the final poem in Thom Gunn's *Moly*, "Sunlight." Gunn works to be precise about the sun in its non-human remoteness and otherness, and yet he also strives to be precise about the exact nature of the sun as an image of our desires. The poem ends in a highly individual address to the sun taken doubly, as it is and as it "outlasts us at the heart."

> Great seedbed, yellow centre of the flower,
> Flower on its own, without a root or stem,
> Giving all colour and all shape their power,
> Still recreating in defining them,
>
> Enable us, altering like you, to enter
> Your passionless love, impartial but intense,
> And kindle in acceptance round your centre,
> Petals of light lost in your innocence.[7]

Although Gunn seems to be in accord with Alvarez's claim that "since Freud, the late Romantic dichotomy between emotion and intelligence has become totally meaningless," he is emphasizing the stress between what one knows and what one desires.[8] It is the pain of holding the known and the desired up against each other that gives "Sunlight" its power. That power, moreover, is enhanced by the way Gunn's sunlight refracts light coming to him from "Burnt Norton" IV ("After the kingfisher's wing/ Has answered light to light, and is silent, the light is still/ At the still point of the turning world") as well as from the last canto of the *Paradiso*. Gunn's "Sunlight" disproves Donald Davie's claim that, along with its violation of the non-human, the process of mass industrialization and suburbanization has so damaged the traditional language of celebration that images like water and wheat have lost their poetic potency.[9]

For Larkin, on the contrary, no object, not even the sun, deserves such adoration. He accepts the debasement of all objects and images and uses even the supreme object, the sun, in such a way as to reduce it to mere words in the service of his special kind of human freedom. That freedom entails a recognition that one cannot rely on anything outside himself as an origin, as a source of value, and that, if one separates himself from his needs and from those aspects of himself which are visible, which "exist openly," he himself can be that which no object, real or ideal, can be, inviolably self-originative. To accomplish this, one must split himself as intelligence off from his needs and emotions. Larkin is willing to do it in order to be uncrushable. When he snaps out "Sod all," or "Books are a load of crap," when he reduces "essential beauty" to a picture slapped up on a billboard, he is not just being mean and nasty, but is insisting that all objects are ultimately unconvincing.

In "Solar," instead of a beholding of the sun with adoration, Larkin offers the hilarious shenanigans of a verbal artist whipping the silly sun about with metaphorical abandon, shaking it like a baby toy. The word "Solar" itself makes the sun small, shrunken in a room with no furniture, a naked bulb, but magical, without wires. It may be a "lion face," but it is a comic one, spilling like a sack of wheat, pouring like a salt shaker. "Continuously exploding" set against "petalled head of flames" is all show, fireworks. The sun's gold is coined, it is just legal tender, solar coinage. The sun, at bottom, is like a picture on a billboard, an illuminated hand unclosing over and over, to which we send our needs and receive them back, unchanged. In its dismissiveness, its mildly sad contempt, the poem is jovial. There is hidden laughter at the loss of one more source of security, for there is such security in one's own self-source. Larkin feels that modernist jazz must be all wrong, because it comes across so clearly as not "the music of happy men." [10] If Larkin's poetry is at times tedious and irritating, it is not because of its chronic sadness, but because of what lies behind it, making it a sham sadness, that is, its gaiety, its jollity, won without effort and held to so jauntily.

In the introduction to the 1966 reprint of his pre-poetic volume of verse, *The North Ship*, Larkin says he woke up poetically when he realized that Hardy's "Thoughts of Phena At News of Her Death" was not a gloomy poem. [11] He also admits that, because the volume of Yeats which so influenced *The North Ship* stopped at "Words for Music Perhaps," he "never absorbed the harsher last poems." If Larkin did, in his maturity, overcome Yeats's influence and write under Hardy's, just as important is the fact that the gaiety which charges Larkin, as it nowhere charges Hardy, resembles that of late harsh poems of Yeats like "Lapus Lazuli," which ends:

> There, on the mountain and the sky,
> On all the tragic scene they stare.
> One asks for mournful melodies;

Accomplished fingers begin to play.
Their eyes mid many wrinkles, their eyes,
Their ancient, glittering eyes, are gay.[12]

Yeats says it and aspires to it; Larkin does it. There is nothing heroic in Larkin, because it requires no effort. The heroic aspect of "Lapus Lazuli" comes from Yeats's feeling that that gaiety is out of his reach, that he is still tied to the natural, dying animal.

It bears repeating, I think, to say that Larkin does not write symbolic poems, only unconvincing translations of them. There are no objective correlatives in his poetry. The sun of "Solar" is shown up as deserving dismissal, as incapable of bodying forth indefinable value. Just so, the sea and "shoreless day" of "Absences," instead of symbolizing mental spaciousness, are made to seem amusingly confined and inadequate, in comparison to the illimitable act of seeing them so. Many of Larkin's poems elude the crushing condescension of unsatisfied critics by crushingly dismissing each and every symbol as inadequate. Alvarez, who quite regularly has the courage to appear in vulnerable ways, called the last poem of *The Less Deceived* "At Grass" (which Larkin considers his first good poem), "a nostalgic re-creation of the Platonic (or *New Yorker*) idea of the English scene, part pastoral, part sporting. His horses are *social* creatures of fashionable race meetings and high style."[13] Alvarez's dismissive tone echoes crudely the delicately dimissive tone of Larkin himself, in the very poem Alvarez is dismissing, "At Grass." It is true that the two horses of the poem are better off at grass than when winning races. At grass they have a freedom not unlike that which is the joy of Larkin's poetry. They stand anonymous, they

Have slipped their names, and stand at ease,
Or gallop for what must be joy,
And not a fieldglass sees them home,
Or curious stop-watch prophesies:
Only the groom, and the groom's boy,
With bridles in the evening come.[14]

Alvarez moves away from the poem uncomprehendingly as a result of placing it next to Hughes's "A Dream of Horses." If it is placed next to "A Blessing" by James Wright, the exquisite edge of "At Grass" will become available, if still invisible. Wright and a friend enter a field where two Indian ponies "come gladly out of the willows" to welcome them. There is a genuine encounter, where the non-human and the human momentarily fuse in a joy so delicate that it cannot quite bear the triumph of the poem's ending:

> Suddenly I realize
> That if I stepped out of my body I would break
> Into blossom. [15]

In "At Grass," Larkin does not approach the horses, but keeps his distance, the eye just barely picking "them out/ From the cold shade they shelter in." If the horses were being offered as representative of a perfect human joy, if a fusion of the human and non-human did occur, then the edge of that moment would turn ironically against the poet, who as author of this poem is not slipping his name but making it, winning the poetry race in England. Larkin, however, is aware that by putting these horses into his poem, he is halting their escape into perfect invisibility and anonymity, their "going down the long slide/ To happiness, endlessly." He is holding them up, a catch, still alive, but corralled within the fence of the poem. Their joy, their freedom, is entirely dependent on the groom and the groom's boy, who "With bridles in the evening come." Even if the reader is merely puzzled by the last two lines, that will be enough to pull him away from the horses, and the poem itself, as objectified, into that condition of aloneness which is identical with oblivion, an identification almost made explicit in the curious little poem, "Wants," also printed in *The Less Deceived*. What often seem like endings that qualify the rest of the poem, the poet turning on himself and getting the whole truth out so that the poem is perfect, are really working in the opposite way, like trick endings which will insure that the reader not take the poem, or the existence within "the garden" of the poem, too seriously. Imagine a dismissive wave of the hand fading out of sight, and you can sense a generosity in Larkin not matched by Marvell, even if their wit is comparable. Larkin wants to be sure that no reader takes his images too seriously. Highly-wrought language, a dazzle which might draw a reader swooning and yet alert into the imaginative experience of a poem, as a refuge where he could live happily apart from the pressures of the daily grind, Larkin will never imperil a reader with such a gawdy trap. What Larkin would share with his reader, ultimately, is the act of dismissing all images, all symbols, all realizations, all artifacts, the world itself, as inadequate, as inferior to the freedom of looking, imagining, thinking dismissively.

What makes not just Larkin's poems, but also his ataraxic stance, his sustained act of looking, imagining, and thinking dismissively, so unstable is that there is only one form of response appropriate to them. Larkin has said that, of "the two tensions from which art springs . . . the tension between the artist and his material, and between the artist and his audience . . . the second of these has slackened or even perished," during the past seventy-five years or so, in the works of those artists and poets known as modernists.[16] Although some poets do unquestionably write poems with no sense of how they will be heard, I should have thought that this was characteristic, not of modernist poets, but of romantic or neo-romantic poets. Modernist poets, in contrast, are, if anything, excessively concerned with their audience. They sense an extreme diversification of the ways in which poetry and art are being responded to, not just hostile ways along with sympathetic ones, but, even more challenging, ways which come out of radically different life conceptions. In both *The Waste Land* and *Mercian Hymns*, the difficulty of the poetry results from its being responsive to conflicting modes of reading, to what, in the visual-auditory experience of poetry, is like a multiple perspectivism in the visual arts. Much of the genius of Eliot and Hill goes into their shaping the poetry so precisely that the unique way in which each hears his words is realized in sharp and often opposing relation to alternate ways in which those words can be heard. As a result, much of the delight of modernist poetry comes from hearing it in several ways at once, in the poet's own unique way, in the ways from which he has differentiated his own, and in one's own way. The poetry is made to allow for, even to encourage and thrive on, multiple modes of hearing and responding. Such charged vitality—in contrast to the relaxed vitality Larkin admires—is not quite the same as Empsonian ambiguity, Wheelwright's polysignificance, or even Umberto Eco's notion of the open work, for it emphasizes the poet's own unique mode of listening as the creative edge of the poem that evokes and keeps alive all the alternate and opposed ways of listening. In modernist poetry the reader feels responsible for listening as the poet listens, but this requires that he also listen in ways the poet sets himself against, and, ultimately, also in his own way.

The strain of creating such polyphonic poetry must lead even the strongest of modernist poets to the verge of disintegration and breakdown. For weaker aspirants it has no doubt led to what Larkin erroneously describes as typically modernist products, "poems resembling the kind of pictures typists make with their machines during the coffee break, or a novel in gibberish, or a play in which the characters sit in dustbins."[17] Collapsing great modernist works, as Larkin does here, with weak evasions from the strain of the modernist predicament into a single junkheap seems, however, to be itself a perilously evasive move. It is, however, consistent with the poetry Larkin writes, a poetry for a single audience, which listens in a single way determined by Larkin as his way. Claiming falsely that all modernist poetry is like so much, say, of Robert Creeley's, not heard at all, Larkin feels even righteous about writing a poetry which is preeminently hearable, in a single, soporific way, indifferent to all other ways, especially thoughtful, reflective, critical ways. The aim is pleasure in the form of ease and comfort. One is invited to set aside his larger, human self in its relations with others and with the complexities of his actual situation and to assume the dream-identity of a single, secure audience, a fictitious cloud of unknowing that takes on real existence only as that into which actual readers and listeners escape. Collingwood was warning forty years ago that entertainment could become so important a part of a person's day that he would cease to live at all except in a make-believe way.

There is, in sum, a weakness in the generosity with which Larkin offers poems that will not disturb his readers. The unstableness of his achievement, moreover, stems from its dependence on his readers' being generous in the same way. The poem "Wants" suggests that Larkin is aware of the instability of the conditions of his poetry:

Beyond all this, the wish to be alone:
However the sky grows dark with invitation-cards
However we follow the printed directions of sex
However the family is photographed under the flagstaff—
Beyond all this, the wish to be alone.

Beneath it all, desire of oblivion runs:
Despite the artful tensions of the calendar,
The life insurance, the tabled fertility rites,
The costly aversion of the eyes from death—
Beneath it all, desire of oblivion runs.[18]

The latent appeal of the poem is that one accept the not quite stated identification of being alone and being in oblivion without reflecting on it or criticizing it. The condition of oblivious aloneness is, to be sure, a delicate one, is, indeed, an aspect of that aloof, dismissive attentiveness which is the inner value of all Larkin's poetry. To be alone but aware of being alone is the painful state of loneliness. In truth, one is not really alone, since he has doubled up into an inner society of being alone and being aware of it. The real aloneness which one desires is an oblivious aloneness, a condition in which others are unaware of one and one is himself unaware of himself as well as of others. The self, moreover, of which one would be unaware is not just the self as one entity among many in the objective world, but also that unidentifiable, unobjectifiable, larger self which is the sustained act of looking at everything dismissively. In the condition of oblivious aloneness, that is, one is dismissive even of one's quintessential dismissiveness.

One is not, of course, to think about this condition, only to experience it, and Larkin, writing from within this condition as from an impregnable fortress, lures the reader who wants what he has with a strikingly subtle technique. At bottom, the technique is the casual lightness of the assertorial tone of the middle three lines of both stanzas. The alternatives to oblivious aloneness are presented not as irritants that make one want to escape into that state and not as attractions in spite of which one wants to make that escape, but as items waved aside and dismissed as negligible. As a result, unless one has read against the grain of the poem, by its end one is himself in the state of oblivious aloneness, unable to remember exactly what it is that he is now beneath and beyond. Properly read, therefore, six of the ten lines of the poem are so forgettable as to be forgotten by the end of the poem: friends, love, family, living with care in time and in thoughtful relation to one's mortality, all such matters are as nothing compared to the comfort of ataraxic aloofness. To think of them would, in fact, destroy the poetic experience, a crucial part of which is the condition of obliviousness.

If a reader begins to fuss, recognizing that there is no hint in the poem that the nature of any of these aspects of living as a human being in the world has been experienced or even thought about by the large, untouchable, uncrushable self dismissing them, so that the dismissal is totally uncompelling and unconvincing, then one will be breaking the implicit contract of the poem, the assumption that the reader shares the poet's wants and will raise no questions if the poem fulfills them. Larkin's own response to such a reader of bad faith is implicit in the following comment which he made in his interview with Ian Hamilton: "There is nothing like writing poems for realizing how low the level of critical understanding is; maybe the average reader can understand what I say, but the above-average often can't."[19] His "average reader" is, in my terms, one who keeps the faith, holding to the contract, submissively. His "above-average" reader is one who raises questions. In Larkin's terms, to raise questions is to read without understanding, to lack the generosity necessary for the reading of his poetry. He remains invulnerable, no matter what the carping of the critic. Yet that critic raises questions because he has read the poems not only with sympathetic understanding, but also with a reflective, critical understanding of their limitations. His discomfort with the poems, his not understanding them Larkin's way, coincides with his understanding them truthfully.

Even though all Larkin's poems share the instability of being dependent on his actual readers' willingness to occupy unquestioningly the passive position he has reserved for them, it is possible to distinguish the more successful from the less. The more successful will be those poems in which the devices used to bring the reader up to the ataraxia of the poet are inconspicuous. For if the reader notices the devices, as devices, he will become more rather than less alert, a ruinous turn for such poetry. Also, those poems will weather best in which Larkin has most effectively hidden the troublesome moral implications inherent in the dismissive attentiveness into which he would lure his audience, for his sort of euphoria cannot tolerate anything worrisome.

On the grounds, then, of the effective concealment of tricks in the means and of moral disturbances in the end, it should be evident that "Here," the opening poem of *The Whitsun Weddings*, will prove more durable than the title poem of that volume. Both poems depend on strategies and a moral flaw which must go unnoticed, if the reader is to enjoy the oblivious aloneness of the poems fully. Above all, readers must be kept from puzzling about the nature of the act of observing which is the basis of both poems. That critics of "Here" have already come close to such puzzling without actually lighting on it is a sign that it has the better chance of surviving undamaged.

The very obviousness of the main device of "Here" has perhaps kept it unnoticed. Grammatically, the first nine lines are a compound dangling modifier. The grammatical "error" goes unnoticed, however, because what dangles grammatically does in truth modify an unspecified, unspecifiable act of aloof attentiveness into which the reader obliviously escapes. Once there, once at one with that anonymous act, he will almost certainly ride out the poem in comfort. Although no critic has to my knowledge noted this quirk in grammar in relation to the invisible act of unreflective awareness, only one, Calvin Bedient, has betrayed a failure to experience it by improperly specifying it as taking place on a train.[20] A casual reading should bring out the inappropriateness of such placement.

HERE

Swerving east, from rich industrial shadows
And traffic all night north; swerving through fields
Too thin and thistled to be called meadows,
And now and then a harsh-named halt, that shields
Workmen at dawn; swerving to solitude
Of skies and scarecrows, haystacks, hares and pheasants,
And the widening river's slow presence,
The piled gold clouds, the shining gull-marked mud,

Gathers to the surprise of a large town:
Here domes and statues, spires and cranes cluster
Beside grain-scattered streets, barge-crowded water,
And residents from raw estates, brought down
The dead straight miles by stealing flat-faced trolleys,
Push through plate-glass swing doors to their desires—
Cheap suits, red kitchen-ware, sharp shoes, iced lollies,
Electric mixers, toasters, washers, driers—

A cut-price crowd, urban yet simple, dwelling
Where only salesmen and relations come
Within a terminate and fishy-smelling
Pastoral of ships up streets, the slave museum,
Tattoo-shops, consulates, grim head-scarfed wives;
And out beyond its mortgaged half-built edges
Fast-shadowed wheat-fields, running high as hedges,
Isolate villages, where removed lives

Loneliness clarifies. Here silence stands
Like heat. Here leaves unnoticed thicken,
Hidden weeds flower, neglected waters quicken,
Luminously-peopled air ascends;
And past the poppies bluish neutral distance
Ends the land suddenly beyond a beach
Of shapes and shingle. Here is unfenced existence:
Facing the sun, untalkative, out of reach.[21]

Though Larkin does ride a train in other poems, in this one, his swerving from "traffic all night north" suggests that his vehicle is a bus, turning off the M-1 in the direction of Hull. The "harsh-named halt" would not be a railway station, but a sheltered bus stop. The vehicle needn't have halted at the halt, however, so it could as well be a car. What is important, however, is the lack of specification, a lack intended to help one feel unseen as he views the scene.

A more sensitive error is John Wain's saying that Larkin's life is one of those "removed lives// Loneliness clarifies," for it nudges one in the right direction, even though it does not bring him to oblivious aloneness, which is altogether superior to anything involving loneliness.[22] Loneliness is a social condition, for the lonely are set apart from the "cut-price crowd"; whereas, as oblivious and alone, Larkin or you or me, any and all aloof, anonymous observers, are secure and at home, though radically alienated, wherever they may be, in the city or in an isolate village. The lonely, it is true, are closer to the alone than the crowd is; that is why they come after the crowd in the movement of the poem, which is meant to lead the reader in a gentle swerve to that condition in the objective world which most nearly resembles the condition of the unobjectifiable act of observing which accompanies invisibly the lines of the poem from beginning to end.

Donald Davie commits an even more sensitive error in suggesting that Larkin has been imprecise in the lines "Here leaves unnoticed thicken,/ Hidden weeds flower, neglected waters quicken".[23] Larkin, he claims, does clearly notice the leaves, and so forth, so how can he call them unnoticed? Perhaps, Davie speculates, he meant to say that they go unnoticed by that "cut-price crowd." But Larkin is not so sloppy as that. What does not get mentioned throughout the poem, the unmentionable anonymous act of noticing, that is the only noticing the leaves get. Larkin himself does not notice them, for he has slipped his name by the time he is at one with that act of noticing. These lines, moreover, are part of Larkin's subtly non-symbolic technique of luring his reader unreflectively into a oneness with that hidden act of negligent noticing. In the last stanza he is simply setting down what is seen, just as he did in the other three stanzas, and what he sees does not in fact seem as interesting, at least in its details, as what has already been observed. But the tone rises, as though something important is happening. Larkin effects the rise in tone mainly by beginning the three sentences of the stanza (the other sentence of the poem covers the other three stanzas) with the title word "Here." "Here" by the end of the poem is "bluish neutral distance," is "unfenced existence:/ Facing the sun, untalkative, out of reach." The proper response to that is a brief, bemused "Hm, so what?", after which one goes about his business, without further thought. This casual, dismissive attitude is what is truly unfenced, even if "bluish neutral distance" comes closer to such freedom than anything else in the objective world does.

Davie, however, almost blows the poem apart with his last comment on it: "In Larkin's poem one detects a perverse determination that the ultimate ('terminate') pastoral shall be among the cut-

price stores, and nowhere else. And the pity felt for the denizens of
that pastoral, the 'residents from raw estates,' is more than a little
contemptuous."²⁴ From the start of the poem, Larkin's aim has
been to ease his reader into the condition of that true "Here" which
is nowhere, that hovering, unspecifiable attending with which the
reader is to identify himself unawares. From such an unlocatable
locus, the attitude taken toward every object, toward everything ob-
jectifiable, not just toward that "cut-price crowd," will be a mixture
of pity and contempt. Except that, in principle, every member of
that crowd might himself be truly at one with the uncrushable act of
observing dismissively, so that, as part of that act, one may be enjoying a false sense of superiority by looking down, as he does,
upon the crowd. Even so, it is Larkin who has lured him into that
falseness, by contrasting the movement of the observing as a
"swerving" to the straight line of the "traffic all night north," and
then emphasizing the straightness of the crowd by having it
"brought down/ The dead straight miles by stealing flat-faced trolleys." He is the one who has made one feel different from and superior to the crowd. He might well weasle, if confronted with this,
saying that he did not really mean the contrast, that it was only a
manner of speaking. Even admitting the truth of that, one may
wonder if it is necessary to the sense of the value of unfenced attending that it be kept in constant contrast to the fenced quality of
everything seen, imagined, or thought. One might even wonder
whether it isn't a moral uneasiness which makes Larkin come out of
the sure comfort of his aloof attentiveness to write poems. Perhaps
he writes them so that he can feel superior to them. Or perhaps his
comfort is unstable enough to need the reassurance of the belief
that others are also of his way of thinking. Perhaps, however,
"Here" would not have given rise to any questions at all, if Davie
had not come at it with the idea that Larkin values the human scene
more than the non-human scene. The truth, rather, is that Larkin
values the human seeing as equally superior to the human and the
non-human scenes. His weakness is that, because of the oblivious
nature of that seeing, he must keep his preference itself hidden, so
that it is imperative that his critics keep making mistakes.

Although "The Whitsun Weddings" was intended by Larkin as
the centerpiece of *The Whitsun Weddings*, it is vulnerable as "Here"

is not, and, for that matter, as its counterparts in *The Less Deceived* and *High Windows*, "Church Going" and "The Building" are not. Because of his deep revulsion for the objective, existent world, Larkin cannot put himself as an identifiable human being into a poem except as an object of revulsion or at least as the butt of his anonymous mockery. In contrast to what he does in those other poems, in "The Whitsun Weddings," Larkin puts himself into the poem as an individual, observable entity, but without the slightest hint of mockery or revulsion. Even worse, toward the end of the poem, because attention is called to the breadth of the "I" 's awareness, in contrast to the self-absorption of those just married, and because of the ostentatious metaphorical flourish with which the poem ends, this "I," who as an entity existent within the objective world of the poem must have limits like its every other entity, is presented as possessing, as a poet, the value which only the illimitable, anonymous act of attending dismissively can have. As a result, the poem is tainted by smugness.

Instead of remaining safely hidden as in "Here," in "The Whitsun Weddings" Larkin recklessly seats himself in a train heading south for London. In his characteristic way of noticing things, he first flattens nature with nature violated by industry ("Wide farms" and "short-shadowed cattle" with "canals with floatings of industrial froth" and "acres of dismantled cars,") and then proceeds to view the wedding participants in the same way he has viewed nonhuman nature and its man-caused violations. The participants are all presented as types ("The fathers with broad belts under their suits/ And seamy foreheads; mothers loud and fat," and so forth) just as animals are noticed according to species and cars lumped together as dismantled. The first direct reference to the brides and bridegrooms, "Fresh couples climbed aboard," might rather be a reference to cattle, and "A dozen marriages got under way" is a manner of speaking more fit for fruit than individual human beings. In themselves, such references scarcely warrant remark, since they are typical of Larkin's attitude toward every object and entity in the existent world.

In this poem, however, they do deserve remark, because of the presence alongside them of the poet himself as just one more such entity who inexplicably and undeservedly escapes any and all dismissive glances and remarks. The reader cannot but observe Larkin looking and looking without ever being looked upon in return. Out the window, as the train leaves another station, he sees girls

> In parodies of fashions, heels and veils,
> All posed irresolutely, watching us go,
>
> As if out on the end of an event
>   Waving goodbye
> To something that survived it.[25]

The "as if" is just a hint that perhaps nothing of a wedding does survive the event. The hint is corroborated two stanzas later; with all the couples aboard, the weddings have turned into "a dozen marriages." The real moral problem, however, does not lie in Larkin's cynicism, but in his observing without being observed. The "us," of course, of "watching us go" is impersonal, referring to the whole train; if those on the platform focus at all, it will be on the married couple they have just seen off. Larkin is in a situation like that of Dante, in the thirteenth canto of the *Purgatorio*, where he and Vergil come upon those doing penance for their envy. They are seated in a row with their backs against the mountainside, the eyelids of each sewn together, so that they cannot see others, about whom they would then say belittling, cynical things, out of envy. Dante turns away from the view, because to him it seems a moral outrage to be looking at others without being looked back upon in turn. Though he may be proud, there is no streak of envy in Dante. In contrast, Larkin keeps staring at people who are unaware he is looking at them and who do not, as a result, gaze back at him. The anonymous, illimitable act by which the "cut-price crowd" of "Here" is dismissively attended to is, in essence, invisible and unobservable. In "The Whitsun Weddings," however, Larkin takes on the sovereign privileges of such invisible, unnameable observing even though he also presents himself as a visible, existent, individual entity. He should have recognized that such a hybrid is inadmissible in poetry like his. By bringing the act of attending into the scene, he has unknowingly committed an obscenity, in the sense that he has brought on stage what by its nature must occur offstage.

The vice is compounded by the self-congratulatory profes-
sionalism of the end of the poem.

> A dozen marriages got under way.
> They watched the landscape, sittng side by side
> —An Odeon went past, a cooling tower,
> And someone running up to bowl—and none
> Thought of the others they would never meet
> Or how their lives would all contain this hour.
> I thought of London spread out in the sun,
> Its postal districts packed like squares of wheat:
>
> There we were aimed. And as we raced across
>   Bright knots of rail
> Past standing Pullmans, walls of blackened moss
> Came close, and it was nearly done, this frail
> Travelling coincidence; and what it held
> Stood ready to be loosed with all the power
> That being changed can give. We slowed again,
> And as the tightened brakes took hold, there swelled
> A sense of falling, like an arrow-shower
> Sent out of sight, somewhere becoming rain.[26]

It is stated as a fact that not one of the dozen couples gave a moment's thought to any of the others. After the statement, however,
its unsettling grounds are provided, inadvertently: "I thought of
London spread out in the sun,/ Its postal districts packed like
squares of wheat." The thoughtlessness of the twelve couples is
not, then, a fact, but rather the claim of this thoughtful "I," who is
calling attention to his own attentiveness by way of contrast with all
those others, who are much like cattle, self-absorbed, looking without seeing. The unsettling aspect of this contrast can be sensed even
in John Wain's praise of it:

> The human actors in this scene, who will set up homes and
> mate and keep the human spectacle going, are unreflective:
> their world is the concrete and the immediate; if we are to have
> any such thing as 'art'—whether poetry or any of the other
> arts—their actions need to be completed and interpreted by a
> brooding imaginative vision playing over them from a point of

detachment. In a sense the poet's involvement is greater than
theirs . . .[27]

The trouble in the passage lies in the turn from art, poetry, a brooding imaginative vision, to "the poet's involvement," at which point
one realizes that Wain is speaking in praise of his friend at the expense of all those others. If Larkin, as I believe, is making for himself, with the poem, the very same claim which Wain makes for
him, then the last six lines of the poem should be read as follows.
Sad it may be, but no significant change has occurred to the married couples. The specialness, the joy, the sacredness of the weddings does not survive the event. The show, the fireworks, the
"arrow-shower," turns to rain. It fructifies, there are droppings of
human babes, the populace grows and grows, naturally and
thoughtlessly, like wheat. The couples copulate, reproduce, and in
time will be fathers and mothers on station platforms, waving
goodbye to their just married offspring. But the rain which the
arrow-shower becomes is also the tears of us superior people, who
observe "The association of man and woman/ In daunsinge, signify-
ing matrimonie—/ A dignified and commodious sacrament" and
think of the unchanging cycle: "Feet rising and falling./ Eating and
drinking. Dung and death."[28] The change that truly gives power is
not that of marriage, but that of poetry. Consider, as the example of
the poem, the change from the weary worker whose "three-
quarters-empty train" pulled out "about/ One-twenty on the sunlit
Saturday" to the "I" of this ending, loosing from his magnificently
broad vision this grand metaphorical display. From just a weary
one he has huffed and puffed till he is so big as to include all of England from Hull to London, all of London, and indeed a vision of all
of life too. It is a very fine thing to be a poet.

Larkin, it is true, wrote the poem for the comfort of his audience, unreflective viewers rather than unreflective actors and carping critics. In the long run, however, even his own audience will
prefer his unpretentious poems, those in which Larkin does not
make the mistake of trying to define what is indefinable, of exhibiting what cannot be put on exhibit, that impersonal, invisible, never
even quite audible act of observing dismissively.

CHAPTER SIX

Stress in Silkin's Poetry and the Healing Emptiness of America

Jon Silkin's poetry hinges on an acute stress between imaginative realization and ideological commitment. As the editor of *Stand*, Silkin himself regards imaginative realization, the intuitive-expressive evocation of self-worlds, with distrust. He thinks of it somewhat as Lukács and Raymond Williams do, as irresponsibly individualistic, as psychologically indulgent, as reactionary Imagism or Modernism. Yet, because of his unmistakable poetic genius, he cannot but be aware that a man devoting himself to stands, with flexed muscles and clenched fist, quickly turns to stone. To be entranced by the image of a rigidly erect, committed individual is to be stunned into stone; to fall into the watery world of Modernism is to drown into madness. A recent anthology of poetry from *Stand*, edited with an introduction by Silkin, is entitled *Poetry of the Committed Individual*.[1] Take the title as the incidence of stress between commitment and poetry, stone and water, land and sea, and it suggests precisely the distinctive quality of Silkin's own finest poems.

The balance is as delicate and difficult to maintain as that of Henry James's Hyacinth Robinson (in *The Princess Casamassima*), so that the unevenness of Silkin's poetry should come as no surprise. I want to thread the fine line of genuine achievement from his first volume, *The Peaceable Kingdom* (1954), his most exuberantly imaginative poetry, to his recent volume, *The Principle of Water* (1974), in which one of the strongest poems ends with these dessicated lines:

Houses and scrap will heap,
and flake, as
if organs of the soil clagged
with shreddings of rust.[2]

The rhythmical counterpoint (which begins with "as/if") draws the effect of "clagging" right into one's mouth.

In the middle of this twenty-year span, in the poems of *Nature with Man* (1965), Silkin is close to strangulation, as if the waters of poetry had withdrawn, leaving him a gaping mouth on the sand. Even in this volume, however, he knows his need and is ready for the healing emptiness of America, where he came for the first time, at the age of thirty-five, in 1965. His American poems (all eight are to be found together in the Chatto and Windus *Amana Grass*, 1971) articulate his release from the confusions of his latest English poetry and at the same time signal a sharp and profound openness and repugnance before the new land. It is true that the series ends with a decisive withdrawal and return to England. But the new English poetry, most finely represented by the "Killhope Wheel" sequence of *The Principle of Water*, is quite different from anything English he had done before.

Before he came to America, his body had been gradually dissolving out from under him (I mean the body of his language and, with that, his own human body and the body of his land). Like so many recent English poets, he seemed to forget that body cannot be taken as a given, but is rather the result of the poet's own constant making and remaking of all that he can take into his own imaginative self-world. By being exposed to the drastically different body of the America he lived in (for three months in 1965, for a year in 1969, along with shorter stays) and by working his way imaginatively into that body, he was able to return to England with a renewed capacity to embody a unique self-world of incomparable edge and vigor. So quickly, however, the delicate air of England turns into a stifling blanket. The poems in *The Principle of Water* which are written out of a settled Englishness, like the long "The People" and "The Malabestia," make one think of phrases like "Shades of the prison-house," "the light of common day," and "And custom lie upon thee with a weight,/ Heavy as frost, and deep almost as life!"

Genuine achievement is what needs emphasizing as against the heaviness to be associated with those "great reticulations of ideas" spread ideologically about the editorials and reviews of *Stand* the past few years.

Silkin's first volume, *The Peaceable Kingdom*, is the finest first volume of poetry written by a living English poet. All the stress, and strength even, of Silkin's maturest poetry can be found in a number of individual poems, and, in addition, the volume itself is a seamless whole, so that the poems are enriched by one another and by the volume in its entirety. In the brief afterword originally written in 1969 and reprinted in the Heron Press edition, I found the unity of the volume in "the way the poet cares for the creatures within it":

> He cares for his creatures by loving them in ignorance, by joining the light of his attention with the darkness of his bafflement. He is concerned for the 'small animals/ With bitter eyes', even though so far as he can tell, they are 'unnecessary beasts.' More precisely, the best of the poems in the volume are full of fear and of a love for what is fearsome. Silkin's music is 'a peaceable music tuned with fear.' The creatures of his kingdom are unfathomable, but the poet loves them even as he recognizes their strangeness and distance from him. His sense of estrangement and his love are, then, inseparable and interdependent.[3]

There is something ignorant about that statement. The ignorance attributed to the poet is really mine. My bent was to emphasize the poet's complete engrossment in the creatures of his kingdom, with no attention to his own position as king of the kingdom. Without my having been aware of it, such a claim suggests that *The Peaceable Kingdom* is at bottom solipsistic, the evocation of a world that is the poet's without a hint that the poet has his limits and that there is a larger world that extends beyond and that may be at odds with, or indifferent to, the poet's world. A reader might infer—with some support from the poetry itself—that the world of the volume is wholly watery, that all the poems occur during the flood (the prologue begins, "All the animals in my poems go into the ark"), that *The Peaceable Kingdom* is modernistically indulgent and decadent.

Even so simple a poem as "A Death to Us" manifests the untruth of that:

> A tiny fly fell down on my page
> Shivered, lay down, and died on my page.
>
> I threw his body onto the floor
> That had laid its frail life next to mine.
>
> His death then became an intrusion on
> My action; he claimed himself as my victim.
>
> His speck of body accused me there
> Without an action, of his small brown death.
>
> And I think now as I barely perceive him
> That his purpose became in dying, a demand
>
> For a murderer of his casual body.
> So I must give his life a meaning
>
> So I must carry his death about me
> Like a large fly, like a large frail purpose.

One might respond to this little poem, which clearly outdoes its counterpart in the *Songs of Experience*, as did Anthony Thwaite to all of Silkin's poetry: "The dogged seriousness of Silkin's concerns (about man's injustice and cruelty, for example) often seem to weigh his poems down with urgently meant but inert abstractions, and in general his admirers appear to be impressed by the gravity of his intentions rather than the actual results."[4] As recently as 1972, in an essay on Geoffrey Hill, Silkin suggested that suffering "is perhaps the only state during which we are innocent."[5] Isn't Silkin simply obsessed, in an inertly abstract way, with the idea that we must care for "the unnecessary beasts"? By accident a fly falls down dead on his page. By accident he sees it. By accident, as a reflex action, he brushes it onto the floor. This has happened to everybody, but no one but Silkin has ever (without even any humor?) blown such a series of accidents up into anything so grave as:

> So I must give his life a meaning
>
> So I must carry his death about me
> Like a large fly, like a large frail purpose.

That might seem so embarrassing that one would want to brush it onto the floor and be done with it, except that the embarrassment ought not to be one's reaction to the poem, because it is a part of the poem. The poet has indulgently observed himself being victimized by the victim; with no action at all, the fly has "claimed himself as my victim." Contrary to my previous readings of the poem, the focus of Silkin's attention is on himself. He sees that he is allowing himself to be coerced into caring for that fly and that he is being swollen up by a sense of self-importance as he takes on this kingly burden. By the end of the poem one is speechless and appalled by the monstrosity of the poet's reaction. He shouldn't be doing that. Something is really wrong with him. He is clearly endangering his sanity by such an excessive response to the fly's "speck of body," which of course does not accuse him of anything at all. The sense of danger belongs to the poet, however, not the reader. The poem suffices the poet in his speechless puzzlement over his peculiar response to the fly. Once it is realized that the puzzlement, the embarrassment, the recognition of monstrousness and fear of insanity, are not the reader's for Silkin, but Silkin's for himself, then and only then is the reader in a position to make the move essential to the reading of all genuine poetry—to respond to and reflect upon the poem himself, instead of simply being its victim and thinking its thoughts as if they were his own.

One's own response to accidental victims is exactly the response that develops within this little poem. One's psyche inflates its own relation to each victim so quickly that he hardly notices it, just because his fear of being wiped out in a meaningless accident, or of losing those he loves in a meaningless accident, is the pervasive emotional undercurrent of life in our time. In contrast to the poet, however, one is apt to brush not only the "casual body" of the fly, but also his own inflating ego in its relation to that fly, out of his mind, because he simply has no time, amid his many chores and his many obligations to other creatures, to dwell upon it. The result is that fly, ego, relation, and growing guilt and fear are dismissed and go unattended. He remains a sane, responsible citizen by allowing himself to fester, insanely, uncared for, inside. Instead of being victimized by his own guilt, Silkin is attending to his monstrous seriousness, not just seriously, but, in the end, even with a touch of hilarity. The speechless astonishment must end with something like a slap of the thigh and an exclamation of "Fantastic!"

Silkin avoids being victimized as a result of his caring by way of attending so acutely to it. Perhaps this aspect, this capaciousness, of "A Death to Us" can be glimpsed best in a less direct way in the following passage from Lawrence's "Europe *v.* America" (written in 1926), in which he observes:

> how much more *tense* the European civilization is, in the Americans, than in the Europeans. The Europeans still have a vague idea that the universe is greater than they are, and isn't going to change very radically, not for all the telling of all men put together. But the Americans are tense, somewhere inside themselves, as if they felt that once they slackened, the world would really collapse. It wouldn't.[6]

Within Europeans, he goes on, "there is still, at the bottom, the old, young insouciance. It isn't that the young *don't care:* it is merely that, at the bottom of them there *isn't* care." Within "A Death to Us," Silkin's relation to the fly is the sort of strangulating caring that Lawrence is so acutely criticizing. Silkin thinks he must turn the most trivial incident into something gravely significant. He has chipped himself free of that encasement, however, by presenting it so vividly. By observing how one's psyche tends to flood the world constantly with its caring, he has freed himself to begin to make adjustments between velleity and genuine desire, between desire and intention, between intention and action, between the American and Freudian tendencies to drown the world in the fluids of the psyche, and the English and Marxist tendencies to dehydrate all psyches and make them stand as stick figures on the desert ground of Society.

Silkin is repudiating neither his own flooding, where he feels his world of poetry flourishing, nor the social desert, where real commitments and actions are alone possible. As Ramon Fernandez in his *De la personnalité* argues so convincingly, to develop into a human personality is to struggle constantly and creatively to make one's actions in the world correspond to the movements of one's inner being,[7] the sort of movements that most of us slight and of which I am claiming Silkin to be extraordinarily aware.

The case for Silkin's self-awareness, even in *The Peaceable King-*

dom, his most lilting volume, may perhaps be made compelling by a brief look at "Carved":

Two small dogs stood by a dead black bird
And the black bird was very dead.

The two dogs stood by the bird like large lions
But they never touched the dead thing, once.

They would like to have eaten the black thing
But it was very dead with red ants

Sawing its neck away like stone masons
And the red ants were very much alive.

So all the time the dogs stood they barked there
Because they couldn't eat the black thing.

Something large about that black bird.
It was being eaten by red death

While the two large-lion small dogs just stood,
Barking: they never touched the black thing,

And the black thing never looked at them, once.
It was indifferent to two small dogs.

Maybe it did not hear those large lions
Or maybe the black bird felt sorry for the small dogs.

Meanwhile the dead went on being dead and the living living.

The title, "Carved," refers, clearly enough, to the quality of the poet's unflinching gaze as he takes in, sensitively and verbally, a scene most of us would flick past with only a momentary spasm of revulsion. Something trivial and yet disturbing, like a dead fly or bird, catches his eye, and he holds it and works it until it flowers, monstrously. He is very busy; he is carving, industriously, just like the red ants. Also, as a poet, he keeps his eyes wide open—he catches ambiguities and nuances, the fierce and the futile aspects of the dogs, and so forth, and he sculpts them in words. He thinks of himself, feels himself, as caring intensely, and yet what does his gaze resemble most if not the indifference, the nonchalance, of the black thing, whose not looking at the dogs is, ambivalently, either the result of his not hearing "those large lions" or of his feeling "sorry for the small dogs." There is the same fearsome sense that poetry is like death, that the capaciousness of poetic awareness is like the indifference in the gaze of the dead that one feels in Cocteau's *The Death of a Poet*. Out of what other feeling, if not that, does the last line, "Meanwhile the dead went on being dead and the living living," come? The poet's not eating the objects of his desire, moreover, his delicately purposive purposelessness, can be felt to be as futile, as unproductive, as the dogs' barking. Just noise. Just words. Perhaps he should become a stonemason (Silkin was a manual laborer, a hod carrier, during this period of his life). Thus, Silkin's courage in "Carved" lies not just in his refusal to flinch before an unsettling scene, but also in his capacity to question, at the very same time, the nature and value of his refusal to flinch and the steady gaze out of which the poem comes. *The Peaceable Kingdom* is no more innocent than the *Songs of Innocence*.

Silkin's most powerful and best-known poem, "Death of a Son (who died in a mental hospital aged one)," might seem to be an exception to this, my revised reading of *The Peaceable Kingdom*. The poem might be read as a purely modernist descent into the abyss of Being, as though, beginning with the father in awe and terror of the inscrutable otherness of his son, the poet moves mystically—in the shift of the son from this inexplicable silence into the deeper silence of death—out of this world. As he does so, he draws his language with him, a swooning of articulateness into the watery realm of death. John Berryman's comments on the poem suggest that he read it in this way. Although the following paragraph (from an essay on Lowell's "Skunk Hour") includes only two sentences about "Death of a Son," the significance of those sentences depends on the rest of the paragraph:

> If the topic seems to anyone theatrical, may I mention suicides: two of the three or four most important early Soviet poets, Essenin and Mayakovsky; while Hart Crane and Vachel Lindsay (and for that matter Sara Teasdale—writing really well toward the end) who destroyed themselves here were not our worst poets. Poets in odd ages have killed themselves or gone mad, Poe and Dylan Thomas as clearly as Swift, Chatterton, Smart, Beddoes, and many have written about it from inside and outside, from Cowper's posthumous "The Castaway" to Miss Bishop's wonderful "Visits to St. Elizabeth's" and Rilke's *"Das Lied des Idioten."* It is better not to feel so strongly:

We poets in our youth begin in gladness,
But thereof comes in the end despondency and madness.
Wordsworth once said that if he had written what he most
deeply felt no reader could have borne it, Coleridge that he
gave up original poetical composition (but the fine, bleak
"Work Without Hope" is late) because he was unable to bear it.
One poem does not edge into the terror but starts there and
stays there: Jon Silkin's "Death of a Son." This you will find in
the Hall-Simpson paperback anthology of recent verse, and it is
as brave, and harrowing, as one might think a piece could be.[8]

(Imagine listening to that siren song of soft modernistic decadence
and then in surprise coming upon your own name as among the
very best of all, among the bravest and profoundest, and this in the
eyes of one of the most vividly legendary suicides of our time!)

No doubt there is a sustained terror in the poem, which develops in momentum from the following lines:

Something has ceased to come along with me.
Something like a person: something very like one.
And there was no nobility in it
Or anything like that.

The momentum builds until the moment of death, when the silence
of the son as "a one year/ Old house, dumb as stone" deepens into
"something religious in his silence":

And then slowly the eye stopped looking
Inward. The silence rose and became still.
The look turned to the outer place and stopped,
With the birds still shrilling around him.
And as if he could speak

He turned over on his side with his one year
Red as a wound
He turned over as if he could be sorry for this
And out of his eyes two great tears rolled, like stones, and he died.

Even so, "Death of a Son" does not fit into the context Berryman
provides for it at all. It has little to do with incipient, suicidal madness, with a harrowing stare into the heart of darkness. The poem is
thoroughly human, a working-out of a father's loving attention to a

defective son who is awesome in his remoteness. The quality of courage in the poem, that is, comes not from the poet's capacity to endure terror, but rather from his capacity to love this creature in ignorance and fear. The uncanny strength of the poem stems from the father-poet's striving to give shape to the otherness of his son, this "house/ Of stones and blood in breathing silence." Because of his love, the poet resists his desire to lessen the terror; he will not violate that which he loves by a single word that would bring it out of its silence and closer to him, that would humanize it or at least make it humanly understandable. In spots, it is true, where the syntax is cracked out of all relation to proper grammatical speech, the poet-father is beside himself in awe and anguish. The fineness of the poem, however, depends on never losing one's sense that an actual father is observing in pain and love his own one-year-old son. The son is more like Wordsworth's Lucy than the "Eye among the blind,/ That, deaf and silent, read'st the eternal deep,/ Haunted for ever by the eternal mind" of the "Intimations Ode."

Even the title, with its parenthetical "who died in a mental hospital aged one," tips one off to the truth that the poet is not aiming for something grand ("And there was no nobility in it/ Or anything like that"), but rather for what only the very greatest poetry achieves: the unique evocation of the unique individuality of a loved creature. It may well be that this poem marks the moment Silkin's career was set, with all its disturbingly discordant commitments, to poetry, to society, to nature, and to other creatures. But it would be wrong to say that those "two great tears" "rolled, like stones," out of the heart of silence, or that Silence and Language have fused in a momentary, mystic flare. It would be wrong to describe the poet's commitment as made against the pact most people have with silence (to leave it behind for the brief span of chattering that life is), as a commitment to dredge the oceanic silence of Being into the stunning light of words. For those tears rolled out of the poet-father's son's eyes. And the poem ends with the son, who has seemed "a breathing silence" that "neither/ Moved nor was still" through most of the poem, actually moving expressively, "as if he could speak," "as if he could be sorry for this." It is as if, and only as if, the father's love was finally being reciprocated. At the approach of death, the son, who had "like a house in mourning/

Kept the eye turned in to watch the silence," has become "Hearing and speaking though he was a house drawn/ Into silence."

Throughout the poem, moreover, it should be kept in mind that the poet-father is aware of other mentally defective creatures attending noisily on his awesomely silent son. They "sang like birds and laughed"; they are "the other birds/ Singing crazy"; even at the moment of death they are, "still shrilling around him." Qualified by these sounds on one side, and by the poet-father's words on the other, which are working poetically to deny themselves as words in order to evoke that which is other than themselves, the son's way of changing his gaze from inwards to outwards and his way of turning over on his side express uniquely the individuality of this awesomely remote creature. If there is a wholeness of being that rises as silence within the son at the moment of death, there is also a wholeness of being in the poet-father's response. He had no need to say: "So I must give his life a meaning// So I must carry his death about me/ Like a large fly, like a large frail purpose." The poem manifests experientially what it is for one human being to love another creature.

There are, it is true, abstract elements in the poem, such as in the following passage:

> I have seen stones: I have seen brick
> But this house was made up of neither bricks nor stone
>> But a house of flesh and blood
>>> With flesh of stone
>> And bricks for blood. A house
> Of stones and blood in breathing silence . . .

In its evocation of the mystery of the relation of body to soul, it echoes the following stanza of Marvell's "A Dialogue between the Soul and Body":

> *Soul*
>> O who shall, from this Dungeon, raise
> A Soul inslav'd so many wayes?
> With bolts of Bones, that fetter'd stands
> In Feet; and manacled in Hands.
> Here blinded with an Eye; and there

Deaf with the drumming of an Ear.
A Soul hung up, as 'twere, in Chains
Of Nerves, and Arteries, and Veins.
Tortur'd, besides each other part,
In a vain Head, and double Heart.[9]

But the movement of thought in Silkin's poem is entirely in the opposite direction. It is not directed towards wittily and analytically exploring the intricacies of the abstract relationship of soul and body but, rather, towards suggesting the uniqueness of this soul-body at that moment when the poet-father is supremely in touch with him.

No one can read "Death of a Son (who died in a mental hospital aged one)" without feeling sure that the father will never abandon his son. Silkin has thus far written five other poems on the child: "For a Child," in *The Re-Ordering of the Stones* (1961); "The Child's Life," "Burying," "The Child," in *Nature with Man* (1965); and the Finn section of "The People" beginning "Air that pricks earth with life," in *The Principle of Water* (1974). These poems exhibit something characteristic of Silkin's poetry after *The Peaceable Kingdom* and through *Nature with Man*: they tend to be incomplete, trailing off from the wholeness of the original. In one, the son is thought of after his death as something like the father-poet's muse, coming to him as an invisible breathing; in another, he is part of the vegetative kingdom of nature; in another, he is the weak link which fails to hold his parents together, his madness the missed connection; in still another, he is the innocent victim of the aloofly efficient, unloving hospital staff into whose care the parents have relinquished him. Or is "this limp and useless going off among" partial statements in truth an abandonment of the son: Silkin fleeing from what he takes to be the watery world of modernistic madness, whereas what he really is fleeing from is that wholeness that is the uniqueness of genuinely creative poetry?

Far be it from me to suggest that the poems of *The Two Freedoms* (1958), *The Re-Ordering of the Stones,* and *Nature with Man* fail because they are heavily discursive. Statements can work poetically (rather than rhetorically, eloquently, imposingly) if they are part of a larger utterance in which words are denied as words to evoke the actual curving of a felt experience, even if it be only an experience of stating (such an utterance—or gesture—can, of course, occur outside poems as well as within them). My concern is rather with the confusion that Silkin fell into over this problem, the need that arose from the confusion, and Silkin's fulfilling that need by way of his exposure to America, as articulated in his eight American poems.

In his earliest editorials in *Stand* (written between 1952 and 1957), Silkin expresses his opposition to all "toy writing, all exercises of the intellect or literary exercises,"[10] all "private intellectualisms, brilliant technics."[11] It would seem that, in contrast to merely witty verse, he was advocating poetry that integrated nature with man, experiencing with imagining, Being with Thinking, a poetry like that of the best poems in *The Peaceable Kingdom*. Conflicting with this apparent conviction, however, Silkin also treats poetry as no more than a means of communication. The poet "must try hard to communicate what he has to say. The only self-respect an artist can have is to be paid by the society he works in as a labourer is paid for his effort."[12] A person "must first live out his life as a human being, not as an artist." No writing is as large as "the *act* of being." "The best that any Art can do is to draw attention to living." The relation of a poet to his poems is the same as that of a lavatory cleaner to the job of cleaning lavatories. "And the worst of it is that in time the man who cleans lavatories *becomes* a lavatory cleaner. That is, he ceases to function on his own and personal level. He sheds his personality like a skin and emerges as the name people call him."[13] Such an analogy, it seems clear, indicates that Silkin is not thinking of a poem as an act in which a man can actualize the full range of his natural and human possibilities. Poems are ways of cleaning up the debris which would "clag" the "shithouses" if they were not attended to. Poems tell us things that matter in ways that interest, as a result of which poets are paid. The living is done elsewhere, not so that one's words can be charged with life, but so that they will have some living already done to which they can draw attention. Poetry is a job. Living, that which is human and personal, has to be done outside it.

Such attitudes would lead quite readily to the notion that effective statements are sufficient to make a poem. Carried out in practice, as it is to some extent in the three volumes of Silkin's under question, the poet in the poems would become mainly mouth and eyes, voice and vision, cut off from the poetic body of his language, from the body of his land, and from his own body. *Nature with Man*, as a volume, is the expression of Silkin's sense of this desperate plight; but the manner of expression remains, on the whole, the very manner that has caused the plight. The poems are attacks on man's having split himself off from nature, and they are obviously urging that the split can and ought to be healed. But the manner, the style, the structure, exhibit—unintentionally—not the cure, but the ailment in its deepest and most personal form.

The title poem, "Nature with Man," opens with the most intensely visualized scene to be found in Silkin's poetry up to that time (and so, in addition to betraying a sickness, it promises a cure):

> The lank summer grass
> As it is, bent and wailing;
> A scorching wind
> Scours a whole plain of it.
> Dust still oppresses. Then
> As if the earth received
> A bruise a pool of brown
> Slime erupts slowly
> From among the stems. Summer mud . . .
> Hot and stagnant. The grass stalks
> Stand pricked without root
> In the rimless mud . . . in what eye.
> On some field of grey stone
> A white sud of saliva,
> So fine it seems a mildew,
> Agonizes over the crop.[14]

It seems unlikely that any American reader at all sensitive to poetry could predict what comes next: thirty-seven lines of allegory about how bad man as the head of nature was to bite through his own neck and then roll as a severed head into the bullrushes, as a result of which "The whole/ Of nature is turning slowly/ Into an eye that searches/ For its most developed/ And treacherous creature, man."

And yet there is trouble even in the first stanza. Reading only the first line, think of Whitman's "I lean and loaf at my ease observing a spear of summer grass," and you will feel how constricted Silkin is around the throat. Add the second line, "As it is, bent and wailing," and think of this comment by Leavis on a passage in *Four Quartets:* "Among the possible effects of starvation, it might be added, is intensity." [15] You realize (1) that "as it is" is meant to say: "bent and wailing" belong to the grass, in and of itself, apart from my way of attending to it, so that there is no pathetic fallacy in what you are being offered, and (2) that just such a split between observer and observed is what it means for a man's head to be severed from his body. Then add Eliot's comment (from his essay on Jonson): "Looking closer, we discover that the blossoms of Beaumont and Fletcher's imagination draw no sustenance from the soil, but are cut and slightly withered flowers stuck into sand," [16] and you are likely to admit that there is much doctrine, too much, even in the startling "The grass stalks/ Stand pricked without root/ In the rimless mud." At the end of the poem this scene is allegorized into the wounded eye of nature, as "perverted into the search" for man. For the poem to have worked, the initial scene needed to be seen ("in what eye") not in the eye of a man, a Moses or Marx who rolled as a "severed head" into the bullrushes, whence he gave out "Great reticulations/ Of ideas, nets wilful and sharp," but in a natural eye, in the eye of a poet, whose head is joined "unto/ The membered flesh." Intention, however, and achievement conflict. Against that deeper poetic impulsion to use all his resources to articulate the individuality of a scene, a creature, an event, a drama, Silkin is committed to a generalizing propensity of mind that merely presupposes the individual (instead of creatively perceiving it). He cannot keep himself from abstracting particulars, identifying them as specific differences, and organizing them into general classes—a propensity that allegory shares with that very English, empirical tradition. Even in its act of condemning, the poem is a symptom of what it condemns.

Another aspect of *Nature with Man* that aggravates Silkin's problem is his increasing tendency to voice his poems heavily and archly—something more characteristic of recent English poetry than its American counterpart. This may be appropriate in "Defence," with its harsh, rasping echoes of Swift, but it seems sour when heard even in the fifteen-poem sequence on flowers. In the finest of these poems, "Moss," the poet asks of the first type of moss, that which grows "in damper places," "With what does it propagate?" The tone of the answer is disturbingly arch, so that, against the movement of the poem, one begins to worry about what is happening to this man who wants to be paid by society for his labors:

> Quiet, of course, it adheres to
> The cracks of waste-pipes, velvets,
> Velours them; an enriching
> Unnatural ruff swathing the urban 'manifestation':
> The urban nature is basemented, semi-dark;
> It musts, it is alone.

Whether the poet within the poem is at all disturbed by that tone is doubtful. But in his essay on Hill, it is evident that, at least after his extended stays in the United States, Silkin had come to recognize the problem: "Even so, a voice cannot itself provide more than a spurious unity, and to put on it work that is beyond its proper capacity produces the strain that exists in a fraction of Hill's work." [17]

Silkin's first American poem, "Brought up with Grass," a one-hundred-and-twenty-two line sequence in four parts, is too programmatic to work, as if the poet had stepped into my essay at this point and said by way of the poem, "Oh, this is how you think I can free myself from *Nature with Man*. First I scotch the notion of any self, ego, or I as a given, as what one can start with. That's easy. Just omit the subject of the first sentence: 'Brought up with grass,/ Fastens under the doorstep, and catches/ Between the toes.' [18] What is brought up, what fastens, what catches? Aha! 'What?' That's the point. Is it weeds or man? Is there a difference, in America?" Such an attitude, towards people and weeds, may be the opposite of the one from which Silkin needs to free himself. But in this instance it smells of burning rubber, as if Silkin were straining too much with his brain to be more than brain. As a whole,

"Brought up with Grass" is flawed in the same way as the first canto of the *Inferno:* the idea is right, but the signs of scissors-and-paste work are too evident. Silkin abhors Eliot enough to want to banish him from England: "Cry what shall I cry?/ All flesh is grass: comprehending/ The Companions of the Bath, the Knights of the British Empire, the Cavaliers,/ O Cavaliers! . . ."[19] There are no such Companions, Knights, or Cavaliers in Silkin's poem, but the human beings of the poem are treated as ingredients in a system of natural forces and desires. They are not very different from grass, or from stone, water, wind, frost, bird, or shark.

While reading the poem, I connect what Silkin is doing with experiences I know he underwent during the months in 1965 he spent in central Ohio. But if the poem is working as a poem, should I be making such connections? Oughtn't the imagining of the poem to pack itself with uniquely shaped experiencing, related of course to living that goes on outside it, but itself determinative of the inner nature, of the quality and feeling, of all the living it evokes? Whereas "Brought Up With Grass" provides mainly the blueprint: the real thing, the actual experience, exists in the past, in events undergone by Silkin, and in the future, in the poems which will realize imaginatively what is only intention and idea here.

After the first sentence with its missing subject, Silkin offers a natural scene which is a close counterpart to the opening stanza of "Nature with Man":

> Not far off
> A cut in the earth's moistened skin.
> The fall's head disinters
> A glutinous liquid congealed
> Round air.
>
> Many dismissive hands
> Are like this dropped water.
>
> Another gorge is close
> Touched with the first's weakness—
> This sheerness
> A dizzying proliferation of dark, green moss
> Dankening the acute
> Corners of shafted stone.

At the bottom are ferns,
Spored and moist. The roof fell
Inwards, and over it, gathering water
Moistens the dissident slab.

It is the water drops.
A man, occasionally.

Here also, a cave
Like half an eye in the ground:
The eye, out; its space, left
With falling into it
A jet of water that splays
Its energy, downward.
In and through which his father
Could be seen.

The scene is meant, I think, to evoke a sense of what it would feel like to be Jon Silkin, an American, living in America (the first entry I know of on Silkin, in the 1973 *MLA International Bibliography*, lists him as an American). One aspect of the feeling is liberation, the freedom of a wilderness that has no jar placed in it in such a way as to center it. This is the first sign of that healing effect American emptiness will have on Silkin's poetry. Space and time are not filled and dominated, as they are in England, by empirical egos living intensely but mainly from the throat up. With his impeccable London English—strictly BBC Received Pronunciation—Silkin could not but receive confirmation of that English truth that Americans speak barbarically because they do not use their mouths and lips enough to make their voices expressive. If this poem is any evidence, however, he also sensed the obverse of this: an American does not use his mouth and lips as much as an Englishman, partly because his speaking rumbles up from his whole body. It is not just Whitman who belched his poetry. Silkin once had a friend, a young American philosopher, Steve Holmes, read this poem as a diversion in one of his own readings, and Silkin's reaction was that the American voice revealed how thoroughly American the poem is. I can find only four notably English lines in the entire poem: "Many dismissive hands/ Are like this dropped water" and "It is the water drops./ A man, occasionally."

You cannot read those lines without pursing and then smacking your lips, and at the same time slightly popping your eyes with a knowing blink. What they suggest is that Americans treat one another in a way that is in harmony with this liberated, uncentered, but weakly, dissipatingly violent scene. The scene is a ravine in a state park in southern Ohio, Old Man's Cave, which Silkin visited with a history teacher and his wife, the man terribly nervous and pinched, out of things in a socially aggressive history department in a small liberal arts college. Indeed, Silkin's first evening in America was spent at one of their festive parties. The one image I retain from that party is of Silkin seated and small in an armchair while a very tall visiting poet towers above him, standing and bouncing muscularly on the soles of his shoes and suggesting that *maybe*, just *maybe*, a reading for the little man could be arranged at his home base, in San Francisco. That poet, it might be added, had a very sensible terror of the emptiness (which I identify with the lack of human caring, the lack of cultivated caring) surrounding him. At his reading (given earlier in the evening before Silkin had arrived), he was clearly trying to break a habit of reading too rapidly and without pauses. So great was his terror, however, that where he left pauses, between lines and stanzas, he hummed a nervous, nasal note. The victim victimizes. That, I would suggest, is what Silkin's antennae were picking up from every direction, in 1965, in central Ohio. On the third day of his visit, at a tea given in his honor, he was told by the local village poetess that she did not mind having left Alabama for good, as she had recently done, because now that Negroes were allowed to use white libraries, the smell made them unuseable. Seeing *Mondo Cane* at some time during those weeks, how could he not have made the connection? It is a dog's world and, at least in America, man is no exception. The following image, by the way, comes from *Mondo Cane:*

> The shark forced by
> Bereaved fishers to take
> A poisoned sea urchin—
> For seven days that melts
> Itself out of the gut.
> A disinterred spike works
> Through the muscle.

The language is undoubtedly smack up against the violence and weakness and emptiness it evokes. But look across the page and you see the same thing in different words:

> The split violet chewing
> A knob of stone to grit.
> The small wren bladed
> With protective anger pierces
> The intruder on the moss.

There is, it seems to me, too much pattern, too much idea, so that one must question Silkin's own claim, in the last section, that, in addition to being an ingredient himself, subject to the impersonal pressures of nature, he is also

> Lens-like to
> The skin's infection, its movement,
> Transist into the meaning of
> The configurated shift of burning wood.

What he provides is not insight, but eye-sight, according to a theory that American experience is a thoroughly naturalistic process, violent and transitory, on top of which he has placed an English-speaking eye for which he seems to claim permanence. There is blood in that eye, but none in the body, which remains theory, idea, though presented with verbal violence.

In his *Love-Hate Relations,* Spender complains that Eliot and Pound did not understand what the English were fighting for in World War I (they were, Spender says, fighting for "gentleness" and "some very green meadow with a stream running through it and willows on its banks; or the cricket match on the village green; or beer or cider in pubs," for friendship, and for laughter "without malice, vindictiveness or triumph") because, like other expatriates from America, they saw Europe "not so much as places where there are people . . . but as civilization." [20] In "Brought up with Grass," it can be said, perhaps, that partly because of the influence of Lawrence and partly because he was staying in a rural part of America, Silkin likewise saw America "not so much as places where there are people," but as the lack of civilization. Even so, it is that

lack of civilization, that bodiliness, that Silkin himself so desper-
ately needs. What disturbs him about America is truly disturbing.
His failure to realize it except as an idea, however, is also disturbing, and the cause of it lies in himself, in what he himself senses to
be a head so cultivated that it has become disembodied.

Before returning to America in 1969 for a much longer stay,
Silkin composed an English counterpart to "Brought up with
Grass." This twenty-six-line poem, entitled "Worm," is the portrait
not of a worm, but of "the worm." Working with something typical, he had no chance himself to get under the soil or to join himself
"unto the membered flesh." Without any intentional humor at all,
the worm turns into a worm-poet:

> It is lowly, useful, pink. It breaks
> Tons of soil, gorging the humus
> Its whole length; its shit a fine cast
> Coiled in heaps, a burial mound, or like a shell
> Made by a dead snail.[21]

Donne's "well wrought urn" has become wormshit. But that is simply a mistake. There must be a better way to join man with nature.
Fixated seeing turns image into idea and necessarily collapses into
allegory, which itself is necessarily disjunctive.

To work out an integral relation between head and body, or individual commitment and imaginative realization, not just in what
he contains within his awareness, but also in the very acts of his
creative perceiving, Silkin knew he must proceed indirectly. Whatever his intentions or plans, Silkin came to America for the deepest
of reasons: to heal the fissure between head and body that made
living in England so dissatisfying. But once he was in America, the
same problem returned. Even within the larger indirection, each
move had to be worked out indirectly. The strategy of "Brought up
with Grass," even though the aim was to get underneath the discursive and strategic aspects of experience, was to face the problem
head-on, the result of which is that the poem comes too close to
being a theory about the need to be more than theoretical. Poetry

simply does not well up out of intention, though it may contain firmly felt intentions, as well as expressions of unqualified commitment.

The seven poems that come out of Silkin's year-long stay in Iowa in 1969 realize with exceptional intensity that insight into America that would free him to return to England renewed. What he discovers is that despite all the studying and investigating and surveying and analyzing that Americans practice upon themselves, their actual lives go on being lived with immense energy and largely unattended to at the public, social, or institutional level. This insight emerges out of Silkin's having eased himself into an ordinary situation, off the superhighways and out of range of the public-relations chatter to which Spender's actual experience in America seems, from what he writes in *Love-Hate Relations* at any rate, to have been confined. As a result, Silkin uncovers the superficiality of Spender's basic sense of American life, a sense summed up as follows:

> What I mean is that America with its air of knowing all the answers and believing that it can solve all problems produces an image of total knowledgeability. One consequence of that is that there seems to be a transparent quality about American life, as though everything has been put under the microscope and talked about over the loudspeakers.[22]

There is, it is true, a shade of irony in Spender's suggestion that American life is transparent and thus as superficial as the mass media and public and scientific accounts make it appear. He does say, however, without irony, that "American man is not so much rational man (an impossibility!) as rationalized man, who breaks his own personality down into questions for which he seeks to provide answers." Or, in the same context, he says, "In a totally Americanized world, everything would be known about everyone, and everyone, since his needs were known could, in theory, and perhaps sometimes even in practice, be provided for."[23] Spender is no further along than Auden was back in 1940 in his "The Unknown Citizen," in which he sets forth "the citizen" as known by public investigation (mostly a matter of statistics) and then concludes, ironically, by suggesting that such knowledge excludes what matters:

Was he free? Was he happy? The question is absurd:
Had anything been wrong, we should certainly have heard.

Because, like Spender's comments, Auden's poem is just talk, and
nothing is realized, one cannot know whether he is hinting that the
unknown citizen did in truth live a life that involved genuine
choice and intense emotions, qualities unknowable by public
means, or that the citizen was a sad slave reduced to what can be
known publicly. What is needed is less English irony playing off
the clichés of sociological, statistical information—a kind of sterile
one-upmanship—and some real poetic knowing, a knowing realized in the second and one of the finest of Silkin's six American
cemetery poems:

From the road, I saw a small, rounded bluff, a cemetery
tufted on it, churchless, and squarely contained by wire fencing;
one more field, increasing in it a short, thick tree.
Its branches emerged, multiplying densely, compacting
an opaque bud of wood and leaves not chinking
light through, or air; populous of itself, impacted.
It had been planted among the dead, or grew
with them, first there perhaps, the dead
put about the tree, in urban grid-like plots.
Since void, that had tissue and bone from them disjoined
into bland nitrogens the tree burgeons in.
Burgeons and thickens, the graves tidied
emptily on its root-veined lumpy wildness;
the graves in distinguishable order,
their territorial bitterness lapsing
into the dense acid wood. Lingeringly
it darkens, and I feel the headstones' life
lengthening past the deads' lives, or any trim, lively care.
The stones split into the shape
the roots strain under with gregarious presence.
The fence's tension snaps, with the grid's.[24]

Silkin begins a note to his most recent sequence, "The Little Time-
Keeper," with this curiously settled, English estimate: "If the universe were stranger than it is we'd go mad."[25] "From the road
. . . ," like his other truly fine poems, is as mad as it is sane, the

stress between imaginative realization and commitment being so intense that, while remaining inexplicably unified, the poem splits into two poems spinning away from each other. The poem realizes Silkin's profoundest insight into the quality of American life and, at the same time, articulates his own self-liberation and renewal.

The scene itself is a thrusting, even from the first line, with "rounded" giving a slight shouldering effect to the bluff, against which the product of man's intentions, the cemetery as a claim for humanity against the destructive forces of nature, of time and weather, is set fragilely ("tufted on it") and awkwardly ("churchless, and squarely contained"). With line seven Silkin stalls the momentum by wondering uncertainly over the relation between the planting of the tree and the burial of the dead, creating a pause before what becomes an onrush. The upsurge of the tree and the straining of the roots then work so unimpededly that the last line, "The fence's tension snaps, with the grid's," is felt mimetically, muscularly. The poem is experienced with awe and empathic identification. Silkin is experiencing an American body, its land and its language, from within. He senses that its stupendous energy is dependent on the slightness and abstractness, on the antiorganic quality of its humane, civilized caring, as manifested in the cemetery, the fence, the "urban grid-like plots," and the headstones. As William Carlos Williams knew, a natural rhythmical energy is impossible unless the reins are left slack. Americans are fascinated with elaborately abstract systems, as the English are not, just because they ride so lightly and casually above the roaring, natural energy which pours up from within.

This American body with its abstract, squaring, nonchalant mentality is not, Silkin recognizes, a body which he, as a man of commitment, could live with. He is pulling back, almost fastidiously, from the scene in phrases like "bland nitrogens" and "lumpy wildness" and "the shape/ the roots strain under with gregarious presence." But living this other language-body-land inwardly, discovering that it is not just a place but is a scene-act, a self-world, a person, Silkin uncovered what was wrong with the relation he had with his own language-body-land. England is so thoroughly humanized and so compactly familial, the very air and clouds being the most sensitively humane air and clouds in the world (the closest one can come to this in America is with certain neurotic dogs which are nature made over in the image of their master or mistress), that it is almost impossible not to live in it as a given, a ground, in no way dependent on one's own actions. Living in the emptiness of America, living inwardly a body not his own, Silkin realized that he himself is not just an actor acting and speaking in a scene, but is rather the scene as well, and that to a be a person is to be one's world as much as one's self.

"From the road . . ." has an English body different from its American body. Put your weight on the distastefulness of the scene-act, and the poem becomes a graveyard poem, a meditation on the dead, a civilized, conventional composition containing a generic aspect not shared by the Williams poems most like it. "Lingeringly/ it darkens" then takes on a new strength and subtlety. The clause suggests the power and domination of the tree. The distaste, however, which comes from the suggestion of evil, the darkening being a sort of staining caused by the territorial bitterness lapsing into the wood from bodies which while alive competed to have and to hold their own private property, works as a tradition into that sense of its being evening, the time for poetic meditation, especially in graveyards, where one observes the shadows of the headstones "lengthening past the deads' lives."

The poem—or at least this second poem spinning off from it—is in fact a poem of withdrawal from America. Silkin's deepest involvement in America was realized in his long "Amana Grass," a poem I have written on elsewhere.[26] "From the road . . ." is a withdrawing of the poet from the awesome scene-act-person, a movement the opposite of the withdrawal of that awesome son in "Death of a Son" from the poet-father. Silkin is pulling so far back at the end of the poem as to hint, with the grotesque image of roots straining "with gregarious presence," at a giant straining to break out of the ground, like the giant in one of Ted Hughes's children's stories. Though the hint cannot but be felt, it should not, in my opinion, be allegorized into an image of American individuals being transformed into a monstrous force out of the control of human intelligence. However that may be, Silkin is clearly withdrawing from the barbarous country cemetery of Iowa to something more like Highgate Cemetery, where, even with all the plantings, the very thought of man's losing battles to nature simply does not occur. That monstrously bodiless marble head of Marx is toppled, periodically, off its pedestal, not by natural forces, but by ideologically committed anti-communists or anarchists.

Of the two sequences of poems Silkin has published since the cemetery poems, only "Killhope Wheel" (eight poems in the original, two extra mistakenly added in the Wesleyan University Press edition of *Amana Grass*, the original eight in *The Principle of Water*) marks a creative leap out of and beyond the American poems. Whenever Silkin returns to England after an extended absence, it seems he is quickly caught up in the rush and business of editing *Stand*. The other sequence, the very long "The People," was, according to my judgment, written out of some such condition. It is a piece of rhetoric constructed along the lines already laid down in his juvenilia, those editorials equating poetry with cleaning lavatories. By intention the poet, as a living person, is barred from the poem. Everything having been thought out beforehand, the poem is then put together as a useful device to give the readers what is good for them in a pleasing enough way to insure that the poet will be paid for his labors. To succeed, the poet must feel that he understands his readers thoroughly, that the England he addresses is, in Raymond Williams' comfortable phrase, a "knowable community," the society transparent (at least, according to Lukácsian thought, for party members, for those whose awareness makes them as subject identical with society as object) exactly the way Spender found America to be. Heard in the summer of 1974 on the BBC, "The People" was a moving experience. One felt the better for it.

The point of stress in "Killhope Wheel," the germinal fount which makes these poems absolutely novel and of incomparable value, is an interplay between Silkin's own serious and austere taking of stands and a large and generous and, at points, almost hilarious recognizing of the limits of those stands. It is not enough to say that the poems are a delicate balance of sobriety and an almost raucous hilarity, because the balance itself, beyond what is being balanced, is so unusual. At the very moment when Silkin's pointing stiffly in the right direction is being unsettled by an almost-laughter, the almost-laughter is being called in question and put in its place by the stiff stance. My concluding aim is to suggest how anything so delicate and fine could have been created.

The discovery Silkin explores and develops in "Killhope Wheel"—and my claim that he glimpsed the germ of this in the cemetery poems might be doubted if it were not for these subsequent poems—is that he is himself both act and scene, both self and world, and that to be a person is to be aware of this self-constituting doubleness and to strive to pull its halves together, and doing all this, moreover, in relation to at least one other human being who is acting with a similar awareness of himself and another. This notion of a person as constituting, in constant striving, self and world, act and scene, individual and society, this growing that includes an attending to, and dramatic interaction with, other persons, other individual-societies, is sharply at odds with any Marxist-Lukácsian-Williamsite idea of the special person, the party member, as the subject identical with the object, the toad that swelled himself into the size of an ox, so that he speaks with the voice of his society ("a facile exercise"). It is no less at odds with the William Carlos Williams plunge of self into world, that modernistic dissolution of self into world, and world into *the* world, which is no less totalitarian and imperialistic and violent than its non-American counterpart.

Such large terms are too heavy and gross for anything so unique as any one among six of the eight "Killhope Wheel" poems. The second, "Small hills, among the fells . . . ," is perhaps the easiest to read in relation to my idea that the interplay between commitment and hilarity comes out of Silkin's growing sense of himself as a fully human person in dramatic relation to another person:

Small hills, among the fells, come apart from the large
where streams drop; the water-flowers
bloom at the edges, or in the shallows, together,
and are white. Whoever comes here, comes, glad, at least
and as they look, it is with some care, you can feel
that on flower, may tree, or dry-stone wall
their gaze collects in a moist, comely pressure.
I feel this, but slog elsewhere.

Swan Hunter's is where we build naval craft;
they emerge: destroyer, the submarine
fitted, at length, by electricians. Their work
is inspected; it is again re-wired. In the heat
men walk high in the hulk on planks, one
of them tips, and he falls the depth of the hold.
It is hot. The shithouses are clagged, the yard's
gates closed for security. The food is not good.
Some people in here are maimed.
I am trying to make again the feeling
plants have, and each creature has, looked at,
demure, exultant. The man who has fallen
looks at me, and looks away.

The world of the poem is split between the natural scene, where human beings and the objects about them are in a mutually health-giving harmony, and the shipyard, where the analogous relationship is perilous and careless. In his act of shaping the poem the poet works to heal the split mainly by way of rhythm and syntax, but also, to some extent, by both the imagery and the way it is looked at. "Where streams drop" is echoed by "and he falls the depth of the hold." The gaze of those who look upon the natural objects collects on them "in a moist, comely pressure," whereas in the shipyard every observation is felt like the recoil of a gun, the observer being rebuffed by the objects ("The shithouses are clagged") so that he swallows with revulsion and swerves into social workers' talk ("The food is not good./ Some people in here are maimed"). The clauses of the natural half of the poem are related in a supple way, so that one moves along smoothly, if thoughtfully, whereas the shipyard syntax is abrupt and assertive, jerky and sharply stopped (the nine lines of natural scenery are in two sentences, the nine concerning the shipyard in seven, and so forth).

What makes the poem (omitting for the moment the last four lines) different from, and more than, a lively, mimetic description of two contrasting scenes depends on the transitional line, "I feel this, but slog elsewhere." The poet, that is, is sustaining and cultivating his memory of the natural scene while he slogs through the shipyard. Just that is enough. He knows that this split world is implicated in an act of his own construction, in an act bringing together two scenes not necessarily related. As he shapes the abrupt lines of the shipyard, he feels the fluid rhythms of the natural scene. He sees and feels and thinks as he does because of the contrast he is making. In his self-world the yard is this way. He notices that a man "falls the depth of the hold." Then he shifts abruptly to noticing the heat. He is careless himself. It is in his own contrast to organic, fluid continuity that everything seems so disconnected, so mechanically and arbitrarily associated. The grounds, therefore, on which the poet makes his final moral assertion, trying to bring expressively into his face the feeling that plants in the natural scene have and thereby trying to act out a judgment against the shipyard, are recognized to be shaky before the assertion is made. I am pointing, of course, not to a weakness, but to Silkin's presence in the poem as a person from the very start, worrying about possible bias in what he sees because of how he sees it. The ending expresses ambivalence:

> I am trying to make again the feeling
> plants have, and each creature has, looked at,
> demure, exultant. The man who has fallen
> looks at me, and looks away.

The ambivalence is built up to by Silkin and is experienced by him first, before the reader, critically and attentively. That is the nature of his satisfaction with the poem. His moral gesture, the expression of plant-human harmony on his face, does, in Silkin's self-world, make the man turn away in shame and despair, in contrast to the "demure, exultant" response of the plants. The emphasis of the lines, however, is not on Silkin's looking at the man (though he is doing that), but on the man's looking at Silkin. What does he see, this man with a life of his own, independent of the contrastive mesh Silkin has woven? Does he see this peculiar little man squidging up his face like a prune, or what? That "and looks away" trails off speculatively, puzzling, as though the man might, within his own self-world, truly be worrying about the odd, impertinent fellow.

Silkin has broken through the glass wall of his self-world, a solipsism that may well characterize the lives of many of us much of the time but which, curiously enough, is never felt and recognized as such until one has broken out of it. The capacity Silkin shows here to be invaded and disrupted by another person, from whom he receives only the one piercing insight, is the germ out of which the human person grows and is made. For it is impossible for one to become a person unless he becomes aware of himself as a person, and that awareness depends upon a breach like the one with which this poem ends. Silkin continues to hope that, having seen his plantlike face, the man who has fallen will quit the shipyard in disgust and become a gamekeeper. He is not shaken morally. He has discovered, however, that he is responsible for the world in which he makes his commitments, as well as for making them. The poem's ending expands capaciously, leaving the poet looking back smilingly on himself as the small prune-faced man. If there is a surge of hilarity, still he must wonder if what he has made as a poet can be as effective as the one small moral gesture he made in that detestable shipyard.

The gesture itself, moreover, is not simply an expression of the poet's commitment to nature over technology, though it is in part that, as Silkin made clear in an interview concerning the sequence, which was written up for *The Guardian* by Raymond Gardner.[27] It is also thoroughly English and uniquely Silkin's. It comes most directly out of this sentence from the first part of the poem:

> Whoever comes here, comes, glad, at least
> and as they look, it is with some care, you can feel
> that on flower, may tree, or dry-stone wall
> their gaze collects in a moist, comely pressure.

The voice anticipates one's sense that there is something precious and affected about a world in which all natural objects appear to be looked at, each being tagged by a human gaze. Silkin now, however, has decided that he can and will live with this weakness, as he could not in "Moss," where disgust prevailed. Instead of fighting, as he did before his American experiences, he accepts it but is keenly aware of its limits. By putting it to work within the action of his poems, he transforms its allegorical blight, which saps its natural energy, into a part of his own personal energy. "I feel this, but slog elsewhere" expresses, in this light, a certain impatience: I feel this but have no intention of dwelling on it, for in itself it represents a very English form of silliness. By the end of the poem, plants that appear to be looked at and a man who looks like a plant are not just silly. They have been made by Silkin into something grotesque but also functional and, though functional, of questionable value.

The earth underneath the yard, in the first poem of the sequence, "Tree," is "disabled, rank," the very opposite of the soil of Iowa in which that "short, thick tree" burgeons. Silkin is going to accept and use and live with English nature, however, even if it is often ridiculous and laughable. So he tries to grow a tree in his house, in a big barrel into which he mixes earth, peat, and dung (a co-editor of *Stand* was quick to point out in conversation that the tree did not survive). In contrast, the tree in Roy Fisher's "City" is made out of steel rods; and the tree in Charles Tomlinson's *The Way In* is simply an imaginary tree the poet places alongside the child he sees shoveling the remains of snow in a totally stoned- and bricked-in city street. Silkin admits:

> I can't fudge up a relationship, but it gladdens
> you, as the sun concentrates it, and I
> want the creature for what it is
> to live beyond me.

"I will work to survive/ With what will work."[28] In "Killhope Wheel" Silkin is working with what he knows may not work. In a poem I quoted from at the beginning of this chapter, "Concerning strength . . . ," he imaginatively perceives the course of the River Wansbeck, which flows into the North Sea not far above Newcastle-on-Tyne:

> The Wansbeck
> shivers over the stone, bits of coal, and where
> it halts a pool fills, oily
> and twitching. Closer to the sea, it drops
> under a bridge, coming to ground
> where the mind opens, and gives uselessly to
> the sun such created heat, the air

cleaves to the flesh,
the bench facing the water, sat on by old men.
If this goes, nothing; this clearness
which draws a supple smell through old skin
making a pause for it.[29]

The poet's concern is with the water, but English water has been gazed at too long to be just water. The course of the river comes to the poet, as to us, already interpreted, as an image of the poetic function. The allegory is not something the poet does, but a part of the water, the land, of England. Even (or mainly?) an American in England can sense that. By accepting that quality of English nature and English awareness, Silkin is then able to shake it loose, to pry it open, to make it questionable. It still comes to one interpreted, allegorized, but a space has been opened up that allows for a clearness and warmth. The metaphor holds, but its two parts have been pried apart. The last sentence of the poem, therefore, is not a cry of horror and despair:

> Houses and scrap will heap,
> and flake, as
> if organs of the soil clagged
> with shreddings of rust.

That is poetic language and not mere talk, not mere discursive language. Its power is to deny itself as merely itself in order to evoke that which is fundamentally other than itself, interpreting in such a way as to evoke that which is not interpreted, along with that which is.

Such creative language is in the service of something larger than individual, nation, or language. That something is a person, tripled into self, world, and attentiveness bridging them under stress, and always, when most heightened, disrupted by forces other than and outside itself. In *The Peaceable Kingdom*, that disruptive other, the fly, the dead bird, the defective child, is marked by inscrutable remoteness. In the "Killhope Wheel" sequence, that other—the man who falls, in "Small hills, among the fells . . ."; a retired plate-layer; a woman whose love was one of the miners bayonetted for striking in 1860 at Killhope Wheel, County

Durham—has become a person who, at least by suggestion, has all the qualities that the poet himself as a person has. One hint of something even finer, of the possibility of a poem's containing a second person as fully and actively realized as the poet himself, may be glimpsed in these two stanzas from "Killhope Wheel, 1860, County Durham":

> A board says that we're free to come in.
> Why should it seem absurd to get
> pain from such permission? Why have
>
> I to see red-coat soldiers prick
> between washed stones, and bayonets
> tugged from the flesh?

Who beyond Silkin himself is raising the question of absurdity? There seems to be a companion, another person who listens to him differently from the way he listens to himself. After those two stanzas that person is resolutely dismissed and Silkin goes on, more comfortably, by himself. Could that other person be the hidden source of the strand of hilarity running through the sequence? Isn't the prospect to be hoped for that of Silkin's realizing poetically such another person—with ears other than his own—so fully as to supersede decisively that inauthentic—because grounded in only one world—drama of which "The People" is a type?

CHAPTER SEVEN

Inner Community in
Thom Gunn's "Misanthropos"

If one attends to his experience of reading poems rather than to that of hearing a poet read poems in a crowded hall, he will, I believe, agree that the performance to which a poem summons him is not so much a public recitation as it is a form of criticism analogous to the performing arts. If the poet is a performing self, as Richard Poirier claims, if no work of art comes alive except in the presence of an audience, as R. G. Collingwood argues, if the reader of poems must accept these claims, nonetheless he will modify them because of his recognition that the poet is always his own first audience.[1]

The echoing quality of all poetic language depends on the presence of this primary audience, on the felt presence of the poet as his own first listener, and this essential echo is drowned out and rendered inaudible by the assumption that the life of poetry depends on its metropolitan audiences which are reached through our great publishing firms and on those crowds who are gathered together by the business of organizing poetry reading circuits. Unless misled by the prospect of a cash reward, no poet would think he was reciting his poems in order that they might be heard. For he could not even compose a poem unless it were heard in the very act of composition. The experience of reading poems to oneself and especially reading them silently must reveal that the listening presence of the poet has to be attended to just as much as his speaking presence. One cannot, in fact, even hear the words of poetry unless he also attends to the echoing into silence which is, at a conceptual level, the poet's act of shaping the poem. A poet works with his words in order to articulate that innermost feeling which determines the quality of his self, his world, and his experience. His words work poetically only in so far as they are the echo of that upsurge of feeling. A reader of those words can respond to them as echoingly resonant only to the extent that he also attends to the echo of that echo, to the over-arching action which is the poet's own attending to his words as echoing the deepest impulsion of his experience.

Words working poetically are neither transitive nor intransitive. They do not, like words used practically or intellectually, have the reason for their being in the conventional patterns and structures and frameworks to which they refer, even though they may include such transitive references. Nor are they self-subsistent, only internally referential, elements of an autonomous artifact, a fiction, a sort of entertaining make-believe. They are rather, in their essential nature, the echo of being as an upsurge of feeling and are in turn echoed by the becoming which is the poet's act of shaping that feeling into an articulated vision.

Quite apart, then, from being read and attended to critically by another person, a poem is itself an active community constituted by the poet as speaker and the poet as listener, by the poet expressing his deepest sense of himself and his world and the poet listening to and criticizing that expression. The poem circles in widening waves, out from its elemental feeling, as the poet speaks listening and, having listened, speaks further until he has made a world adequate to his own deepest impulsion.

For at least the past twenty-five years, as part of the macadamization of literary studies, critics have been busy crushing out the communal life of the poem by reducing its being and its becoming, its feeling and its thinking, to what I should call its non-being, its status as a self-subsistent object. Once objectified in this way, the poem may then be said to have, in René Wellek's terms, a single structure of determination, the grasp of which leads us to its proper meaning.[2] Once reduced to an artifact, the poem calls for an interpretation in the manner of E. D. Hirsch, Jr., a delimitation of its intrinsic and extrinsic genres, accomplished by reference to the linguistic ambience of the poem, now treated as an object among objects. With the poem rendered lifeless and the process of interpretation itself doing nothing to revive it, critics have been led unavoidably, in order to retain some sense of themselves as alive, into widening circles of entrapment. Hirsch himself will locate Wordsworth's Intimations Ode within the vast framework of Schelling's philosophy. Raymond Williams, like many another neo-historicist, will view each objectified literary work in the light of a massive social and political movement, his version of which he calls The Long Revolution. Northrop Frye, radical structuralist that he is, will back away from the painting fixed on the wall until it blurs with more and more of its neighbors, "all reduced to one form and one size," to a single structure, a repetition, only, with variations, capped by his favorite myth. With the poem's echoing in widening waves blocked out, the critic must undertake his own spiralling out, with the consequence that the warmth and light of the poem diminishes to the point where it averages out with all other poems in grains of dust. There are, of course, secondary values accruing from such critical strategies. But all rest upon a deep-seated error, the conception of the poem as a corpus, the direct touch of which is death. The pain of that touch, or a horror at its numbness, when it should have been so vital, is what set them off on their long slow trips, on which they passed no humans, until each arrived, a final man upon a final hill, in a state of ataraxia, of apatheia, unperturbed by the touch of the dead poem or by any recollection of the joyful pain of touching a living poem.

If we do leave the green slopes of our isolation and vacate the empty centers of our structuralistic, historicistic, phenomenological webs, and approach a genuine poem with some sense of its vital activeness, we will find in its smallness an illumined largeness realizing, as few other experiences can, the full being of human community. The experience must surely be a painful one, partly because of our own bad habits, but also because of the painful element in all genuine community. We may even have to learn to memorize poetry again, so that we can truly join our breath with the poet's, giving the poem time to germinate in the dust of our own natures until we feel its deep surge and over-arching action. The closer we get to a poem, the more fully we experience the world as it is in the articulation of the poet, the more painful our sense of his otherness from ourselves is almost sure to become. At some point in our attention not just to what the poet says, but also to the way in which he attends to what he says, we will be forced to recognize that neither his mouth nor his ears are ours and, even while at one with the poem, we will move out of it into our own sense of experience in the effort to hear and feel its resonances as distinct from and at times at odds with those of the poem. At this stage, in this *concordia discors*, at one with the poem and distinct from it, opening up to ourselves our own natures as part of our experience of opening up the innermost nature of the poet and his world, with the poem qualifying and judging us as we qualify and judge it, in this vital interplay we will experience the living pulse of human community as it is and as it might be, but ah, as it is, as it is. And then, at last, we will be ready to perform the poem critically.

It is not possible to work out the critical performance of a poem by means of direct encounter, by what children call a "stare-down," and thus it is that I have moved with indirection towards Thom Gunn's "Misanthropos," in spite of the lines with which Gunn concludes the poem:

> You must
> If you can, pause; and, paused,
>
> Turn out toward others, meeting their look at full,
>   Until you have completely stared
> On all there is to see. Immeasurable,
>   The dust yet to be shared.

Each of the seventeen poems of which "Misanthropos" is composed echoes the others, and all of them interinanimate each other. But if one would sense the surge of feeling that gives life and unity to the whole, he must attend to the interlinking action of Gunn's mind. Just as the final man of the poem, who has become its first man, can affirm that you must "Turn out toward others, meeting their look at full,/ Until you have completely stared/ On all there is to see," only if you have the capacity to pause, so we can stare into these final lines of the poem with understanding only if we can pause to hear the deepest echoes of the whole as they roll up and break into this final affirmation.

The skeletal pattern of "Misanthropos" is not hard to discern nor is discerning it important, when compared to the question, "do these bones live?" But noting it has mnemonic value and is a first step in coming as close to the poem as possible. The pattern is derived ultimately from Vico's eternal course and recourse of nations. The decadence of any nation or civilization is a state of disintegration. In the final stage of Rome, the citizens retreat to the hills, each one a final man upon his final hill. The accepted hierarchy of value collapses, each man carries off his own fragmentary version of it to his own hill, no one sees anyone else, and it is only the wind that utters ambiguous orders from the plain. Chaucer's pilgrims may stand as representative of another such recourse of decadence. But such decadence is virtually indistinguishable from the innocence with which a new recourse of nations begins. Thus, as Toynbee has shown, the Holy Roman Empire springs out of the isolated monasteries and mountain citadels and Germanic tribes which represent the final stage of the fall of the Roman Empire. And Chaucer's pilgrims are full of innocent exuberance and self-confidence. Now Gunn, in "Misanthropos," is working with just this moment of transition in the eternal course and recourse of nations, the moment of decadence as it turns into the moment of innocence.

But Gunn responds to this pattern in an extremely personal way. He feels, and I think he is right to feel so, that all his poetry written prior to the volume *Touch* (London: Faber and Faber, 1967), in which "Misanthropos" is the central poem, was fundamentally decadent. His first volume, *Fighting Terms* (1954), was written while he was still an undergraduate, and Charles Tomlinson found it to be clever and precious, an adolescent forcing of talent, much as F. R. Leavis found Auden's early verse to be.[3] His first poem of that volume, "Carnal Knowledge," beings with the clause, "Even in bed I pose," and includes the line, "You know I know you know I know you know," which should sum up adequately the cleverness and preciosity of the early Gunn.[4] In the third poem of "Misanthropos," Gunn as listener recognizes the similarity between the early Gunn and the final man in these lines:

> But the curled darling who survives the war
> Has merely lost the admirers of those curls

That always lavished most warmth on his neck;
Though no one sees him, though it is the wind
Utters ambiguous orders from the plain,
Though nodding foxgloves are his only girls,
His poverty is a sort of uniform.

Even in isolation he adopts a role and poses. He remains the same
as the one who "Curled my hair,/ wore gloves in my cap." By wear-
ing dark glasses, he was able to stand, "an armed angel among
men." He fussed affectedly over the question of whether he was
spy or spied on, "master/ or the world's abject servant." I do not
intend, by noting these echoes in "Misanthropos" from earlier
poems, to suggest that the poem is basically a conversation with
those poems. Contrary to the position of Thomas Whitaker, I am
convinced that no genuine poem is such a conversation.[5] A poem is
essentially a dialectical dialogue between the poet speaking and the
poet listening, the poet expressing and the poet criticizing; any
conversational echoes with other poems which it may include are
strictly subordinate to that primary dialogue. Thus the man referred
to in "Misanthropos" as "the curled darling who survives the war,"
though he resembles a Gunn who could say "Even in bed I pose,"
is transformed by a feeling of loathing and disgust which is absent
from the earlier poem. If it were insisted that the poem is a conversation with another poem outside it, then one would be forced to
say that in the poem itself the conversation is fraudulently partisan,
and whatever genuine conversation one claimed to exist would be
the concoction of the critic rather than the creation of the poet.

When Gunn came to America in 1954 he avoided that deepen-
ing of affectation to which Auden succumbed, by going to Stanford
and coming under the severe tutelage of Yvor Winters. Once there
Gunn peeled off that delicate fastidiousness which would cause
Philip Larkin to be terrified of riding a motorcycle for fear he might
tear his pants. Gunn heard the call, "Man, you gotta Go," and
joined the Boys, "In goggles, donned impersonality." It is clear
that, in *The Sense of Movement* (1957), Gunn does not "strap in
doubt," as the Boys do, but the last lines of "On the Move,"

At worst, one is in motion; and at best,
Reaching no absolute, in which to rest,
One is always nearer by not keeping still.

indicate that, for all his doubt, for all his knowledge that the Boys are "Small, black, as flies hanging in heat," he can come up with no alternative to riding in the "direction where the tires press," and thus accepts their way even though with a despairing cynicism. The passage echoing "On the Move" in the fifth poem of "Misanthropos" is dominated by a quite different feeling:

> thickets
> crowd in on the brown earth gap
> in green which is the path made
>
> by his repeated tread, which,
> enacting the wish to move,
> is defined by avoidance
> of loose ground, of rock and ditch,
> of thorn-brimmed hollows, and of
> poisoned beds. The ground hardens.
>
> Bare within limits. The trick
> is to stay free within them.
> The path branches, branches still,
> returning to itself, like
> a discovering system,
> or process made visible.

Here Gunn places the despairing cynicism of his decadence with a fine, discriminating disgust. The Boys were really just going around in circles. And their act was craven. Like our master structuralists, concocting patterns as remote as possible from the thickets of genuine poetry, they treaded out their discovering systems, returning upon themselves, merely to avoid the fearful things moving at the edges of their minds. Nor is there, in "Misanthropos," any of that sentimental indulgence with which "Lines for a Book" closes:

> I think of all the toughs through history
> And thank heaven they lived, continually.

Gunn has achieved that moral discrimination of which Leavis despaired in Auden and which Tomlinson feared Gunn would not attain.

He has even surpassed the hard heroizing of the title poem of his next volume, *My Sad Captains* (1961):

                    They were men
who, I thought, lived only to
renew the wasteful force they
spent with each hot convulsion.
They remind me, distant now.

True, they are not at rest yet,
but now that they are indeed
apart, winnowed from failures,
they withdraw to an orbit
and turn with disinterested
hard energy, like the stars.

As early as the fourth poem of "Misanthropos," Gunn recognizes that such heroes are modelled on the movement of the moon ("And steady in the orbit it must go") and the Milky Way ("A luminous field that swings across the sky") and that they represent an "envy for the inanimate." In the fourteenth poem, the first man's desire to be "Inhuman as a star, as cold, as white,/ Freed from all dust" is placed as a form of cowardice, an unwillingness to accept the dust of life itself. Yvor Winters complained that the Gunn of *The Sense of Movement* and *My Sad Captains* usually had a "dead ear."[6] If his own sense of experience had not been so close to that of Gunn's, Winters might have realized, as Gunn does in "Misanthropos," that the deadness went much deeper than the ear.

It was not, however, the Viconian pattern or Gunn's personalization of that pattern which sprung him free of his deadness, but rather, I think, his discovery that his decadence was "wholly representative." Gunn makes that recognition throughout "Misanthropos." His withdrawal first into affectation and then into isolated hardness ran parallel to a mass reaction to the Second World War. When the relief of the end of the war had exhausted itself, men turned away from each other in disgust. The humanized air which held the nation together in its united war effort suddenly became dry and empty. Even hitchhikers were abandoned to themselves. "Each colourless hard grain" was "now distinct,/ In no way to its neighbour linked." College students writing essays about what sort of man they would like to have survive a nuclear holocaust were in truth working out the desire to be "The final man upon a final hill." It was not their fear of the future but their disgust for the past which made them open this "disused channel/ to the onset of hatred." Nor was the hysterical construction of fall-out shelters, an act usually accompanied by an image of oneself gunning down his improvident neighbors who implored him for a breath of unpoisoned air, really a sign of providence so much as it was an expression of misanthropy, a dream in which one was at last free of the smudge of other men. Some such realization resounds throughout "Misanthropos": we had all withdrawn into an isolated state of ataraxia where we could live imperturbably, untouched by pain, "evil's external mark," unaware that if pain is the mark of evil, it is also the mark of goodness, the mark of "A man who burnt from sympathy alone."

That Gunn could find a way out of such a state, in which he had "grown/ As stony as a lizard poised on stone," is not so remarkable as it might at first appear, especially to Americans. For, unlike us, he had behind him an experience in England following upon the First World War much like what happened to us only after the Second. Think, for example, of Yeats's ataraxic "An Irish Airman Foresees His Death" or of his desire to be taken up in the stone mosaics of Byzantium. Think too of Ezra Pound's major English poem, "Hugh Selwyn Mauberley," a poem written out of a state of paralysis from which there seemed to be no exit, whether into a Pre-Raphaelite dream world or into an impossibly depraved society run by the Mr. Nixons. Or consider whether the most influential English poem of the century, Eliot's *Four Quartets*, is not in truth written out of a deep state of ataraxia, being the sustained and repeatedly realized withdrawal from earthly, engaged experience, even a withdrawal from the crumbling language of the poem itself. Once Eliot had abandoned personal, sexual love in the poem "La Figlia che Piange," mustn't he be viewed as the exemplary final man upon the final hill, for whom every personal face is but a mask beyond which one moves into "the still point of the turning world"?

Even more important to the change that takes place for Gunn in "Misanthropos" is the criticism of F. R. Leavis and of the journal *Scrutiny*, which was a focus of literary intelligence in England from 1932 to 1952. Nothing in American criticism is comparable to Leavis' battle against the disintegration of his society and the impersonalization of both its social experience and its art. Leavis fought these heavy driftings not from the outside, rebelliously and violently, but from within, burning with good will and sympathy. He has never, for example, reneged on his claim that Eliot is one of the greatest of English poets. Compare his cautious and tentative and delicate criticism of Eliot with the blasts of Yvor Winters or with Quentin Anderson's recent claim, bordering as it does on hysteria: "The notion of the impersonality of art became the refuge of the infantile demand to rule the whole world."[7] Anderson's immediate targets are Emerson, Thoreau, Whitman, and Henry James, and the hundreds of thousands who gathered at Woodstock. But he is being exacerbated by the hidden foe of foes, T. S. Eliot. At least when set beside Leavis, Anderson seems to have no capacity to pause, and, having paused, to turn out toward others. In spite of himself, he appears as one more imperial self raging against imperial selves. Not, of course, that Gunn has found the way out of his stony isolation simply by following Leavis' precepts. He is an original poet, and, for all the resemblances between his recent poetry and the ideals Leavis advocates and certain poems by Hill, Silkin, and Tomlinson, the beating impulsion and the curve of action of "Misanthropos" are distinctly Gunn's own.

Even so, if Gunn had not had in his background Leavis' opposition to the impersonality and self-abnegation of Eliot, it seems likely that he would have fallen under the spell of that peculiarly imperialistic form of misanthropy to be found in so much of the very finest of contemporary American poetry. He could easily have turned into the path of Robert Bly, as James Wright did, temporarily, and tried to abandon his keen intellect and self-awareness. Bly would have us abandon ourselves utterly in order to move to the deepest point of our brain, where it dissolves into oneness with the God in Nature. He would have us move back to that still point at the heart of the wilderness and live and write poetry out of that impersonal center. Or Gunn might have followed Gary Snyder beyond the high point of his mountain retreats into an oriental form of ataraxia. At the very least he would have fallen in with Allen Ginsberg's feeling that "All separate identities are bankrupt." Without Leavis' constant warnings he would have missed the odd likeness between the violence at the center of the vision of those poets who reject our society and the destructive acts committed in the name of that society. He would have missed the similarity between the perspective those poets take on the society they reject and the perspective of that society on the basis of which its leaders make it move.

With all his misanthropy and with all the sympathy he shows for this American form of misanthropy, Gunn is able to resist this deepest revulsion for men with a disgust more intense than the sympathy he feels for it. Gunn articulates this complex mixture of sympathy and disgust in the twelfth poem, "Elegy on the Dust," which is the high point of "Misanthropos," the point at which the last man turns into the first man. The poem is a stunning articulation of the vision of men in society as a bowl of dust, "vexed with constant loss and gain," "a vaguely heaving sea," a graveyard which is a sea of dust. At the beginning of "Misanthropos," the final man was being a contemporary Englishman in his refusal to build a watch tower. But here he has moved to America and looks outward from his retreat, taking into his view the hill, the wooded slope, and the vast expanse of dust beyond it. He has made the transfer which Lawrence's Lou Witt makes at the end of "St. Mawr."[8]

"Elegy on the Dust" ends with this visionary judgment on man in a modern mass nation state:

> Each colourless hard grain is now distinct,
>   In no way to its neighbour linked,
> Yet from wind's unpremeditated labours
>   It drifts in concord with its neighbours,
> Perfect community in its behaviour.
>   It yields to what it sought, a saviour:
> Scattered and gathered, irregularly blown,
>   Now sheltered by a ridge or stone,
> Now lifted on strong upper winds, and hurled
>   In endless hurry round the world.

The poem might seem to be merely a vision of man's ultimate form of decadence, that last stage in a Platonic cycle of degeneration at which a mobocracy turns into tyranny. Men are seen in the poem at their very lowest, averaged out in indistinguishable "grains of dust/

Too light to act, too small to harm, too fine/ To simper or betray or whine." In such a mobocracy, where even those who sought distinction are levelled with the rabble, in absolute uniformity, men are ready for a savior, a tyrant, who will windily hurl them "In endless hurry round the world." But instead of sharing this vision of Marcuse of the complete bankruptcy of our civilization, Gunn attends to its articulation with his keen, critical ear and turns the poem into a condemnation of that vision for which he has so much sympathy. The ultimate form of decadence turns out to be not what is seen, but the vision itself. As Raymond Williams has argued so persuasively, men exist as a mass only in the eye of the beholder. It is the beholding of men as a bowl of dust, as a mobocracy turning into a tyranny, not the men beheld in such a way, which is decadent.

One senses the special judgmental turn which Gunn is giving the vision in the way he works certain allusions into the poem. For example, in this part of the second stanza:

> Beneath it, glare and silence cow the brain
> Where, troughed between the hill and plain,
> The expanse of dust waits: acres calm and deep,
> Swathes folded on themselves in sleep
> Or waves that, as if frozen in mid-roll
> Hang in ridged rows.

Gunn is clearly echoing Wordsworth, and especially in the "acres calm and deep" the line "Ne'er saw I, never felt, a calm so deep!" from the sonnet "Composed upon Westminster Bridge." But he is doing more than simply alluding to the line; he is also judging Wordsworth's vision of London as organically beautiful only when all its citizens are asleep as an expression of imperialistic misanthropy. With Wordsworth so deeply studied and felt, Gunn could not fail to recognize the way in which the viewer personally determines the nature of the view. That the line "And vexed with constant loss and gain" in the next stanza echoes Wordsworth's sonnet "The world is too much with us" simply confirms how Gunn has learned from but then gone beyond the poet whom Galway Kinnell is now echoing somewhat uncritically. Of course, Marvell is present

too, especially in the allusions to his most misanthropic and mis-
ogynous poem, "The Garden," as the lines "Interdependent in that
shade" and "Are all reduced to one form and one size" echo the
lines "Annihilating all that's made/ To a green thought in a green
shade." But the dominant allusion of the second of Gunn's lines
just quoted is to Pound's "Hugh Selwyn Mauberley."

> here
> The graveyard is the sea, material things
> —From stone to claw, scale, pelt and wings—
> Are all reduced to one form and one size

echo these lines from Pound's "Envoi":

> I would bid them [the woman's graces] live
> As roses might, in magic amber laid,
> Red overwrought with orange and all made
> One substance and one colour
> Braving time.

Gunn senses that Pound's advocacy of the eternal beauty of art over
the transiency of ordinary experience, summed up as it is as "Siftings on siftings in oblivion," is just a step short of going off to Italy
and becoming an advocate of the Duce. It is Gunn's disgust for this
disgust for men in society that turns the "Elegy on the Dust" away
from being just one more imperial vision and into an extremely personal expression of Gunn's revulsion for such imperialism. It is the
vision of men as a smudge of dust, this way of seeing men, which
must be buried, the reducing of men to such a state, not men thus
reduced, which must be abandoned. Gunn knows too much about
Pound, he knows what Leavis recognized in him and what Donald
Davie, following Leavis' lead, demonstrated in his book *Ezra Pound:
Poet as Sculptor*, to be willing to follow after Ginsberg, Snyder, and
Bly.

My reading of the "Elegy" as an expression of disgust for the
vision of men as a bowl of dust instead of as a direct expression of
that vision is reinforced by echoes in the "Elegy" from the poem just
before it, the Epitaph for Anton Schmidt, and by the echoes of the

"Elegy" itself in the poem which follows it, "The First Man." There is no irony in Gunn's admiration for Anton Schmidt, whose greatness depends on his not having mistaken "the men he saw,/ As others did, for gods or vermin." The vision of the "Elegy" clearly mistakes the men viewed for vermin and the viewer for a god. Furthermore, the first man of the thirteenth poem is presented as Gunn's vision of the man who has had the vision of the "Elegy," "An unreflecting organ of perception." That man can perceive men as a disgusting smudge because he does not reflect on what such a vision implies about himself. What it implies for Gunn is that, just as the men viewed in the "Elegy" disappear into the dust of a society blown "In endless hurry round the world" by a windy tyrant, so the visionary of the "Elegy," that imperial self, that "transcendental eyeball," is finally to be seen "darkening in the heavy shade/ Of trunks that thicken in the ivy's grip." And this image of the first man, of this American innocent, this barbarian who may be what must follow after the decadence of Europe, this appalls Gunn as much as it did the poet here being echoed, Wallace Stevens. The eleventh poem of Stevens' "The Man with the Blue Guitar" is the rejection of its vision of men dissolving into a thicket of time, where they are caught as flies, "Wingless and withered, but living alive." At this point Gunn must make his final choice: to accept the disappearance of man as an individual into the dust of society or the heavy shade of nature or to reaffirm the value of that man as distinctive. His choice, as is obvious from the fourteenth poem, is the second: he must stare upon men as a smudge until they come so close to him that the outlines of the smudge break away from it and the men turn into individuals.

Only as a result of doing this does he realize in direct experience that as he gazes upon a man, he is himself gazed upon, as he touches another, he is himself touched, and that his own self and his whole world are enlarged and enlivened by this interaction. Gunn does not simply assert this but works it out experientially by means of echoes. The first man's affirming in the seventeenth poem that you must pause, if you can, echoes and is even learned from the scratched man's pausing in the sixteenth poem. The first man's revulsion from the stale stench, the hang-dog eyes and the pursed mouth of the scratched man in the sixteenth poem echoes the scratched man's response to the first man when he first sees him in the fifteenth poem:

> The creature sees him, jumps back, staggers, calls,
> Then, losing balance on the pebbles, falls.

The effect of Gunn's restraint in this passage—we aren't quite sure what the lines imply and may even feel them to be empty—is that our sense of the repulsiveness of the first man and Gunn's sense of his own repulsiveness coincide with the first man's momentary revulsion from the scratched man even as he grips his arm. Although Gunn's movement out of isolation at the end of "Misanthropos" includes such moments of felt insight, it is harsh and painful. There is no moment of explosive joy as there is at the end of Stevens' "Esthétique du Mal," when Stevens realizes that human life is made up of

> So many selves, so many sensuous worlds,
> As if the air, the mid-day air, was swarming
> With the metaphysical changes that occur,
> Merely in living as and where we live.

Gunn's use of the word "stared" to express the way in which we must connect with others suggests harshness. And his last words, "Immeasurable/ The dust yet to be shared" come out with a grudging sigh. But Gunn has made his recognition and affirmation. And the poems which follow "Misanthropos" in *Touch*, especially the last one, "Back to Life," and many poems in his most recent volume, *Moly*, show that he meant it.

The innermost sense of experience which forces Gunn to pull himself out of his isolation still remains to be explained. What forces him to affirm the value of human community is, I believe, his sense that his own nature as an individual is communal, even when he is most isolated. Observing the first man, in the thirteenth poem, "darkening in the heavy shade/ Of trunks that thicken in the ivy's grip," he sees that his very existence as an individual, composed of himself as self-aware observer and himself as a rudimentary man, is about to be annihilated. It is his commitment to himself as a community, as both spy and spied on, which forces him

finally to turn out toward others. The final choice is between dissolving into nature and rejoining men. Gunn chooses the second
because of his growing awareness that the very essence of himself
as an individual is communal and that he will not survive in any
form at all if he becomes one with nature.

As early as the second poem of "Misanthropos," Gunn reveals
the doubleness of his individuality as poet and the last man quite
emphatically. In contrast to the first poem of the sequence, in which
Gunn as poet talks out his sense of himself as the last man, presented in the third person, in the second poem Gunn speaks as the
last man in the first person to his echo, which of course is Gunn as
poet. This conversation concludes thus:

> Is there no feeling, then, that I can trust,
> In spite of what we have discussed?
> > Disgust.

The form of the whole of "Misanthropos" is implicit in these lines.
The experience of the last man is based upon disgust, upon misanthropy. But the nature of this disgust is articulated in marvellously
varied discussions carried on between the last man and his echo or,
to reverse the coin, between Gunn as poet and himself as last man.
Gunn's shifting from poem to poem between the last man as objectively third person and as subjectively first person can be explained
in no other way. It is in passing through "what we have discussed"
that Gunn is enabled to move from disgust to trust and thus begin
the last poem with:

> Others approach. Well, this one may show trust
> Around whose arms his fingers fit.

The trust of this last poem never breaks free from a need that it be
discussed or even, for that matter, from an element of disgust.
Thus, the poet, in expressing the last-man-become-first-man's willingness to trust the scratched man, also implies his grave doubts as
to whether the man is worthy of such trust. Even the internal community of the second poem, moreover, is itself full of disgust. To
get the tone of the poem right one needs to add to each echoing
word the phrase "you poor fool." Thus, even though the basic

movement of "Misanthropos" is from isolated disgust through discussion to communal trust, there is an internal community involved
in the initial disgust just as there is an element of disgust in the
trust of the final external community.

Once the reader recognizes the explicitly communal nature of
the isolated individual as presented in the second poem, he can
then see this community as implicitly present even in the first
poem, which begins:

> He avoids the momentous rhythm
> of the sea, one hill suffices him
> who has the entire world to choose from.
>
> He melts through the brown and green silence
> inspecting his traps, is lost in dense
> thicket, or appears among great stones.

Although one probably begins the poem merely spying on the last
man, who "lives like/ the birds, self-contained they hop and peck,"
further readings are sure to convince him that the poem contains,
along with the man we spy on, its own spy, the echoing controlling
presence of the poet. Unlike the last man, the last man's echo, the
poet Thom Gunn, proves himself capable of the momentous rhythm
of the sea. The first clause of the poem, with its anapestic rhythm
and with the first line running on into the second is a sealike
rhythm. But having set this rhythm in motion, the poet then drops
it abruptly, with the second clause, "one hill suffices him," working
iambically and in a syntax at odds with that of the first clause, so
that there is no build-up by way of clauses rhythmically and syntac-
tically parallel. Similarly, in the second stanza the first line is a return to the momentous rhythm of sea-like anapests, but here the expected run-on effect of the first stanza is frustrated; one must pause
after "silence" and begin again with "inspecting his traps." The
poet as spy does, in other words, have a watch tower. He is not
self-contained as the spied-upon man is; he looks beyond that self-
containment to glimpse the rhythm the last man avoids, introducing it only to break it down, so that we sense not just the isolation
of the man, but also that from which he is isolated.

The communal nature of "Misanthropos" is shared, it seems to me, by all genuine poems, and is why John Crowe Ransom was wrong when he said: one cannot write a love poem while he is in love and that is why Elizabeth Barrett Browning's sonnets are loving but unpoetic. The truth is rather that one must be both in love and out of love to write a love poem. To write a poem on himself as a man who widens his solitude till it is absolute, Gunn had to be both in that solitude and in community. In other words, the very writing of the poem forces him into internal communal relations which work against his desire for absolute solitude. "Misanthropos" is distinctive because it is a genuine poem based upon the realization of the communal doubleness inherent in all poetic sincerity. The very form of the poem, the way its parts echo each other, grows out of Gunn's sense that the poet's individuality, in the act of composing the poem, is communal. And it is this sense of the communal nature of the poet as individual, even when pushed to an extreme isolation by disgust, which leads Gunn to reject the American desire for dissolving into nature and to turn out toward other human beings.

Gunn's "Misanthropos" has a cinematic counterpart in Antonioni's *Zabriskie Point*. Like Gunn, Antonioni explored with fascination our desire to be "on the move" and to throw ourselves into simple, bodily love affairs, and he found them to be expressive of the deeper desire to end up in "this universal knacker's yard," at point zero, all levelled in dissolute copulation on the desert. Though Antonioni draws back from this lure to dissolution, the vision he moves back to is very much like the imperially decadent vision of Gunn's "Elegy on the Dust." This explains, I think, why *Zabriskie Point* disgusted its American audiences but was extremely popular in Europe. Gunn, in contrast, rejects not just the "vaguely heaving sea" of dust which is America seen from a final hill, but also the vision itself, as a deeper form of decadence than that which it contains and repudiates. Even so, Gunn's final position is not so very stirring. "Misanthropos" is pitched at a thin high extreme of self-consciousness. It is clear that the man who wrote this poem is the same man who wrote "The Corridor," in which the "I" spies through a keyhole at two people making love and then realizes that he the spy is himself being spied upon by a figure in a mirror at the end of the hall. But though the poem is resolutely self-conscious, it does move with the force of necessity beyond itself and into communion with others, whose otherness is more painful and also more vital than the otherness contained within the poet's individuality. The community achieved is minimal, but it is also essential.

One cannot leave the poem without a glancing reminder of what it implies about the critical maneuvers that have been so popular during the past twenty-five years. Once the poem is taken into the blood stream, wouldn't a critic be too ashamed to wear dark glasses and, "Between the dart of colours" to wear a darkening and perceive "an exact structure,/ a chart of the world"? Too many things are moving "at the edges of the mind" to leave him content to be treading out a path "like/ a discovering system,/ or process made visible." Nor, once he has watched with Gunn's disgust the paradisal

> cells swimming in concert
> like nebulae, calm, without effort,
>
> great clear globes, pink and white.

is he likely to be satisfied with utopian and visionary criticism or, like Harold Bloom, to condemn Yeats's "Sailing to Byzantium" on the grounds that it fails to achieve oneness with the visionary company.[9] He would recognize that Yeats's poem comes alive just because the visionary company, the "great clear globes," and the ladies of Byzantium are violated by "the intruder with blurred outline" who touches and holds "in an act of/ enfolding, possessing, merging love." The intruder may cause pain like a devil, but, without such a spark of fire, even sympathy cannot burn.

Criticism that moves to touch and hold a poem will be not only interpretive, but also appreciative. Interpretation alone is more like memorizing notes than performing them. A musician does not try simply to get the notes right. He must play in such a way as to articulate the living value of the notes, to realize, far beyond the score itself, the vital act of sound in movement which is the composer's creation. It is true, of course, that a critical performance lacks the immediacy of a musical performance. For the critic and his audience must always return to the text of the poem itself and work out the values in it which the critic can at best only hint at and point toward. Even so, I agree with Roger Sessions that, in their purpose and value, literary criticism and musical performance are fundamentally the same.[10] What the critic may learn from the musician is that he can expose and evoke a poem with any fullness only if he is willing to evoke and expose himself at the very same time. The critic who fashions for himself a frock from the skins of mole and rabbit, who writes in hiding, with sovereign impersonality, who tries to interpret and appreciate a poem in such a way that the poem is not permitted in turn to interpret and judge him, will touch neither the poem nor himself. He must listen long and carefully not just to the poem but also to himself until he too speaks with a voice of his own, if he would ever hope to converse with the intimate dialogue that every genuine poem is. He can learn from the musician that he himself must venture creatively if he would hope to touch the creativity of the poems of his concern. I am not suggesting that schools of criticism should model themselves on the great conservatories. But to the extent that those conservatories are committed not to technical perfection, but to a form of performance in which one realizes himself in the very act of evoking the living composition in all its otherness, it does seem to me that they provide a vital and meaningful model worthy of our emulation.[11]

CHAPTER EIGHT

Intuition vs. Perception:
On Charles Tomlinson's
"Under the Moon's Reign"

The source of both the energy and significance of the most ambitious poem Charles Tomlinson has written to date, "Under the Moon's Reign," a sequence of four closely related poems (125 lines in all) occupying the second section of *The Way In* (Oxford, 1974), is the relation between what can be called perception and intuition. As I read the poem, it is a conflict between two fundamental modes of awareness or two basic forms of poetry, a poetry of perception and poetry as intuition, and of the analogous ways of interpreting and criticizing poetry. The idea of poetic intuition is simply not in use today in either American or English criticism, so that I am forced, for the sake of clarity and precision, to use what is basically a Crocean conception of it.[1] Croce's concept of poetic intuition has more affinities with what is going on in Tomlinson's poem than its nearest rival, the phenomenological thought of Dufrenne, does, largely because Croce's thought was forged in direct relation to poetry on which Croce was engaged in writing criticism. An additional though perhaps incidental reason for introducing Croce into a study by an American critic of a poem by an English poet is that his presence may refine and deepen what is in danger of becoming a crudely adversary relationship, the "love-hate relations" which Stephen Spender has analyzed as holding between English and American sensibilities and which Donald Davie, in a review of Spender's book, has even more aggressively affirmed to be a necessary antagonism.

Poetic perception, at least as it works in much of Tomlinson's earlier poetry, is a form of awareness presupposing and depending upon a series of fundamental distinctions, those between the real and the unreal, world and self, space and time, exterior and interior, and the necessary and the contingent. The title of Tomlinson's second book, *Seeing Is Believing* (Oxford, 1960), means in effect that, if one looks with care and alertness, he will see what is really there, he will see objectively and not subjectively, the world and not the self. In tachist painting—at least as Zola saw it when thinking about Manet or as Pollock saw it when thinking about his own painting— one must start with the blob of paint on the canvas, that blob being an object or thing in a field instead of a subject or feeling in a void. What may seem to be the crucial choices or questions, that is, have already been answered even before one begins. Curiously enough, this conception of poetic or artistic perception is the reverse of Schiller's distinction between simple and sentimental poetry. Sentimental poetry was thought to be subjective and sophisticated in contrast to the objective and primitive nature of simple poetry. A poetry of perception is objective and elemental, just as simple poetry was said to be, but it is based upon an elaborate set of philosophical distinctions; it is thoroughly civilized.

Poetic intuition is a mode of awareness more primitive than, yet also inclusive of, the distinctions that make up the presupposed basis of a poetry of perception. As poetic intuitions, Hart Crane's "the dry sound of bees/ Stretching across a lucid space" (from "Praise for an Urn") and Wallace Stevens' "As a calm darkens among water-lights" (from "Sunday Morning") fuse feeling and image immediately and uniquely. At least as they work in their respective poems, these lines have the power to draw one behind conventional forms of experience. They break down and fold into themselves whatever code, language system, and framework of perception one might for a moment have thought them to be part of. The awesome stillness and brilliance of Crane's space, strung together by the dry hum of golden immortality, is at one with his anguished desire to eternalize the dead man he loves. One is pulled into a new place and time and becomes one with its desperate beauty. At first, he may think he is seeing and hearing double: that is, the words will retain the stain of their conventional usage, but will be suffused and irradiated by a primogenitive light of intuitive awareness. As he meditates within this intuitive moment, however, it will come to enfold and absorb and revitalize the conventional world, that world will become Crane's world, and one will see everything afresh, colored by a lucid pain as never before. Such poetic intuitions are elementally simple and can be analyzed endlessly.

Poetic intuitions swarm with questions. They seem to be the fount of questioning itself. No matter how refined and intricate the discriminations within them may be, they retain an aura of wonder and marvel, as if all forms of intuitive awareness are versions of "mirando," of "beholding," of looking with awe. In a poetry of perception, in contrast, even questions are basically answers; that is, all asking takes place within a systematic framework in which the basic questions have been taken care of. If considered at all, primary convictions are treated as if they were settled. Thus, in what reads much like a manifesto, the sixth part of "Antecedents" (in *Seeing Is Believing*), Tomlinson declares:

> Out of the shut cell of that solitude there is
> One egress, past point of interrogation.
> Sun is, because it is not you; you are
> Since you are self, and self delimited
> Regarding sun.

The way to escape one's separateness is to accept as dogma the separateness of one's self and the sun; if one insists on a oneness of self and sun, by that very insistence he is locked in isolation. The declaration itself, both in what it affirms and in what it negates, is thoughtful and subtle. But is escaping separateness by accepting it the "one egress," and is it truly "past point of interrogation"? Nothing in intuitive poetry is "past point of interrogation." Whereas, however subtle Tomlinson's perceptions may be, they suggest that he is stamping his foot and insisting that there shall be no more questioning. If only, when at Cambridge, he had heard I. A. Richards' anecdote about G. E. Moore and the setting sun. Moore believed that the green spot on the card which he held up here and now was objectively real, a point of departure (like Hume's "impressions") instead of a mere part of a presupposed system of space and time and color. He had also, it appears from what Richards says, declared that the setting sun as seen by him is really there and in no way dependent on how or by whom it is looked at. One day a physicist, A. A. Robb, visited the class and at the appropriate moment observed:

> about sunset, you can't see the sun. The sun is below the horizon. It's the refraction of the earth's atmosphere which enables you to see an image of the sun. Quite a different location from where the sun is.[2]

Richards recalls that, upon hearing this, Moore then "went nearly helpless with rage. 'I can't see the sun,' he cried. 'I can't see the sun!' Everything broke down; that was what we were used to." Even though it is in verse, Tomlinson's dogmatic slumber is as provocative as Moore's. "Self" and "sun" within the lines are related by the self's regarding the sun. What, one wonders, is the relation between the self thinking through and writing down the lines of verse and the self and sun referred to in the lines? Is it simply another "regarding": self regarding self regarding sun? But can Tomlinson still say "you are self"? Mustn't he rather say "you are two selves"? And isn't it possible that the second self, that actual self that was doing the thinking and the writing, that self hidden from Tomlinson because of the dogmatic form of his seeing, is the sun not only of his "self delimited," but also of that sun which he says he is regarding? Such questions must be brought to poems of perception by their readers, whereas they are intrinsic to intuitive poetry.

In a sense perceptive poetry can be taken as a translation of the questioning of intuitive poetry into an answer which satisfies the intelligence. The truth of this idea depends, of course, on its not being taken too literally or construed as a theory of poetic composition. A sufficiently simple and also loose example of this would be Tomlinson's early "How Still the Hawk" taken as a perceptive poem in which the wild questioning of Tennyson's "The Eagle" has been tamed and domesticated. Tennyson's poem, it should be noted, was composed when it was still possible for an Englishman to have unsettled notions and feelings concerning imperialism.

THE EAGLE

He clasps the crag with crooked hands:
Close to the sun in lonely lands,
Ringed with the azure world, he stands.

The wrinkled sea beneath him crawls;
He watches from his mountain walls,
And like a thunderbolt he falls.

This awesome intuition is all questions, to be lived in as a fount
both of energy and light and of violence and oblivion. The event of
the poem is simple and definite enough: a predatory bird is aloof
and then it strikes. Beyond that, however, everything is rich with
the uncertainty of experience at its keenest. The first line lures the
reader into the poem so that he is both at one with and distinct
from the bird, and as a result the bird, though still a bird, is something more too. Even the question of why it leaves its self-sufficient
center allows for no simple answer. True enough, the plunge must
be predatory, and yet it is also like a magnetized fall, perhaps the
result of vertigo caused not so much by height as by the taint of
disease and obscenity in the fourth line, "The wrinkled sea beneath
him crawls." The questions with which the poem swarms are definite enough, but they are not answered and so they do not lose
their energy or cancel each other out. There is simply no single conceptual framework into which the poem can be comfortably fitted.

Whereas a poem like the following fits into place very neatly. It
gives the effect of being a tidying up and sweeping things clean.

How still the hawk
Hangs innocent above
Its native wood:
Distance, that purifies the act
Of all intent, has graced
Intent with beauty.
Beauty must lie
As innocence must harm
Whose end (sited,
Held) is naked
Like the map it cowers on.

And the doom drops:
Plummet of peace
To him who does not share
The nearness and the need,
The shrivelled circle
Of magnetic fear.[3]

One is to see things exactly, and one is to maintain his proper position. The poet's vision depends as much on his keeping his distance as on the accuracy with which he details what he sees. His
perception, his delimitation of thinking self regarding predatory
hawk, is part of a network of conceptions concerning the nature of
space, of objects, and of observers, civilized and otherwise. As
likely as not, the poet is thinking of a "let's pretend" poem, Ted
Hughes's "Hawk Roosting," and is carrying on a civilized argument with it. He is, it is true, omitting that which he is arguing
against, but such an omission is typical of perceptive poetry, as it is
not of intuitive poetry, which is self-sufficient, containing what it
negates within itself. While Hughes pretends that he is a hawk and
so enjoys being wicked innocently:

My manners are tearing off heads—

The allotment of death.
For the one path of my flight is direct
Through the bones of the living.
No argument asserts my right:

The sun is behind me.
Nothing has changed since I began.
My eye has permitted no change.
I am going to keep things like this.[4]

Tomlinson, without any such huffing and puffing and hoo-hoo-
hooing, shows the essential cruelty of proper perception. He is arguing that there is no point in getting excited about these creatures
which assert their rights without arguing. Just keep still and give
them a good stare. You get your thrills (cooled perhaps by the distance: "The shrivelled circle/ Of magnetic fear"), you can savor the
beauty of it cold, and you can feel as guilty and wicked as you like,

because of the element of indifference for the victim which the dis-interestedness of your observation entails (see Tomlinson's "Wind," in *American Scenes*, Oxford, 1966, for a similar argument with Hughes's "Wind"). The poetry of perception is fundamentally conceptual; it manifests intelligence, but not the originality of intu-itive poetry. Its perceptions are part of a conventional system, just as the words studied by structural linguists are part of a language system. In "the science of the concrete" (to modify a point made in Calvin Bedient's remarkable essay on Tomlinson), whether in the prose of Lévi-Strauss or the poetry of Tomlinson, discovery is painless and somewhat easy, because everything that matters has already been decided upon and is being presupposed. What is ab-sent is the creative impulsion of poetic intuition.

The crucial question for me about the best of Tomlinson's re-cent poems is whether they are intuitions broken down and re-duced to a perception or perceptions caught up and revitalized as part of an intuition. Many of the poems have the effect of a sketch, as if Tomlinson had begun with a *tache* (a spot of paint, perceived to be totally independent of the man who works it) or a *macchia* (an incipient flash of intuition, feeling and image, subject and object, fused), in any case with a blob, worked it about a bit, and then left it for whatever it was.[5] Is he just playing around with what can be abstracted from the genuine poetry of someone else, or is this the play, with that touch of wild gaiety, to be felt in all intuitive poetry? The impression given by the title poem of *The Way In*, for example, is that Tomlinson took a blob of white (from Larkin's "Here") and a blob of black (from Lowell's "For the Union Dead"), mixed them together, and came up with a grey of his own, a genuinely intuitive poem that teeters uneasily in a living and not peaceful harmony.

The first poem of "Under the Moon's Reign," itself bearing the title of the sequence, either is a poem of perception concerning the supremacy of intuition over various forms of perception, or it is an intuitive conflict in which even such a triumph, of intuition over perception, is still open to question.

UNDER THE MOON'S REIGN

Twilight was a going of the gods: the air
  Hung weightlessly now—its own
Inviolable sign. From habit, we
  Were looking still for what we could not see—
The inside of the outside, for some spirit flung
  From the burning of that Götterdämmerung
And suffused in the obscurity. Scraps
  Of the bare-twigged scene were floating
Scattered across scraps of water—mirrors
  Shivered and stuck into a landscape
That drifted visibly to darkness. The pools
  Restrained the disappearing shapes, as all around
The dusk was gaining: too many images
  Beckoned from that thronging shade
None of which belonged there. And then the moon
  Drawing all into more than daylight height
Had taken the zenith, the summit branches
  Caught as by steady lightning, and each sign
Transformed, but by no more miracle than the place
  It occupied and the eye that saw it
Gathered into the momentary perfection of the scene
  Under transfigured heavens, under the moon's reign.[6]

If read as primarily a poem of perception, with its images fitting
into a conventional framework of ideas, then its form will turn out
to be that of an allegorical narrative. The story goes something like
this. We once lived in a world of accepted perceptions, in the common light of day, bathed in a sea of sunny faith, a luminous mirror
with the sun in the center and everything in its reflected-upon, conceptual place. At twilight, *fin de siècle*, that sense of a center, of a
single source of energy for man and nature, was lost; the sun-cen-
tered mirror split into innumerable pieces, each of which reflected
the wintry, bare-twigged scene from its own perspective. Even
worse, these mirror-slivers were being drawn into "that thronging
shade" of utter darkness, where each poet, isolated in the empty
dark, would mirror only himself: imagistic poetry was being replaced by confessional. Then a miracle occurred, "a revolution in

human sensibility," as J. Hillis Miller calls the transformation that occurred to one of Tomlinson's main precursors, William Carlos Williams, at the age of twenty.[7] Williams said, "I resigned, I gave up." Miller translates this "nameless religious experience" (as a result of which, Williams himself said, "I decided there was nothing else in life for me but to work"),[8] into the notion that Williams abandoned "his private consciousness, that hollow bubble in the midst of the solidity of the world." As a result of this abandonment, still according to Miller, "consciousness permeates the world, and the world has entered into the mind. It is 'an identity—it can't be/ otherwise—an/ interpenetration, both ways' (*Paterson*, 12)."

This sort of reading is not implausible, even if inadequate. It may indeed be because of Williams that Tomlinson's presentation of his encounter with the moon is so different from, say, Wordsworth's account of his in the last book of *The Prelude*. The blazing illumination Wordsworth experienced when climbing Mount Snowden is followed by an elaborate translation of images into concepts, the moon, the mist, the sea, all being made to stand for certain aspects of the self and mighty intellect of man. Even in our time, according to what Tomlinson said some ten years ago in an interview with an American disciple of Williams, Robert Creeley, the English tend to read and interpret poetic images in that way, making them stand for something abstractly human. It can be said with reason that Tomlinson, in contrast, as a person who had much to do with getting Williams' works published in England, has taken part in that anti-romantic revolution described in such apocalyptic terms by Miller. "The act by which man turns the world inside-out into his mind [what Wordsworth does in the last book of *The Prelude*] leads to nihilism" (to Nietzsche, that is, and that "emptiness left after the death of God," the result of which is that "man becomes the sovereign valuer, the measure of all things"). Miller claims that such nihilism "can be escaped only by a counter-revolution in which man turns himself inside out and steps, as Wallace Stevens puts it, 'barefoot into reality.' "

> To walk barefoot into reality means abandoning the independence of the ego. Instead of making everything an object for the self, the mind must efface itself before reality, or plunge into the density of an exterior world, dispersing itself in a milieu

which exceeds it and which it has not made. The effacement of the ego before reality means abandoning the will to power over things. . . . Only through an abnegation of the will can objects begin to manifest themselves as they are, in the integrity of their presence. When man is willing to let things be then they appear in a space which is no longer that of an objective world opposed to the mind. In the new space the mind is dispersed everywhere in things and forms one with them.[9]

Miller might be describing that triumph of intuition, that perfect pastoral, with which "Under the Moon's Reign" ends: the moon, the place (including all the signs in it) and the eye that saw it, all are "gathered into the momentary perfection," a oneness of mind and world. Read in this way, the poem is an allegorical explanation of the origin of that "new aestheticism" of which Donald Davie takes Tomlinson to be a prime example. When speaking of Manet, Zola said that the whole personality of the artist consists in the way in which his eye is organized. Tomlinson has delimited himself so that he is no more than "the eye that saw it," he has in effect become what he sees, he has taken part in that "revolution of human sensibility."[10]

Such a reading, however, stirs up enough contradictions to suggest that either it is inadequate or the poem a mess. "Twilight was a going of the gods: the air/ Hung weightlessly now—its own/ Inviolable sign." How could Tomlinson begin the poem by suggesting that the air is now free of all conceptual weight and then proceed to burden it as a recurrent sign for an allegorical narrative concerning the changes from imagistic to confessional poetry and from that to a poetry of reality? How, for that matter, could he affirm a mode of awareness dependent on the self's being abnegated before the scene by means of a poetry in which he as poet, spinning an allegorical web, uses the scene as material for his story? How, that is, write a poem affirming the rightness of letting things be, but in such a manner as to dominate them? It is possible, of course, that the manner of the poem contradicts its content.

Or perhaps the manner of the poem is not finally allegorical; perhaps the poem is not a poem of perception. Tomlinson's recent graphics are not visual so much as they are "an imaginative experience of total activity," to use a phrase of R. G. Collingwood (the English proponent of Croce's concept of art and poetry as intuition rather than perception). Tomlinson could not, at least as a painter, dissent from this statement by Collingwood:

> Of course Cézanne was right. Painting can never be a visual art. A man paints with his hands, not with his eyes. The Impressionist doctrine that what one paints is light was a pedantry which failed to destroy the painters it enslaved only because they remained painters in defiance of the doctrine: men of their hands, men who did their work with fingers and wrist and arm, and even (as they walked about the studio) with their legs and toes. What one paints is what can be painted; no one can do more; and what can be painted must stand in some relation to the muscular activity of painting it.[11]

To treat a poem or painting as primarily visual, as perception, is, in effect, the same as treating it allegorically. To disconnect a phenomenon from the act of its making is to turn it into the sign of an idea, even if the idea is that it, the phenomenon, is not the sign of an idea. An image that is "let be" is turned into a perception, as distinct from anything imaginary or fanciful; it is no longer so rich and fine as an intuition, but is necessarily, just because it is "let be," violated by an idea. If, in contrast, "Under the Moon's Reign" is read not as a perception, but as an intuition, as "an imaginative experience of total activity," its allegory will be caught up in the expanding act of the poet's making and will cease to be allegory, and the final transfiguration will be experienced not assertively, but questioningly, with a sense of its possible limitations.

More specifically, Tomlinson is presenting the allegory as cancelled. It is experienced as effectively there, but there as a subjective imposition. A spirit does suffuse the obscurity of the scene, but it is Tomlinson's, not at all an "objective" inside of the outside. He hints at this subversion of the objective allegory near the beginning by saying that we kept looking for that inside "from habit." In truth, it is Tomlinson's own act of looking that provides all the inside the scene has. The spirit left over and suffusing the obscurity is not one of the gods, but is Tomlinson's personal, imaginative, searching self. Out of personal feeling and without any allegorical justification, it is Tomlinson who feels that "too many images/ Beckoned from that thronging shade," and it is Tomlinson, the avowedly anti-confessional poet, who says that none of those images "belonged there." Finally, even the momentary perfection at the end of the poem is suffused by Tomlinson's own subjective luminess, as he calls even that quality of perfection into question. The vivid phrase, "the summit branches/ Caught as by steady lightning" is brittle with death; the branches are skeletal and they are caught as if they are being electrocuted. Tomlinson's intuition is neither visual nor visionary (as Wordsworth's was). It is a vision being doubted and called in question.

Tomlinson's discovery is not that his world is false or illusory or fanciful or even merely subjectivistic. He is affirming his world and he is affirming the "momentary perfection" in which moon, scene, and eye are luminously and joyously at one. The falseness lies in the notion that this experience of oneness is truly between oneself and the world, so that one's mouth and eyes and mind have dilated to become the mouth and eyes and mind of the world. That falseness evokes the *frisson*, the hint at an electrocution, that cancelled, unheard cry of "The horror, the horror!"

From *The Necklace* (1955) up to *The Way of a World* (1969), and including the poems of *Seeing is Believing* (1960), *A Peopled Landscape* (1964), and *American Scenes* (1966), Tomlinson has been effacing himself so that the sun may be regarded as separate from and unaffected by his way of regarding it. From 1957 on he has been assimilating and accepting the Williams of whom Miller says:

> The resignation to existence which makes Williams' poetry possible is the exact reverse of the Cartesian Cogito. Descartes puts everything in question in order to establish the existence of his separate self, an existence built on the power of detached thinking. Williams gives himself up in despair and establishes a self beyond personality, a self coextensive with the universe.[12]

"A self coextensive with the universe." Miller goes on to say that, after Williams plunges into the Passaic, "he possesses all time and space and has complete knowledge of everything: 'I knew all—it became me.'" There is no pun on "became": Williams and Miller are serious. But, at some time, Tomlinson must have read the passage—or one like it—and wakened from his dogmatic slumber with

a cry like Kurtz's "The horror, the horror!" at the imperialistic nature of the contemplativeness he had been cultivating for so long.

The following statement by Calvin Bedient may be true of Tomlinson's earlier poetry:

> For Tomlinson wisdom is acquiescence, acquiescence an allow-
> ing of the inward and the outward to meet and be each stilled
> in the other, and fulfilled there. For this is what contemplation
> is, this mutual calming. . . . No poet has ever seemed at once
> so intelligent and immune to anxiety as Tomlinson. His mind
> is superbly serene, inhumanly human. He descends upon ap-
> pearances like a calm of love.[13]

But the mutual calming, the serene acquiescence, at the end of
"Under the Moon's Reign" is under severe, acidic interrogation.
Perhaps it was words like Bedient's that stung Tomlinson into asking: am I as arrogant and complacent as he says, as the Williams
Miller is describing? For in his selection of critical studies on Williams, Tomlinson admits that Williams "remains in some ways a
very egocentric poet"; and of Miller's claim that Williams marks the
climax "of the development so far of twentieth-century poetry" he
says: "This seems an absurd way of looking at art, not least because
it ignores the uniqueness of talents very different from Williams."[14]

Miller, of course, is not alone in attributing to a poet the prophetic authority Fundamentalists reserve for the authors of the
books of the Bible. Charles Singleton has claimed as much for Dante
(and claimed that Dante claimed it for himself). And Pasolini recently claimed it for films, including his own (they are, he stupify-
ingly asserts, reality being presented as reality).[15] Between the despair of such dogmatism and the despair of that nihilism it is a
reaction to, Tomlinson has truly come into his own with the realization that his world is not the world, but a world, his world, and
that every other unique talent has its distinctive world. Such mul-
tifariousness is not available to perception. It can only be experienced intuitively, questioningly. Indeed, such an awareness is the
question with which Wallace Stevens' "Esthétique du Mal" ends:

> And out of what one sees and hears and out
> Of what one feels, who could have thought to make
> So many selves, so many sensuous worlds,

As if the air, the mid-day air, was swarming
With the metaphysical changes that occur,
Merely in living as and where we live.

The achievement of "Under the Moon's Reign" is not so much
in what it frees Tomlinson from as in what it frees him for. His
steady aim from *The Necklace* on has been to evoke a sense of otherness, of that which is unassimilable to the ordinary concerns of humanity. Even though his poems may only rarely betray a latent imperialism, he has regularly failed in his aim, largely because the
world he has etched for the purpose of evoking otherness turned
out again and again to be at one with his self. This need to evoke
and sustain a sense of otherness, and the virtual impossibility of
doing so, is something peculiarly English. Wherever one turns in
England the land bears the mark of human hands. Even the air, the
clouds themselves, move in patterns that seem providential. Unlike
his American counterpart, an Englishman of some sensitivity cannot simply set aside the conceptual framework according to and
within which he runs his daily life and step into empty air. The air
that bathes England is steeped in the breath of the dead. Even in a
cemetery most Americans would have to treat such an idea as fanciful. Lawrence's treatment of the difference between English and
American space, especially in "St. Mawr," is so fine and vivid that
the point needs no pressing.

"Under the Moon's Reign" realizes electrifyingly the lack of
otherness in the scene presented "under transfigured heavens"; the
world is all in his eye; and his whole personality inheres in the organization of his eye. To recognize that his world is his self, no
matter how often he may insist that the other is other, it is this recognition that frees Tomlinson at last to strive to evoke what is genuinely other. "Foxes' Moon," the second poem of the sequence, is
based upon his realization that to face genuine otherness and to
have even a chance of evoking it as truly other, he must bear his
own world with him. His self is his world; to present otherness as
genuinely so, he must present it in relation to that which it is not,
to that self-world which he has realized and affirmed as his. What
Tomlinson is doing, then, and necessarily doing, is bearing "Under
the Moon's Reign" into "Foxes' Moon."

> Night over England's interrupted pastoral,
> And moonlight on the frigid lattices
> Of pylons.

The poem opens with a jab of doubleness. England's pastoral is what Tomlinson has just liberated himself from, a condition in which men take their world to be the world; nature made over in the image of man, the farmland gradually being taken over by the towns, the end of night being announced by "the coming red" of "the beams of early cars" as much as by that of the sunrise. It is a social-welfare-state pastoral, England industrialized and urbanized, in which all men are accepted equally and indifferently, the nights of which are devoted to variations of those dreams, easy enough since they are so undistinguished.

It is Tomlinson's pastoral, that "momentary perfection" edged by doubt and here given its proper poetic name, which interrupts England's. The sarcasm of the poem—heightened perhaps by a touch of envy at the popularity of Larkin, the main representative of "England's interrupted pastoral"—arises from this clash of pastorals, the one anxious and edgy, the other fat and sassy, the one like Tasso, the other like Boucher: the one sordid and damp, cluttered with pylons, the "row of the approaching town," "the garbage of the yards," the "daily view," the "early cars," and the "windows, asphalt, wires"; the other "under the moon's reign," the daily view having undergone "a white displacement," with everything given an edge and refined by a drying wind, and all dominated by the foxes, which "bring/ Flint hearts and sharpened senses to/ This desolation of grisaille," their "thin volpine bark" being caught but then lost by the warm sleepers "to the babbling undertow they swim." For a brief time, till the end of the poem, Tomlinson's pastoral dominates the other:

> These
> Are the fox hours, cleansed
> Of all the meanings we can use
> And so refuse them. Foxes glow,
> Ghosts unacknowledged in the moonlight
> Of the suburb, and like ghosts they flow
> Back, racing the coming red, the beams

Of early cars, a world not theirs
Gleaming from kindled windows, asphalt, wires.

But it does so in such a way as to accentuate the repulsiveness, the absolute otherness, of present-day England viewed in its own common light. Tomlinson's acceptance of the scene as cleansed, as "a white displacement," is at one with his repudiation of the scene as "a daily view." From Westminster Bridge, Wordsworth could assimilate London only because it was asleep (his London, not Londoners' London). Only as a subdued suggestion is it evident that the city as a working machine would have been repugnant to him. Tomlinson heightens the clash in a way quite uncharacteristic of Wordsworth. If "Under the Moon's Reign" is written under the crossed-out sign of Wordsworth, it is in memory of Leopardi that "Foxes' Moon" is written.

The doubleness of the poem is what calls Leopardi to mind most forcefully. True, his "Canto notturno" has a purity and an acerbity something like Tomlinson's poem, and "La Ginestra" is as sarcastic a repudiation of notions of politics and progress in Leopardi's day as Tomlinson's poem is of the sordidness of contemporary England. At bottom, however, it is the evocation of a way of life that is repudiated by its double, it is that curiously realized otherness as contemptible that defines in both Leopardi and Tomlinson a purity and simplicity which is anything but classical. If it were a matter of simply seeing double instead of a new form of anguishing intuition, then no doubt Croce would be right in saying that whenever Leopardi turns sarcastic, he ceases to write poetry. The sarcasm can work poetically, I think, as part of an intuitive fusing of seeing and imagining. Perhaps this is Leopardi's most explicit statement on the subject:

For a sensitive and imaginative person, who lives, as I have for a long time, mainly by his senses and his imagination, the world and its objects are in a certain way double. He will see with his eyes a tower, a field; he will hear with his ears the sound of a bell; and at the same time, with his imagination, he will see another tower, another field, he will hear another sound. All the beauty and pleasantness of things lies in this second kind of object. It is a sad life (and it is the common life) which does not see and hear and sense anything but simple objects, those of which the eyes, ears and other senses receive the sensation.[16]

Croce thinks that in the finest poems only the imaginative object is present, whereas for me both objects are regularly present and a poem works intuitively when the imaginative object prevails. Then the poem is beautiful, the experience pleasurable, and the objects of daily view are present as so ugly as to be repudiated, so that their otherness, their unassimilable ugliness, is evoked as it is. The beauty of the great idylls depends on such ugliness, and "Foxes' Moon" is aimed at something very much like that.

The doubleness is a matter of language as well as of scene and feeling. Ungaretti (Tomlinson has translated a number of his poems) makes the case for Leopardi in a brief statement of his own poetics issued not long before his death. As Ungaretti sees it, Leopardi was the first to distinguish the indeterminate, vague sense of poetic words from their literal and material meaning:

> In the form of a poem those words are poetic which have been impelled by the force of inspiration to open and enlarge not only their proper meanings, but also an infinite margin within which the poetry will be able to extend itself without ever being definable. On one side, tradition, history, memory appear indispensable to the birth of a poem; on the other, the frontiers, the limits, of tradition are abolished—an innocence is recovered. Poetry exists then through elegance, by wisdom and knowledge, an old language attains the belief that it has become again primitive and has recovered its innocence.[17]

Tomlinson is clearly working for a poetic sense of language "always a thought" beyond "the meanings we can use." Indeed, he is contemptuous of "the meanings we can use," of words that are merely useful and communicative. His own words nonetheless contain the meanings of common usage, even if edged acidly with Tomlinson's sense of his own "daily discontent." The "white displacement" does not exclude the garbage; the poetic sense does not exclude the usable meanings; the edges of purity are jagged with sarcasm. The poetic quality of "Foxes' Moon" is severely threatened, if not compromised, by the ugliness and sarcasm it provokes. The same can be said, however, for several of Leopardi's finest poems.

Yet, according to Croce, there can be no doubt or sarcasm in a poetic intuition. If he is right, in "Under the Moon's Reign" and "Foxes' Moon" Tomlinson is doing what cannot be done. In the third poem of the sequence, "The Dream," he confronts this seeming contradiction directly and offers his own intuitive definition of intuition, his dreaming delimitation of dreaming. Worse and worse, Croce would have said, further and further from authentic poetry. Croce knew, however, that what is special about poets is that they do the impossible; only, he thought his aesthetics took that into account, so that it would never be necessary for a poet to do what is impossible according to it. In a sense Collingwood anticipated Tomlinson, for in his modification of Croce's aesthetics he breaks down the distinction between poetic intuition and philosophical thinking. Philosophically, however, it is just that, a breakdown. The most one is left with is the dissatisfaction Collingwood felt over the lack of self-awareness in intuitive experience as conceived by Croce.[18]

Without being in any way a philosophical answer, Tomlinson's "The Dream" succeeds poetically where Collingwood failed. It is a self-conscious intuition. From the first it is clear that the dream will differ from the somnolent dreams of the "warm sleepers" of "Foxes' Moon." The poem begins with the mind of the dreamer held down by a dream "that blinded him/ To all except the closed-in warmth/ Of his own present being." The poet, in contrast, is not blind to what the dreamer was blinded to: that his dream took place

> Under that benign calm eye that sees
> Nothing of the vista of land and sky
> It brings to light; under the interminably
> Branching night, of street and city,
> Vein and artery . . .

In his dream, however, the dreamer experiences something closely analogous to what the poem presents as outside him. He follows a hope that "swayed into palpability like a wall." By following it he comes upon his freedom; his freedom, that is, is following it; and it, the constricted hope that "Swayed into a palpability like a wall," becomes "this tense fluidity/ Always a thought beyond him." Accepting within himself an otherness that is always a thought beyond him, doing that is his liberation and it is essentially what poetic intuition is: accepting and attending acutely to otherness without translating it into a thought, without explaining it, without putting it into a conceptual framework. Not self-consciousness, but hermeneutical interpretation, the propensity to allegorize felt images into perceptions is what violates intuitive imagining. With this new courage, this willingness to follow and attend to what he cannot place and understand, the dreamer is in effect resurrected. He had been buried by a reality that too much defined him, by a reality he accepted as given. By breaking free of that perceptual presupposition, he is treated to a spaciousness opening around him; his dream turns into the branching streets and passageways of a city. He experiences what Tomlinson elsewhere calls Eden's "radial avenues of light," with everything in felt, integral but unexplained relation to everything else. This is "The dream of a city under the city's dream"; it is the "white displacement" of "Foxes' Moon" without the "daily view" it is the displacement of. Unlike Crocean intuition, however, Tomlinsonian intuition does not stop there. It is a dream dreamed and looked upon and thought about dreamingly. At the end of the poem, the dream vision is recognized as having been

> Proportioned to the man whom sleep replenishes
> To stand reading with opened eyes
> The intricacies of the imagined spaces there
> Strange and familiar as the lines that map a hand.

And that man, of course, is the man who had the dream and has now written this poem about it. The fundamental awareness is analogical: between dreamer and poet, between the blind seeing of the moon ("that benign calm eye that sees/ Nothing of the vista of land and sky/ It brings to light"), the blind seeing of the dreamer, and the intuitive seeing of the poet; between the intricate lines within the dream, those lines the moon shines upon, and those lines the poet alone is aware of, "the lines that map a hand." Although the poem presents a dream that took place in the past, the end of the dream issues into the present of the poem: the poem illuminates the dream and is illuminated by it. They are one and yet they are different, though not logically so.

In the most artistically sensitive and profound tradition of aesthetics, that running from Vico to Croce, poetic intuition has been thought of much as Tomlinson presents it in "The Dream." It is the blind seeing of the moon, genuinely exploratory, being carried out in ignorance, without the supportive framework of any accepted set of presuppositions. It is essentially creative and original, that form of activity which lifts man out of the bestial and toward the human, out of chaos and toward order, out of darkness and toward light. As Baumgarten, who along with Vico discovered that genuine poetry is not intellectual and perceptual, but a *cognitio sensitiva*, says (in that study in which he gave what has become the philosophical discipline of aesthetics its proper name): aesthetic experience is not clear and distinct, as logical thought is, nor is it dark and obscure as sensuous experience is. It is rather that middle ground, "Sed conditio sine qua non, inveniendae veritatis, ubi natura non facit saltum ex obscuritate in distinctionem" (*Aesthetica*, para. 7, 1758). Aesthetic experience is sensuous cognition, that without which no truths are discovered; nature makes no leap from obscurity into lucidity; it passes from sensation through intuition to clear and distinct perception. As Montale says, in essential poetry, in the waking dream, dark things tend toward clarity, "Tendono alla chiarità le cose oscure," with the emphasis on the tending, on *tendono*.[19]

Tomlinson, however, is not simply re-enacting the transition from Neo-Classical verse to Romantic poetry, from the clear mirroring of Nature, of what is accepted as out there, to the obscure expression of the darkness within. He is too deeply and tenaciously committed to the light and opposed to the darkness. His dilemma has been that he will not relinquish his motto that "seeing is believing," he will not close his eyes, hold his nose, and let himself sink into the oceanic depths; and yet he has discovered that perception, even the most exacting perception, is not enough to make a poem, that not even the perception of an intuition is enough. He knows that he must see blindly, but he refuses to see darkly. As a poetic intuition, "The Dream" is clear, but not conceptualized, and yet it is self-aware, it includes the sense that it is clear, but not logically distinct, it in effect judges itself to be a poetic intuition, but doing this in an intuitive rather than a perceptive or logical way.

In other words, Tomlinson is not giving up the virtues of his poetry of perception, those aspects of his early verse which Donald Davie praised so highly in what must be the most famous London literary conversation of the sixties, his talk with Alvarez about "The New Aestheticism?". Alvarez had complained that Tomlinson slighted the human. Davie's defense runs as follows:

> Tomlinson most of the time is talking about the sort of reality which there is in him, the sort of reality that there is in that stone wall, the relation that is set up between him and that stone wall . . . I daresay that you would agree that the cardinal rule in human relations is for one partner in the relation to respect the integrity of the other person, not to attempt to violate it, not to attempt to dominate it, not to attempt to possess. . . . We ask 'how do we learn to do this, how do we learn not to dominate, not to be aggressive?' Simply a resolution: 'I will not dominate', is not good enough. And it seems to me that the sort of thing which Tomlinson in certain poems in a sense recommends—realizing this stone wall as different from all other stone walls—in its otherness, its thusness, its quiddity. To see things in this way, to see a tree thus, to see a stone wall thus, affords a sort of model which you can then apply to human relations.[20]

In "The Dream," Tomlinson is still striving to realize the stone wall in its otherness, but he has learned that all Davie's "Thou Shalt Not" 's result, not in the realizing of the otherness of any thing or person, but only in the blindness of fixed staring, a habit that has caused nothing but harm to English art. Antonioni explores the vice in *Blow Up*, showing the folly of the attempt to get at reality by means of fixed staring (with the camera in this instance instead of the eye) and by enlarging the image. Aldous Huxley actually was on the verge of blindness as a result of such staring; his *The Art of Seeing* is a manual of exercises for getting one's eyes in motion and for learning to see with one's whole body and not just with the eyes. What a trap Moore's "green spot here and now" could be. But behind it one thinks of the hysteria in the visual intensity of some of Ruskin's late writings (e.g., "The Storm-Cloud of the Nineteenth Century"), and, behind that, of Hume's presupposing the elemental reality of impressions, and, even further back, of the curiously sharp visual imagery in early sixteenth-century English translations of Petrarch. Tomlinson has learned that "to see a stone wall thus" is to presuppose its reality, to take it for granted, and thus to leave it out of one's seeing.

In "The Tree" and in the title poem of *The Way In* Tomlinson develops his discovery that the way out is the way in. By facing outward, by looking closely at the way in which what is truly other, Bristol, say, has turned into a rendering plant, with neighborhood after neighborhood being dismantled to make room for the "mannerless high rises," he comes upon the margin of his inner self. He recognizes that he is a victim of this process which is wiping out the last marks of civility and style; he realizes also that in the very act of driving a car he is taking part in the destruction of what he values. Most important, however, is his discovery that there is a radical distinction between this truly other world, which he detests, and that world he has come to love, what he had previously felt to be truly other, but now finds to be at one with his self—a world not his self, to be sure, but not not his self, not truly other.

Having broken down the notion that there is a simple, objective world the laws of which scientists determine and the surfaces of which a scientific painter like Constable explores, having recognized that the world he has regarded with love is not *the* world, but his world, and that the detestable other is not *the* other, but just other, Tomlinson has deprived himself of all reason not to explore his inner world, his dream world. So long as he was committed to perception, he thought the exterior world was far richer and more intricate than any interior. He would have nothing to do with dreams, not because he realized that dreams are simply not available to "that antarctic blaze" of analytical perception, as Hart Crane does in "Paraphrase," but because he thought of dreams only as explicated, as perceived, as rendered conceptually by one theory of dream or another. In "The Night-Train" he spoofs dream poetry, surreal poetry, self-expressive poetry, on the grounds that it is so common, every dream being pretty much the same as every other: the train is "freighted tight/ with a million/ miniscule statuettes/ of La Notte (Night)," and when day breaks, the train turns into "white/ white white—/ the snow-plough/ that refuses to go." [21]

Dreams as dreams are indistinguishably black (not pulsating rhythms thrown off by the beat of one's heart, as in Crane's "Paraphrase") and dreams as analyzed are much the same, indistinguishably white, just "a white paraphrase" without even the "bruised roses" "on the papered wall."

Having lost his steady grip on the difference between real and unreal and outer and inner, however, Tomlinson could no longer dismiss the inner world with such confidence. If the way out is the way in, if by exposing oneself to the full brunt of the detestably other one discovers the living edge of his self, perhaps the way in is the way out, an inner journey the way to come upon the living otherness of something like a stone wall. His first effort at such a journey, sections III and IV of "Movements" is as weak, I think, as any verse he has published in the past twenty years. The third section begins as follows:

> Man, in an interior, sits down
>   Before an audience of none, to improvise:
> He is biding his time, for the rhymes
>   That will arise at the threshold of his mind—
> Pass-words into the castle-keep,
>   The city of sleepers. Wakened by him,
> Stanza by stanza (room by room)
>   They will take him deeper in. Door
> Opens on door, rhyme on rhyme,
>   And the circling stair is always nearer
> The further it goes.[22]

A comparison of these two sections of "Movements" with "The Dream" reveals that the earlier verse is something like a perceptual, discursive version of the poetry of "The Dream." Whether Tomlinson is trying for perceptions about something which he recognizes to be intuitive or whether he is still thinking of dreams only as explicated cannot be determined, but no hint of anything intuitive or dream-like comes through. What Tomlinson needed was a nudge to recognize that not all dreams are common sewage. Perhaps he received this help from Philippe Jaccottet's discussion of dreams in *La Semaison* (Gallimard, 1971), a book Tomlinson praises with startling lavishness.[23] Jaccottet observes that his ordinary dreams are distant

from his books. The material of his dreams is that of the newspa-
pers, "des 'mauvais' journaux. Sexe et violence." His dreams often
take a cinematic form, with crude plots and obvious allegories, and
they may be prison experiences or have to do with stories
"d'espionnage, de gangs, ridicules, brutales, angoissantes."[24] In
sum, by dreaming "one rejoins that low, common material of which
history is also made, today as always." After apologizing that his
own poetry probably neglects unduly "ces étages inférieurs," Jaccottet then offers two dreams of a very different kind. In the second
of these, he is walking in a large, dark, and empty house and comes
upon a woman who points at a door in a wall through which he is
supposed to proceed. At that point he wakened, not, he says, as
one might expect with a sense of escaping a nightmare, but rather
as from "une beauté solennelle, souveraine." The door, he concludes, led into death, but also into an attractive other world, like
Dante's Inferno. Such dreaming, it would seem, is at the heart of all
essential, intuitive poetry. In it one dies to the conventional world
in which self and other are discreetly distinct and where words are
only useful signs for abstract meanings, as in sections III and IV of
"Movements," and enters into a new space, that of intuition, where
feeling and image are fused, immediately and uniquely.

Yet another influence, then: Wordsworth and Williams in
"Under the Moon's Reign," Leopardi and Ungaretti in "Foxes'
Moon," and Jaccottet in "The Dream." The problem needs facing if
only because the question Ian Hamilton asked of Tomlinson ten
years ago ("You mention all these other artists. People have spoken
of there being a danger of too much influence in your work. What
do you feel about this?") has been turned into an affectedly arch
and ugly judgment ("one might more rudely say that he is a bit of
a cultural magpie") by Anthony Thwaite in so solemn a place as the
British Council's *Poetry Today: 1960–1973*.[25] Tomlinson's reply to
Hamilton was:

> That's Alvarez, not 'people'. You can't have too much influence
> if you know what to do with it—look at Picasso, or, just as strik-
> ing in a different way, the American-Armenian painter, Gorky.
> The trouble with most critics is that they have such shallow no-
> tions of originality. A measure of the real artist is his capacity
> for discipleship.[26]

Such a capacity means the ability to respond with imaginative sympathy to the genius of another and yet with enough genius of one's own so as not to be overwhelmed and dominated by that other. In his poetry of perception Tomlinson is always arguing with someone or other so that, if one tracks him down, that poetry turns out to be a series of human encounters, an action as human as one could hope for, even if the content of the poetry includes only stones and trees and no people.

In perceptual poetry such dramatic encounters, however, are between one poem and another; they are not realized within either poem itself. As a result, the reality of the drama lies only in the mind of that reader who makes the connection. In essential, intuitive poetry, in contrast, there is no such duality. The master's influence is incorporated into the unique intuition of the disciple and becomes seamlessly at one with it. Conflicts, contrasts, arguments are all internal to the poetic intuition. Croce, it is true, would have said that in genuine poetry there are no real conflicts or arguments, that intuitive fusion is so thorough that it is experienced as utter oneness. Tomlinson's poetic intuition, however, as realized and defined in "The Dream," is different. The intuition is experienced as such and at the same time reflected upon intuitively. Tomlinson does not puncture his dream with an interpretive idea like Death, as Jaccottet did. His reflective awareness is as much a blind seeing as the dreaming attention he reflects upon is. The dreamer is following a constricted hope that has become a stone wall always a thought beyond him. The hope-wall-tense fluidity has an opaqueness even in its vibrant livingness that makes it possible for the dreamer to follow it by feeling for it as a flank of stone. As he does this a space opens up around him that turns into "The dream of a city under the city's dream," a space that seems itself somewhat opaque and impenetrable, even to the attention of the poet, who in the past was that dreamer. Finally, the image of the dreamer turned poet, with which the poem ends (the man who stands "reading with opened eyes/ The intricacies of the imagined spaces there/ Strange and familiar as the lines that map a hand"), has an opaqueness (in those eyes which have been replenished, filled, by sleep, to become prophetic) comparable to the opaqueness of the spaces he is reading. The dreamer, the dream, the poet, the moon, each is "strange and familiar" to the other: each is opaque to the others; all are radically, intuitively identical.

"The Dream" is Tomlinson's first major effort to turn inward for the purpose of exploring that inner self the margin of which he had discovered in "Under the Moon's Reign" and "Foxes' Moon." The self of "The Dream" is no less than a mediated immediacy, a dialectical intuition. The self Tomlinson has discovered is a community composed of a dreamer, a city, a moon, and a discovering poet, all individually opaque and yet somehow identical, so different from anything in his previous, conventionally perceptual experience, that that self can be said to have turned out to be quintessentially other, inscrutably strange even if as "familiar as the lines that map a hand."

Quite possibly Croce would have been converted by the success of "The Dream," for he had himself striven to activate intuition by making it internally mediate without compromising the immediacy essential to its nature as an intuition. The move, however, which Tomlinson makes in "After a Death," the last poem of "Under the Moon's Reign," would surely have confounded him. For Tomlinson begins the poem with one line of perceptive verse and then tries to work that perception, as a perception, into the rest of the poem, which is predominately intuitive. "Under the Moon's Reign" realizes an intuitive vision called in question and doubted; "Foxes' Moon" presents an intuitive pastoral so tinged with sarcasm that it evokes its ugly opposite as repulsed; "The Dream" works out an intuition which is self-reflective, an intuition which judges itself intuitively to be an intuition. Poem by poem, intuition by intuition, Tomlinson has forced another concession from the Crocean position: yes, an intuition can be self-doubting, fringed with sarcasm, and even self-reflective. But a poem in which perception and intuition stand side by side, neither giving way to the other; or, even worse, an intuitive poem containing lines of perceptive verse? That is what it means for a poem to fail.

Even if they have been triumphant, Tomlinson's advances have been made at the expense of his long-standing commitment to a poetry of perception. In "After A Death," if he still insists on a single perception as invulnerable to poetic intuition, nevertheless he is conceding that perceptive verse is at its very heart empty and dead. He is granting almost everything to Croce even as he shakes his aesthetic intuition to pieces. The one perception Tomlinson will not give up is the perception of death. Death is a fact. Death as a fact, as a perception, is not the same as death in intuitive poetry. In poetry a person dies, he is buried, and then he is resurrected. Once a month

> The husk of moon, risking the whole of space,
> Seemingly sails it, frailly launched
> To its own death and fulness.

But when a person one loves dies, he stays dead. That is a fact.

> We buried
> A little ash. Time so broke you down,
>   Your lost eyes, dry beneath
> Their matted lashes, a painted rose
>   Seems both to memorialize and mock
> What you became. It picks your name out
>   Written on the roll beside a verse—
> Obstinate words: measured against the blue,
>   They cannot conjure with the dead.

Just these words that I have quoted, along with three or perhaps four more lines, are the dead, perceptual spots which Tomlinson has worked into the otherwise intuitive poetry of "After a Death." They do not flower. It is as if Tomlinson has set Lear's

> And my poor fool is hang'd! No, no, no life!
> Why should a dog, a horse, a rat, have life,
> And thou no breath at all? Thou'lt come no more,
> Never, never, never, never, never!

against *The Divine Comedy*. That empty raving against such a luminous vision. And two things then happen at once: Dante's entire vision collapses into empty words; Lear's words expand to the magnitude of Dante's vision and become its dark side, an emptiness so awesome as to match its fullness.

The opening of "After a Death" indicates that Tomlinson is try-ing for an irreconcilable contrast like this, or perhaps like the re-verse of it, with none of the sublimity that results from imagining an encounter between Dante and Shakespeare.

> A little ash, a painted rose, a name.
>   A moonshell that the blinding sky
> Puts out with winter blue, hangs
>   Fragile at the edge of visibility. That space
> Drawing the eye up to its sudden frontier
>   Asks for a sense to read the whole
> Reverted side of things.

The first line is a perception. A person the poet loves has died and been cremated. All that is left is "a little ash," a roll of parchment with a verse, the dead person's name, and a painted rose beside that name. Mere facts in empty words. With the second line Tom-linson deftly launches the poem proper, the poetic intuition, by doubling perspective, by imagining himself as drawn up to where the moonshell "hangs/ Fragile at the edge of visibility," looking backwards upon the earth and its surrounding space, and reading "the whole/ Reverted side of things." He was prepared for this feat by "The Dream," by discovering how much more spacious even his own self is than ordinary perception can allow. He can stay put and yet at the same time move imaginatively to the edge of space, from which point he can comprehend all that waste of air intuitively. Tomlinson is not, however, ignoring the death of line one as he enjoys this intuitive expansiveness. Even though he wins "that height and prospect such as music brings," he also remains grounded:

> This burial place straddles a green hill,
> Chimneys and steeples plot the distances
>   Spread vague below: only the sky
> In its upper reaches keeps
>   An untarnished January colour. Verse
> Fronting that blaze, that blade,
>   Turns to retrace the path of its dissatisfactions,
> Thought coiled on thought, and only certain that

> Whatever can make bearable or bridge
> The waste of air, a poem cannot.

Perceptive verse cannot "make bearable or bridge/ The waste of air." Its words are empty of any air to make bearable or to bridge. Intuitive poetry cannot bridge or make bearable the waste of air, but it can realize the sense of that waste of air as unbearable and as not to be bridged. That is the glory of "After a Death": the vast grandeur, the desolate emptiness. The magnitude of poetic intuition is pushed so far as to reveal its limits. By its means one experiences empty space so intimately as to know in the very marrow of his bones that he is inconsolable. Even worse, or better, the poem ends with a perfection comparable to the end of "Under the Moon's Reign," and yet it is of no comfort either to the dead or to oneself as the bereaved.

> The imageless unnaming upper blue
>   Defines a world, all images
> Of endeavours uncompleted. Torn levels
>   Of the land drop, street by street,
> Pitted and pooled, its wounds
>   Cleansed by a light, dealt out .
> With such impartiality you'd call it kindness,
>   Blindly assuaging where assuagement goes unfelt.

The poet, in the act of "reading with opened eyes/ The intricacies of the imagined spaces there," is at one with "the imageless unnaming upper blue," and, as part of that indefinable act of defining, he is also at one with that cleansing, impartial, "blindly assuaging" effect the light of the moon has. So cosmic an intuition does not assuage so much as it exacerbates the pain of the poet who as a man knows that his loved one is no more than a little ash. The light blindly assuages the burial place. That is the one place "where assuagement goes unfelt." It goes unfelt, obviously, by the one who has been reduced to ash. It goes unfelt, too, by the poet who evokes the awesome abyss of empty air, because he has remained in addition a man who stubbornly clings to that last perception, that death is an unmodifiable fact.

   If the notion of "After a Death" as a poetic intuition that includes several unmodified and therefore dead spots of perception seems fanciful, then a glance should be given to three of Tomlinson's paintings which are printed in *Words and Images* (London: Covent Garden Press 1972): "Origins of the Milky Way" (p. 5), "Centrifugal" (p. 23), and "Small Galaxy" (p. 29). Each of these has an intricate texture, full of depth and movement, worked out by the painter's rubbing or brushing. In all three paintings, dead white, milky droplets are laid over the texture of depth and movement in which they take no part, into which they most emphatically do not sink.

Croce would say that a poetic intuition is infinitely expansive and infinitely absorbent, so that whatever is brought close to it is caught up and fused into it. This is why all intuitive poetry, no matter how limited its subject, gives the effect of something like cosmic totality. To limit a poetic intuition with a spot of dead perception automatically turns the intuition into another spot of dead perception. Intuition is delicate. Expose it to a perceptual glare and it will be electrocuted, shrivelled to "a bare-twigged scene." Tomlinson is using the glare of his last perception in order to empty his intuitive words of their vitally expansive sense and meaning. He is doing this in order to replace the sense and meaning with a sense of utter desolation and cosmic emptiness—all this, it should be noted, this elegy without rival, for a loved person whose name the poet has withheld, this poet so often criticized for being more interested in stones and trees than in people.

The unsettled quality of "Under the Moon's Reign" suggests that concluding assertions must be extremely tentative. In one sense, a poem of such magnitude and intensity may redefine the entire career of its maker: perhaps it marks the culmination of Tomlinson's career, putting all else he has done in its proper and subordinate place; or perhaps it signals the beginning of his career as a major poet, in the light of whose work our very conceptions of poetry must be redefined. In another sense, however, when one reminds himself that Tomlinson is alive and writing and painting much as he was before "Under the Moon's Reign," it seems that the poem may signify little or nothing in relation to his career.

Quite possibly he will continue to admire verse composed of detailed perceptions, verse calling to mind the photograph of Williams at his microscope or Marianne Moore's fascination with biological detail.[27] Reinforced by his admiration for the works of Pollock, de Kooning, and Gorky, he may continue to turn out technical things according to the tachist notion that one throws a blob onto a canvas and after a spell of doodling it becomes, magically, spontaneously, the vital germ of a living work.[28] This excerpt from a poem printed as recently as 1972 supports that prediction:

STONE SPEECH

Crowding this beach
are milkstones, white
teardrops; flints
edged out of flinthood
into smoothness chafe
against grainy ovals,
pitted pieces, nosestones,
stoppers and saddles;
[. . . .]
a mob of grindings,
groundlings, scatterings
from a million necklaces
mined under sea-hills, the pebbles
are as various as the people.[29]

The sad little allegorical tag at the end exaggerates the deadness of what has gone before. Nevertheless, even though he continues such play, it seems unlikely that he could again contrast his own poetry with that of Stevens in the way he did in 1964:

I first read "Thirteen Ways of Looking at a Blackbird" in Oscar Williams' anthology late in '49. It was a case of being haunted rather than of cold imitation. I was also a painter and this meant that I had far more interest in the particulars of a landscape or an object than Stevens. Stevens rarely makes one *see* anything in detail for all his talk about a physical universe.[30]

He must know now that Stevens does make one see, really see, but creatively and intuitively, not in the inert, if detailed manner of his own imitations of "Thirteen Ways" in *The Necklace*. He would admit that this little poem by W. S. Merwin is altogether superior to his own "Stone Speech":

EYES OF SUMMER

All the stones have been us
and will be again
as the sun touches them you can feel
sun
and remember waking with no face
knowing that it was summer
still
when the witnesses
day after day are blinded
so that they will forget nothing.[31]

Perhaps, however, such distinctions are more dangerous than not and may turn one to stone and make one utterly sombre. As Tomlinson himself said, the spirit of poetry "blows where it listeth, not to accomodate the Sunday *Observer*." In November 1972 Jaccottet wrote to Cid Corman: "I haven't written any poems since *Lessons* (that is, since October 1967), I don't know at all how that is made, a poem. I still try, sometimes, quite in vain."[32] In his '64 interview with Ian Hamilton, Larkin prefaced an answer with: "Well, I speak to you as someone who hasn't written a poem for eighteen months. The whole business seems terribly remote and I have to remember what it was like."[33] Who can guess just what would be the best way for a poet who has written a major poem to wait for the return of the spirit of poetry? Perhaps one can at least say that he should at all costs avoid foundering under sombreness, that weight "heavy as frost, and deep almost as life!" Perhaps like Wordsworth's philosopher he should be a "little actor," conning part after part. Perhaps his way of waiting should be to be "a bit of a cultural magpie."

CHAPTER NINE

The Authentic Duplicity of
Thom Gunn's Recent Poetry

J*ack Straw's Castle*, Thom Gunn's most recent volume, both sharpens and develops Richard Howard's findings on *Moly*, Gunn's next-to-last volume:

> The effort—and in such poems as "The Color Machine," "The Fair in the Woods," "The Garden of the Gods," "The Messenger," and, chiefly, "At the Center," the effort is not only made but mastered—is to get beyond definition, questions like "what place is this," "what am I," and into identification, into that surrender of the separating will which may then merely—merely!—acknowledge, acquiesce. [1]

All the best poems except "Autobiography" in *Jack Straw's Castle* divide into a non-verbal experience of surrendering and the words of the separating will, acknowledging, acquiescing. The words remain words, finely textured, steeped in the tradition of English poetry, and they somehow loft the non-verbal experience, which drifts and floats away from them. Before Gunn's third-from-last volume, *Touch*, he wrote mainly verse, words of the will only. *Touch*, in contrast, contains major poetry, in which words and experience interact. Since *Touch*, the tendons holding words and experience in tensile relation have been snapped and the words are textured so as to hold them, aloof and fastidious, away from the non-verbal experience which even so, is evoked and set afloat.

So much recent English verse is no more than that, just verse, words, all ears and mouth, that even a fine critic like John Bayley, in reviewing *Jack Straw's Castle*, seems to be on the lookout for nothing more. From what he says, he was so busy browsing through volumes and attending poetry readings, in the hope that something would make his ears prick up and his mouth drop open, that the real thing, genuine poems, the best of Gunn's volume, slid by without recognition. He is simply offended, even by the very funny, though unsettling, "Yoko," which is the least of the best. Gunn has given himself up to an hour or so as experienced by a dog, but the poem is made up of the dog's speaking out the experience to himself in words. The grotesqueness of the words as the dog's speaking splits the words and the dog's experience apart. The speaking dog, that is, is just words without experience, but because the words have been worked over so as to come as close as possible to the non-verbal experience of the dog, in turning on themselves as just words, they also loft the non-verbal experience of the dog so that it floats free of their funnily grotesque verbalness. There is, in other words, no integration of the canine and language as there is, say, of the gallinaceous and language in "The Nun's Priest's Tale," in which Chaunticleer is a cocky man or manly cock who never splits apart into cock and man. Bayley, who is sniffing about for poems that prick up his ears, is so unsettled as to say: "By declining, so to speak, to be a poem as a turd is a turd, each poem deliberately prevents us from being a reader as a dog is a dog."[2] He is right, but wrong to complain, for this is genuine, original poetry, which invariably exceeds one's expectations and disallows one's "being a reader as a dog is a dog."

Before considering the best of what is characteristic of *Jack Straw's Castle*, a sequence of four poems entitled "The Geysers," I wish to look at something even finer, the short "Autobiography," which may be the presage of a major advance in Gunn's work:

AUTOBIOGRAPHY

The sniff of the real, that's
what I'd want to get
        how it felt
to sit on Parliament
Hill on a May evening
studying for exams   skinny
seventeen   dissatisfied
        yet sniffing such

> a potent air, smell of
> grass in heat from
> the day's sun
>
> I'd been walking through the damp
> rich ways by the ponds
> and now lay on the upper
>
> grass with Lamartine's poems
> life seemed all
> loss, and what was more
> I'd lost whatever it was
> before I'd even had it
>
> a green dry prospect
> distant babble of children
> and beyond, distinct at
> the end of the glow
> St Paul's like a stone thimble
>
> longing so hard to make
> inclusions that the longing
> has become   in memory
> an inclusion[3]

If one stays close to the words of the poem, he will experience the youth's longing as an inclusion in the memory of the adult. The longing, that is, will be included in memory not as a longing, but as an inclusion, an item recollected dryly. The first two lines show that the adult's relation to himself as seventeen will exclude the real thing, what it really felt like:

> The sniff of the real, that's
> what I'd want to get

He's at his business, doing his job as a poet, out getting things he wants to get. What he wants to get is the opposite of what he takes it to be in his words "The sniff of the real'; it is the ache and anguish of longing to embrace Lamartine and the smell of grass at the same moment. There is something dismissively doggy in the adult's phrase, though that quality is receding by the time of "yet sniffing such/ a potent air." And by the time he arrives in memory at

> life seemed all
> loss, and what was more
> I'd lost whatever it was
> before I'd even had it

the adult himself has softened and senses in the form of winsome regret what is in reality the excluded, crushingly emotional grief which could never be "got" in rhetorically moving syntax. Because, however, the adult has moved not just as an investigator, but with a charge of feeling, toward that youthful pain, he provokes one's sense of its uncontainable wordlessness, so that the next stanza is to be read doubly, with longing, grievously included as beyond one's dearest hope, but also as framed, dry-eyed, the exact scene reviewed by the poet at work.

What has happened, as I read the poem, is that it has doubled up or split apart dramatically: the poet includes in his way the youth, but he cannot include the real youth and that youth we sense as excluded so that he, in his turn, in his yearning comes to include the adult as the rather monstrously desiccated final product of his own intense longing. Gunn as poet, that is, has evoked and released another person, who includes in his world the poet as the poet includes that person in his world. The drama suffuses the entire poem, though it certainly reaches its peak in the next-to-last stanza, in which the single scene is experienced doubly, in mutually exclusive ways.

> a green dry prospect
> distant babble of children
> and beyond, distinct at
> the end of the glow
> St Paul's like a stone thimble

Such an unlikely bringing together of longing and inclusion, of intense feeling and cool ordering, is the heart of poetic creativity, but, in this instance, in an entirely unexpected form, with such promise for Gunn's future and his readers'. The last stanza sunders what was momentarily simultaneous. The first line, "longing so hard to make," comes straight out of the adolescent anguish, but there is a real fall into the second line and then, especially with the pause in the middle of the third line, the longing settles into sediment, into a mere inclusion.

Like so many recent poets, Gunn tends to be trapped by a model of experience in which there can be but one investigator with a field to be investigated, a Kantian model re-inforced by most forms of phenomenology. In this poem, Gunn breaks out of that solipsistic trap as the "field" turns into a second investigator who includes, indirectly, the first investigator in his field. Once this happens, the investigator-field model is exploded into actuality, a dramatic encounter between two persons, two self-worlds. Gunn's doing this even once is a partial fulfillment of the promise of "Misanthropos," the major poem in *Touch*. "Autobiography" is, though, the only such fulfillment to be found in Gunn's last two volumes. Only in focussing exclusively on himself does he succeed imaginatively in putting two live persons or self-worlds into a poem. If, however, he can do it once, with himself as the community of two, then he must have the capacity to do it again, and with other persons. The promise of "Misanthropos" will not have been made good until he does that.

Set afloat in your imagination a composite portrait made up of the Hart Crane of "Voyages" and the Yvor Winters of "The Significance of The Bridge, or What are We to Think of Professor X," and you will be in the right frame of mind to read the four-poem sequence, "The Geysers," the finest of the characteristic poems in *Jack Straw's Castle*. The poems of the sequence tend to overlay one another as Crane's six "Voyages" do, but, with Winters' stern tutelage as a permanent black hole or star or conscience at the center of his compositional life, Gunn is not about to give himself up to any entropic disintegration like the regression from the first to the last of the "Voyages." Crane, unlike the brilliant self-loving kids, who fondle their "shells and sticks" in the first voyage, truly does give himself up to the bottom of the sea. The whole of him, including his language, is drenched in the oceanic oneness of the experience of unqualified love for and by another person. The affair, needless to say, does not last. In the sixth poem of Crane's sequence, he feels like the sea's "derelict and blinded guest," hoping at most for "some splintered garland." At the end, with the lover gone forever, he is left with only "the imaged Word," "that holds/ Hushed willows anchored in its glow." It alone is "the unbetrayable reply/ Whose accent no farewell can know."

Gunn wants to sink to the bottom of the sea, to become one with the very quick of life itself, sunk in hot mud, then "stretching my coils on coils," and he wants to experience complete emotional, bodily oneness with other human beings. The fourth and last of "The Geysers" acts out such a submergence of self-identity as the imaginative transformation of a communal experience. Gunn wants, however, at the same time, to be totally at one with absolute compositional control. The experience of that oneness, with the "gray and bare" jar which Stevens, the Stevens admired by Winters, placed on a hill in Tennessee so as to make "the slovenly wilderness/ Surround that hill," Gunn acts out in the third of "The Geysers." As a whole, moreover, "The Geysers" is to be read as double, an experience of verbal delight, the words textured finely so that they have the feel of felt, and an untextured experience of emotional oneness with a natural situation and with other human beings. It is a bit like *The Faerie Queene*, which almost requires a double reading, one for the experience and one for the words, though ideally the two ought to go on at once. Or, it is like a performance the Boston Symphony gave several years ago in Ames of Mahler's Fifth Symphony, with Michael Tilson Thomas not so much conducting as doing a dancing out of the music, just a fraction of a second behind it, as if to help an uncouth audience stay alert. The words, that is, do not sink into and become drenched with emotional experience, as Crane's words do. It is like hearing in one ear Landowska playing *The Well-Tempered Clavier* while hearing that Boston Symphony performance with the other.

Consider these lines, for instance, from the third of "The Geysers":

Heat from the sky, and from the rubble of stones.

The higher the more close-picked are Earth's bones:
A climb through moonland, tortured pocked and grey.
Beside the steep path where I make my way
Small puffs of steam bloom out at intervals,

And hot deposit seeps from soggy holes
Scabbing to yellow or wet reddish brown.

I reach the top: the geyser on the crown
Which from the distance was a smart panache
Is merely a searing column of steam from ash.[4]

The experientially repulsive, what the eyes are attending to if they look denotatively through such words as "soggy holes/ Scabbing to yellow" or "a searing column of steam," is being presented in a language as lush as that of Keats's Odes. The first two lines of the poem, as quoted above, provide the key both of the song and of the experience. The first line is as little language as possible; it simply points to the two sources of the heat felt (though as part of the sequence as a whole, it suggests the doubleness of Gunn's sense of himself as a man and poet and prefigures the final words, "I am raw meat/ I am a God"). The second line, in contrast, calls attention to itself as poetic language, and, though it rhymes with a clang with the first line, Gunn emphasizes the doubleness, the separateness, by the stanza break after only the first line. The compressed, inverted syntax of the second line, moreover, requires that it be read with the mind and the lips, as poetry, that is, not as experience. Thereafter, the textural richness of the passage is astonishing as words touch each other in all directions with tonal tangs. Notice how "higher" touches in assonance "sky" in the line above it and "climb" in the line below, and how "path" touches alliteratively "pocked" above it and "puffs" below it. Meanwhile, as one savors the delicious language, he is being repulsed by what he is experiencing. What looks so attractive, "a smart panache," is just hot air, painful ("searing") and sterile ("from ash").

The experience itself is thoroughly American. A naked man, who has come with friends to this area of geysers in Sonoma County, California, not so long before 1973, climbs a hill in the heat of the day and he reacts and thinks as he walks. Though the words are letting one into that experience, they themselves stay aloof from it and build up, along with tonal richness, a sense of what it means to be the man and poet who has this experience and writes this poem. The last line of the poem, "Up here a man might shrivel in his source," although it floats one away from it as a line into that experience of a fearful shrinking from the barrenness and emptiness of the place, also builds up within itself, as language, the phoenix sense of poetry, the sense that, having undergone an experience, after giving oneself up to it wholly, one must die into poetry, one must annihilate oneself, evacuate the rubble of bones one's remains have become, and blaze forth Apollo-like, like the new sun of day, with its "smart panache," even though, experientially, one has been reduced to nothing more than hot air, "a searing column of steam from ash." The poem thus heightens, excruciatingly, a doubleness it shares in its peculiar way with all authentic poetry. The relation between the poetic language and the experience is not to be thought, it itself exceeds inclusion, either by way of experience or by way of language, it is "too simple and big to comprehend,/ Like a beginning, also like an end." It is a death and birth, a blackness between experiential longing and poetic inclusion.

Even though this third of "The Geysers" poems is limited to the experience of Thom Gunn as man and poet, even though it excludes any other activated originative center and thus lacks the drama of "Autobiography," it does seem to be one of the finest poems Gunn has written, perhaps even that any living poet has written. And if one has the endurance to allow his seeing and hearing and experiencing to be stretched to the point of breaking into utter doubleness, the other three of "The Geysers" poems will be found to sustain that fineness. The experiences of the first two poems are not repugnant, as that of the third one is; indeed they verge on the Edenic, except that both involve such a strain and stretch, including as experience intense alertness and emotional and bodily insouciance. But the language itself dances away from the experience like the notes of a harpsichord that are stars not seen but felt inwardly. The doubleness of the experiences themselves is enough to prove amazing, but what makes the sequence unique and great poetry is the doubleness between the poetic language and the experiences.

Gunn himself, I should imagine, finds this doubleness in himself as man and poet to be baffling and all but intolerable. As if as an admission of this fact, in its first form "The Geysers" included a fifth poem "Discourse from the Deck," which Gunn placed between the third poem and what is now, in *Jack Straw's Castle*, the fourth and last poem.[5] It is difficult to imagine a worse poem than "Discourse from the Deck," at least as written by Thom Gunn, though it is possible to guess why it was written, even printed, before Gunn realized that it must be withdrawn and silenced. It is an indulgent poem, in which experience and language are conspicuously and almost slangily at one. As experience, to be sure, the poem fits into the sequence, as it tries to bring together an astronaut's view of America as "One great brave luminous green-gold meeting place" with the view the naked men have as they loll about on "a certain wooden deck/ Outside a bath house falling into wreck." "Fig-musk pervades the thought of everyone": experientially that line effectively unifies alert thinking with relaxed, sensuous openness. By allowing the language, however, to sink into the "Ambiguous perfume!" of "the figtree's smell," Gunn undoubtedly found that he had made an ass of himself, not composing as a poet at all. The very quick of "The Geysers" is divisiveness, a quality so painful that Gunn almost ruined it with the smear and blur of the now discarded piece. The badness of "Discourse from the Deck" stems from a longing close to that which led Wallace Stevens to write "Owl's Clover," a poem in which he tried to be at one with the multitude and to speak with their voice. As is well known, after first printing "Owl's Clover" along with "The Man with the Blue Guitar," in which Stevens writes as the intelligence of the monster but never as the monster, he then wisely kept the mess out of his *Collected Poems*.[6] In their badness "Owl's Clover" and "Discourse from the Deck" betray the intense pain which is the cost of great poetry.

"The Geysers" may well be the perfection possible for postmodernist poetry, if it is conceived as the rejection of the multiple perspectivism of modernism and the acceptance of a single investigator/field model of experience after the manner of William Carlos Williams. Without creating imaginatively that which is truly other than himself, a second investigator different from himself and with a field other than his field but including him as he includes that investigator in his field, Gunn has nonetheless created a poetic society of two independent but non-communicating selves: an experiential self, reaching out to others, allowing himself to be absorbed by his scene, yet also always watching himself; and a poetic, compositional self, weaving words that strangely evoke that other self by withdrawing and turning away from it. With such radical divisiveness as that of "The Geysers" and, for that matter, *Jack Straw's Castle* taken as a whole, Gunn is at the dead center of himself. This is what he must exceed, if he is to transcend himself as he showed that he can in "Autobiography"; this is what he was groping for without success in *Moly*.

Most of the poems of *Moly* are, it is true, severed as those of *Jack Straw's Castle* are, but Gunn is neglectful, if not downright oblivious, of the doubleness because he is so intent on trying to bring together in single experiences acts of participation and acts of attentiveness. As a result, the doubleness between poems and experiences makes for either falseness or clumsiness or both. Gunn is well beyond the attitude he was expressing in 1966, in a review on Gary Snyder: "often in Snyder, as in the Pound of Canto 47, we find the rituals of the life-cycle presented without pedantry or patronage, rather with a simple fidelity in the recording which is the equivalent to participation."[7] As though he himself is in entire accord, he says that in Snyder, as in Williams, attentiveness is a moral discipline: "The act of attentiveness is, too, one in which you can fully live, and its analogues are to be found in the deer running, the mussels sucking, the man and woman making love, and the labourer at his job. These acts are a means of 'unifying categories and interpenetrating things'."[8] The way these words echo the last stanza of Stevens' "Of Modern Poetry" suggests that Gunn is himself not far from recognizing that what he is finding admirable in Snyder, Pound, and Williams, is too simple a model for him to live and write by. By the time of *Moly*, in any case, he is committed to participation as much as to attentiveness, having realized that they are not at all equivalents and that the act of attentiveness is simply not an act in which one can fully live. He seems, however, at the time of *Moly*, to be thinking of the relation between his experience and his poetry as indistinguishable from the relation between attention and participation. His efforts to bring attending and participating together in single experiences make him feel that he can also bring his poems into oneness with those experiences, as though they were just another form of attentiveness that could sink into oneness with the experiences they are efforts to evoke. Such a blurring reductiveness can be glimpsed, I think, in the following comment made in a letter to William Meredith. I am guessing that Meredith had asked why Gunn kept using metre even while writing poems that suggest that he was trying, like Snyder and Williams, to meld poetic rhythms into the rhythms of attentive experiences (still taken to be the equivalents of acts of participation):

> One reason I write metrically is very simple: I do this better than I do in the more open forms. But I think I have a more deliberate choice behind it: from first to last most of my poems have dealt with violent or extreme or non-verbal experience. Fitting such experience through a fairly fixed form helps me to more firmly re-create it, and so to come to terms with it, possibly even to partially understand it. The openness of the experience is brought into relation with the structures of the mind.[9]

As intelligent as that is, it is too simple for the poems even of *Moly*, though the presence of thinking very much like it in the poems may explain recurrent blurs and blanks in even the finest poems of that volume. For the experiences that occur within the poems of *Moly* already include both acts of participation and acts of attentiveness, the openness of experience and structures of the mind, even before consideration is given to Gunn's act of poetic shaping. He is, in other words, discussing an experiential relationship on which he may work poetically as though it were the relationship between experience and poetry. Such a blurring is at the heart of the volume. The poems exhibit a doubleness between Gunn's experience as man and his poetry, but they are written as though there is no such doubleness, as though a poem and its experience are as firmly and comprehensibly related as are the participation and the attentiveness of the experience. Gunn continues to be his own difficult, divisive self, even as he proceeds as though he is as uncomplicated as Snyder or Williams.

The short poem "Words" not only shows the kind of limitation marring *Moly*, but also pairs closely with a poem in *Jack Straw's Castle*, "Thomas Bewick," in which Gunn senses the distinctness of the act of shaping a poem in words from an experience in which one both participates in his immediate surroundings and is attentive to them. In "Words" the attentiveness and the poetic shaping are blurred, to the disadvantage of both:

WORDS

The shadow of a pine-branch quivered
On a sunlit bank of pale unflowering weed.
I watched, more solid by the pine,
The dark exactitude that light delivered,
    And, from obsession, or from greed,
        Labored to make it mine.

In looking for the words, I found
Bright tendrils, round which that sharp outline faltered:
    Limber detail, no bloom disclosed.
I was still separate on the shadow's ground
    But, charged with growth, was being altered,
        Composing uncomposed.[10]

Despite the past tense of the poem, the shaping poet is working as if he and the "I" of the poem are basically at one, so that the "I"'s search for words within the experience of the poem is made to seem to have issued in the poem itself. The clang, however, of the rhyme with which the poem ends, "uncomposed" with "disclosed," disconcertingly calls attention to how nicely composed poem and poet are. Instead of evoking a sharp, striking contrast between poetic composure and experiential discomposure, this conclusion fixes the poem with so hard a glaze that everything experiential is distanced to the point of disappearance. This is the fault of most of Gunn's early poetry as it is of most of Yvor Winters' poems. "Words" stands out, however, in its effort to pull one into the very experience from which its glaze excludes one. The experience in the poem seems meant to be the experience of the poem: by his attentiveness the "I" is said to achieve a participation in the scene while still remaining aloofly attentive. Such attentiveness is blurred into the attentiveness of the poet in his compositional act as a result of the main point being made in the poem. As in "The Rooftop," another poem in *Moly*, Gunn is making the point against the too painterly poet, Charles Tomlinson, who, for all his practice with words, cannot shake off the notion that seeing is believing. In one of the finest poems of *The Way of a World*, "Adam," Tomlinson is suggesting that truly Edenic, poetic words are elicited somehow by that which they name, and that words which are not derivative in this way but rather creative, self-originative, are, in their possessiveness of that which they name, reenactments of Adam's original sin. As a poet, Gunn is not so presumptuous or self-righteous. He does not know whether it is from poetic obsession or animalistic greed that he seeks to render the exact relation between light and shadow in the scene before him. He knows, however, as Tomlinson seems not to know, that, whichever it is, the rendering does not occur as the passive reception of a gift, but unavoidably entails labor and an element of possessiveness. Moreover—and here Gunn as poet is chastising Tomlinson for his eye-idolatry—it is in his search for words that Gunn discovers the true intricacies of appearances. It is words that break down the falsely sharp outline between light and dark and, more important, between field and observer, so that the outer growth becomes an inner charge and the composer is uncomposed by the scene he thought to compose. The poet, that is, makes visual discoveries which enhance his own nature as the result of his acts of composing with words. That is what is given as the experience of the poem, only it is not given as experience, only as theory, as assertion. The reason for the failure would be a mystery if it were not for a poem like "Thomas Bewick," in which Gunn himself shows what was wrong. He is too much a man of words, in the great tradition of English poetry, to give his words, his lines, his rhythms and rhymes and stanzas up to imitative forms, to give up poetic attentiveness and making to experiential attentiveness. Under the lure of Snyder and Williams, in *Moly* he tends to blur the distinction between poem and experience, or at least to neglect it; the poems are written as if their attention was the attention within them, even though they are in fact written in such a way as to block out rather than evoke that which Gunn is trying to merge them with.

The only way Thom Gunn can get experience and poetry into a poem is by separating them. The power of "Thomas Bewick" comes from the fact that Gunn is recognizing this truth about himself as man and poet even as he realizes it imaginatively in the poem. The separateness of the experience and the poetry of the poem can be understood only if the poem is read and considered in its entirety.

THOMAS BEWICK

I think of a man on foot
going through thick woods,

a buckle on his brimmed hat,
a stick in his hand.

He comes on from the deep
shadow now to the gladed parts
where light speckles the ground
like scoops out of darkness.

Gnarled branches reaching down
their green gifts; weed reaching up
milky flower and damp leaf.

I think of a man fording
a pebbly stream. A rock
is covered in places with
minute crops of moss
—frail stalks of yellow rising
from the green, each
bloom of it distinct, as
he notices. He notices
the bee's many-jointed legs and its
papery wings veined like leaf,
or the rise of a frog's back
into double peaks, and this morning
by a stile he noticed ferns
afloat on air.

   Drinking from
clear stream and resting
on the rock he loses himself
in detail,
   he reverts
to an earlier self, not yet
separate from what it sees,

a selfless self as difficult
to recover and hold as to
capture the exact way
a burly bluetit grips
its branch (leaning forward)
over this rock
    and in
The History of British Birds.[11]

The poem itself sets forth in words an imaginary walk through thick woods by Thomas Bewick, and it then concludes with generalizations about the two kinds of experience Gunn thinks Bewick would have had to have in order to write *The History of British Birds* and engrave its marvellously exact illustrations. The experience of the poem, however, is quite another matter, and only when it has been evoked and re-enacted is the reader going to be reading the poem as poetry, as both words and the felt qualities of lived experience. The crux of the poem, as I read it, resides in that experience the poem evokes as other than and at a distance from itself. This experience alone allows one to sense the rightness, say, of the "I think of" in the first lines of stanzas one and four, of the "on" of "He comes on" in line one of the second stanza, of the "as/ he notices. He notices" in stanza four, and, perhaps most crucially, the "and in/ The History of British Birds" with which the poem ends. Until one has the experience evoked by but other than the poem, he is bound to find such phrases oddly off, affected, or ineffectively clever.

The experience is far enough from the poem so that it is difficult to pin down exactly how it is that the poem leads one away from itself evocatively. My conjecture as to how it occurs is as follows. As one puzzles over the relationship between Bewick's recovering and holding that "selfless self," "not yet/ separate from what it sees," and his capturing "the exact way/ a burly bluetit grips/ its branch," one recalls that, before he made his very exact notations in stanza four, Bewick was said to come "on from the deep/ shadow now to the gladed parts/ where light speckles the ground/ like scoops out of darkness." To make his minute observations, Bewick must be coming out of deep shadow into the gladed parts, he must have reverted to an earlier self from which he then emerges to make his notations, and he must undergo the same reversion and re-emergence in order to make his engravings. By making the connection between the concluding generalizations about Bewick and the opening lines concerning his walk, one is apt to be thrown into that experience which is other than but interdependent with the poem.

The poem, that is, does in truth evoke the experience, but the experience makes the poem genuinely poetic. The experience goes this way: Gunn has been studying Bewick's book, reading it and looking at its illustrations. So hard has he looked that finally he loses himself in the details Bewick has engraved and he reverts to a oneness with Bewick, a selfless self. The dark shadow of that reversion, of Gunn's falling into a oneness with the source, the author, of the book he was studying is then the experiential otherness the light of the poem's words speckles. Only if the "I think of" 's are sensed as emerging out of that dark selfless revery can they sound right, and once they are read rightly, one is ready to revert himself into such darkness in the center of the line "he notices. He notices". Of course, the "as/ he notices" has a finality to it calling for a pause which encourages the lapsing into darkness that alone can reveal the rightness of the repeated "He notices." Finally, the "and in/ The History of British Birds" is to be experienced as an awakening out of the trance-like alternation between experiential darkness and verbal lightness, as the poet fixes, again, his attention on the book which he had left behind in his recovering and holding of that selfless self in which he was one not with the book but with the experience that led up to the book, Bewick's own reversions and re-emergences. It is such a small, dry, meticulous poem, and yet the otherness it evokes has a largeness not unlike that of Stevens' "The Idea of Order at Key West."

The largeness of Stevens' finest poems comes from a oneness of poetry and experience made possible by Stevens' sense that life is pluricentric, that it is made up of dramatic encounters between sensuous selves each with its own sensuous world.[12] "The Idea of Order at Key West" implicates and allows to be felt the movement of the "ever-hooded, tragic-gestured sea," the gestures of the woman singing solitary by the shore, the meditative acts of thought of Stevens and his companion, who are intent on the sea and the woman's song of the sea from a removed position, and even the compositional act of Stevens as poet and his sense of the critical act of attending to the poem.[13] The poem includes such variety of action because Stevens' world is not centered, but inclusive of numerous self-worlds, each self-originative, its feelings and images and sounds flowing outward and overlapping with the inner-originated but outer-directed sensuous worlds of other sensuous selves. The grandeur results from the integration of a subtle, lavish imagination and a profound belief in freedom and diversity.

In contrast to Stevens, Gunn believes that ultimate value, that oneness as experience, must involve total identification, utter merger, a single center. Even in *Jack Straw's Castle*, this belief tends to work as a stultifying force, so that, except for "Autobiography," the poems which succeed do so in spite of or in contradiction to that belief. The belief is, at bottom, that postmodernist single observer/field model of experience. In "Thomas Bewick," for example, there is plenty of variety in appearances: the woods with its shadows and lights, the burly bluetit gripping its branch, Bewick in the woods studying the bluetit and at his book capturing the exact way of its grip, and Gunn himself as poet recovering Bewick's recovering of the bird's act. But the variety is believed to be only apparent. Stevens' "The Idea of Order at Key West" is, it is true, made up of the interacting of various self-worlds each of whose acts is included, in the end, under the exclamation "Oh! Blessed rage for order." But the din and conflict drown out the sense of oneness in the phrase; its oneness is essentially, dramatically manifold. In contrast, to the extent that Gunn succeeds in realizing his belief, he reenacts Bewick's reversion to a selfless self, in total participation, then emerging into keen attentiveness which itself is but an illustration of that participation-attentiveness experience the subject of which, Bewick's reversion and emergence, is itself but another illustration of that ur-experience. Gunn's mentor, Yvor Winters, believed that human value depends on one's becoming identical with pure mind and right judgment. Though such value for Gunn resides in a less heady identification, not with pure mind, but with impersonal acts of participation and attentiveness, ultimate value does, nonetheless, reside in utter identification.

Despite his belief, Gunn writes poems out of a love for language that is so intensely personal that the poems become exquisitely permanent gestures of defiance of the notion that they are no more than illustrations of a paradigm of experience just as effectively illustrated by the likes of Bewick's book. Gunn believes that an impersonal all-mind, all-river writes his poems, or else they are a curse, divided at their very source. So long as he works under the single observer/field model, so that every sentient, self-originative center must be identical with that all-mind, all-river, or else it would be only an item in the field attended to, his poems can succeed only in so far as they split divisively into poem and experience. Moreover, to read Gunn's poem according to his belief, one would have to submit to the coercion of the overshadowing paradigm and so become but another illustration of it. But the finely textured language of the poem has such evocative power that one knows, as he lets it float him away from itself and into the non-verbal experience of participating attentively, that the value of this strangely double experience is inseparable from the uniqueness of Gunn's compositional genius. As a result, in accord with Gunn's genius but at odds with his belief, one cannot but worry in his own way over the incongruity of Gunn's succeeding only to the extent that he fails.

The poems of *Moly* seem larger, more ambitious, and even richer than those of *Jack Straw's Castle*, more like Stevens' big poems, that is. But they lack what makes Stevens' poems work and so they finally sour, or appear flatulent, as is true of many of Duncan's poems. Consider even the middle section of "At the Center," the center-piece of *Moly*, in which Richard Howard felt that Gunn truly achieves the full surrender of the separating will. Having taken LSD, Gunn had, in the first section, climbed to the roof of a building and begun observing, in fascination, "the lighted sign above Hamm's Brewery":

2

What is this steady pouring that
                    Oh, wonder.
The blue line bleeds and on the gold one draws.
Currents of image widen, braid, and blend
—Pouring in cascade over me and under—
To one all-river. Fleet it does not pause,
The sinewy flux pours without start or end.

What place is this
               And what is it that broods
Barely beyond its own creation's course,
And not abstracted from it, not the Word,
But overlapping like the wet low clouds

The rivering images—their unstopped source,
Its roar unheard from being always heard.

What am
            Though in the river, I abstract
Fence, word, and notion. On the stream at full
A flurry, where the mind rides separate!
But this brief cresting, sharpened and exact,
Is fluid too, is open to the pull
And on the underside twined deep with it.[14]

Though the section is meant to be pure, immediate experience, it turns out to be no more than pure, abstract doctrine, with rhetorical devices like "Oh, wonder" to make one feel like Miranda, with a few inscrutable phrases which resonate only to the extent that they border on cliché—"steady pouring," "one all-river," "the sinewy flux"—and with the feeble fiction that one is simultaneously undergoing some massive influx, and yet keeping keenly alert and getting the nature of what's happening expressed in words, all it seems made possible because one has become indistinguishable from the universal "all-river," and one's mind indistinguishable from "the mind." At the center of "At the Center" there is an imputed "all-river," "the pouring we are of," but actually there is a null.

It might be argued that the last stanza of the poem suggests that Gunn himself, at least as the poet of the poem, realizes the emptiness of the apparent fullness of the center section:

Later, downstairs and at the kitchen table,
I look round at my friends. Through light we move
Like foam. We started choosing long ago
—Clearly and capably as we were able—
Hostages from the pouring we are of.
The faces are as bright now as fresh snow.

His commitment, then, would be to what is "bright now as fresh snow," to lives as transient foam, when seen after an immersion in "the pouring we are of." I think, in contrast, that that "pouring" is meant to be taken as magnificent, must in fact be taken so, as soon as it is recognized that "the mind" is a part of it. "The mind," in contrast to any individual ego with a face of its own, "Is fluid too, is open to the pull/ And on the underside twined deep with it." But because the "pouring" is really a null, the faces of the last stanza, which are meant to seem like mere foam, come across in a wobbly form as more substantial than the mighty river they are said to be no more than an ephemeral part of. Thus, instead of feeling sentimentally poignant, as Gunn would have one, a reader is apt rather to feel rebellious, to be disinclined to share even imaginatively this stipulated Foucault-like death of man as individual. The language of the poem is so coarse because Gunn is mistakenly thinking of it as at one with the participating-attentive experience the poem is about. In *Moly* as a whole, Gunn fails to split off from that mistaken belief as he succeeds in doing in *Jack Straw's Castle* as the result of his renewed delight in his extremely personal verbal genius.

Perhaps the exquisite first poem of "The Geysers" is the perfect counterpart to the heavy coarseness of "At the Center." "Sleep by the Hot Stream" is the consummation of what can come out of the dead center of Gunn as man and poet, out of what strikes me as his authentic duplicity.

> Gentle as breathing
> down to us it spills
> From geysers heard but hidden in the hills.
> Those starlit scalps are parched blond; where we lie,
> The small flat patch of earth fed evenly
> By warmth and wet, there's dark grass fine as hair.
>
> This our bedroom, where we learn the air,
> Our sleeping bags laid out in the valley's crotch.
> I lie an arm-length from the stream and watch
> Arcs fading between stars. There
> bright! faint! gone!
> More meteors than I've ever set eyes on:
> The flash-head vanishing as it is defined,
> Its own end streaking like a wake behind.
>
> I must have been asleep when morning came.
> The v-sides of our shadowed valley frame
> The tall hill fair with sunshine opposite.

Live-oaks are of it yet crest separate,
In heavy festooned arches. Now it's day
We get up naked as we intend to stay.

Gentle as breathing
                Sleep by the hot stream, broken.
Bright, faint, and gone. What I am now has woken.[15]

In a recent article on *Moly* and *To the Air* (which includes the first version of "The Geysers") Catharine R. Stimpson complains that Gunn is trying to do the impossible:

> How can the flesh, of man, woman, or nature, become word? The poet who wants to translate the physical, the sensible, the sensuous, the sensual, into language struggles against impossibility. Though language is inseparable from the physicalities of sight and sound, it is involved with the physical world rather as a ghost is. The poet who metamorphizes place into text must, as he writes, feel the solid melt away, and the reader, as he acts as a random perturbation of the system of the text, enters, not material, but mental spaces.[16]

John Bayley agrees as to what Gunn was trying to do and to his failure, though he thinks Gunn fails not because the aim was impossible, as Stimpson claims, but because Gunn still had in him too much of the poet, of the word man, the man made of ears and mouth, to get wholly caught up in bodiliness.[17] Their diagnosis strikes me as accurate for *Moly*, in which Gunn was working under the illusion that bringing experience and poetry together in a poem was the same as, or even just a part of, integrating participation and attentiveness in a single experience.

    "Sleep by the Hot Stream," however, is a different matter, a genuine poem, a doing of the impossible, in Gunn's inimitably duplicitous way, an exquisitely textured verbal context which evokes that from which it remains divided, a fully lived experience in which one participates with his whole body, emotionally, insouciantly, with the natural scene, even as he is attentive, with star-like keenness, to all that is happening. In its magnificent doubleness, the poem is comparable to the ecstatic oneness of the second of Crane's "Voyages," which even the harshest of critics, Yvor Winters, conceded to be "one of the most powerful and one of the most nearly perfect poems of the past two hundred years."[18] Gunn himself must have sensed the specialness of the poem, since he had it published first accompanied only by "Autobiography," on the facing page.[19] Because of its strangeness, however, the poem's greatness could not be recognized immediately, even by the most sympathetic reader.

That reader could not but have been lured into the rich verbal texture of the poem, which dances out a softness in balance with a still keenness even from the first, split line.

> Gentle as breathing
>   down to us it spills

But even as he was internalizing its rhythms and memorizing its texture, he was being lured into forgetting them and entering into a non-verbal experience, a physical oneness with the valley's warmth ("earth fed evenly/ By warmth and wet") and the lulling breathing of the geysers ("heard but hidden in the hills"), along with, at the same time, an amazed attentiveness to the meteoric display, in which lights disappear just as they appear ("The flash-head vanishing as it is defined,/ Its own end streaking like a wake behind"), a phenomenon the likes of which have not been experienced in a poem since Stevens' "The Auroras of Autumn." The living out of these unheard melodies is related only by a moment of oblivion to the heard melodies of the verbal texture of the poem. The stretch of the poem exceeds that even of the most demanding of string quartets, which calls for a listening to each independent voice separately, but also in its relations to the other three. A sympathetic reader of the poem is inclined to pull away from the words and forget them, whereas a sharp reader would be likely to enclose himself within the verbal texture, analyzing out intricate tonal patterns and also the stunning sexual imagery, which peaks no doubt near the end as the oaks are at one with the hill and yet separate from it, as the hill is with the valley.

If the doubleness of the poem is finally experienced in its divided wholeness, its ending, "What I am now has woken," will have a forcefulness like that of the ending of "Voyages II," "The seal's wide spindrift gaze toward paradise." Gunn's statement is simple and plain, beside the splurging effect of Crane's line, so that the way it contains the power and keenness, the lapsing into dark softness and the assertive, even defensive rising in strength, of the entire poem, might easily be missed. There is a harsh, almost abrasive quality to the language of "Now it's day/ We get up naked as we intend to stay." Such decisiveness is touched with defiance. And yet it is then followed by the most lulling of phrases, especially in its repetition:

> Gentle as breathing
> > Sleep by the hot stream, broken.
> Bright, faint, and gone. What I am now has woken.

Geysers and meteors, along with the sleep, are felt to be left behind as the "I" wakes and yet to be carried forward into his waking experience, as the "valley's crotch" and the meteors of the night scene were carried analogously into the day scene of the "shadowed valley" and the "tall hill fair with sunshine." Sleep was broken yet its calm strength is carried into the day; and, miraculously, "What I am now has woken" evokes the experience of nakedness, not as tainted by externality and so by the weakness of defiance, but inwardly, as a sense of awesome opening, something not far from that "wide spindrift gaze toward paradise." Crane, however, felt a latent suicidal desperateness, even at his most ecstatic. The nakedness of "Sleep by the Hot Stream" is undoubtedly learned. But it is not experienced at the end as learned, and so is perfect.

The perfect experience, however, is broken away from that last rhyming, and in no other genuine poem has the relation between word and evocation been so dark as to make authentic duplicity seem an accurate descriptive phrase. That darkness is what makes it so easy to feel that one is being offered only place or text, only material space or mental space, instead of what Gunn has so masterfully realized, a doubleness which leaves such pedestrian distinctions far behind in their limp inertness.

CHAPTER TEN

The Idea of Communal Creativity in F. R. Leavis' Recent Criticism

Acreativity that is fundamentally communal is the innermost impulsion of the finest recent English poetry and also the guiding insight in the literary criticism of F. R. Leavis during the past twenty years. According to this idea of communal creativity, in contrast to ordinary speech-act situations, in which speaker and listener are entirely different individuals behaving according to the rules provided by their single, shared linguistic ambience, the speech of a poem, its expressiveness, originates in dramatic conflict with a critical attentiveness just as original and individual as it itself is. Even before any reader of poems, in the ordinary sense, makes his appearance, the act of the poem is an interplay between poetic expressiveness and critical listening, is, in effect, a dramatic community.

The best of recent English poems, moreover, the "double lyrics" of Hill, Silkin, Gunn, and Tomlinson, are communally creative in an even more radical way. They explode the last element of authorial singleness, the notion of the singleness of the act of poetic shaping, even that act which is a communal, dramatic interplay between expressing and listening. They set in dramatic conflict what seem to be two authentic poems, two communal interplays of expressing and attending, with each poem including the other in its world or ground or field, so that the very notion of "dramatic conflict" is doubled up, being one thing for one poem, another for the other. Such realizations of communal creativity are the most original and profound form humanity has taken in recent times. They are the primary creative thrust against the tyranny and coerciveness of a model of experience that permeates modern culture, the model of experience as a single field, whether geographical or historical or a combination of the two, with a single unlocatable and inaudible and unobservable observer or listener. Visionary, scholarly investigator, the Mind, the single subject of its object, the Lukácsian dictatorship of the proletariat, whatever form this hidden tyrant may take, his sublime, untouchable aloofness is the most perilous enemy of what I am calling communal creativity. His presence may be felt as created and discovered approvingly everywhere in the *Four Quartets*. Philip Larkin's finest poem, "Here," offers that same invisible, inaudible presence in a more comfortable and complacent form.

The poetic renewal which I take the double lyrics of Hill, Silkin, Gunn, and Tomlinson to be runs parallel to a comparably original form of literary and cultural criticism, the collaborative criticism which F. R. Leavis advocated and practiced during the past twenty years. Leavis himself, it must be admitted, said, as recently as 1976, that no English poetry of importance has been written since Eliot finished "Little Gidding" "and gave up poetry," so that he offers no overt support for my claim that his most recent criticism is analogous to recent poems of authentic greatness.[1] It is, furthermore, only in his recent criticism that Leavis refined and integrated his notions of creativity and community to the point where he achieves work comparable to the finest of recent English poetry. It would, therefore, be inaccurate to call Leavis' criticism an important influence on that poetry, as though he had actually accomplished what Matthew Arnold was trying, without success, to do a hundred years ago. It might rather be said that the poetic renewal brought about by Hill, Silkin, Gunn, and Tomlinson, like the critical renewal brought about in Leavis' recent criticism, is set quite resolutely against Leavis' own criticism written during the *Scrutiny* period, from 1933 to 1953, and including a large part of what Leavis wrote after *New Bearings in English Poetry* and before his "T. S. Eliot as Critic" of 1958.[2]

Although *New Bearings* exhibits remarkable critical genius and also contains the main elements of Leavis' recent criticism, nothing in the book gives consistency to Leavis' condemnation of the dreamworlds of late nineteenth- and early twentieth-century English poetry, which he presents as part of the sterile cultural situation in which poetry could not be taken seriously, and his unqualified praise for the dreamworld of Eliot's "Ash Wednesday." Some such inconsistency is at the heart of the entire book, which, even so, is impressively organic in the way it unfolds out of and is turned back upon the poem at its center, "Hugh Selwyn Mauberley." The critical judgments of the book are what is acted out poetically by Pound's poem. Incongruously, however, the poem acts out the impossibility of a poem's being written in the cultural situation in which it itself purports to have been written. In *New Bearings*, the cultural situation within Pound's poem is set forth as the cultural situation in which Pound's and Eliot's early poetry was written. The situation is sterile, maiming Yeats among others, and yet it was in that situation that Pound and Eliot did what it disallowed. The impasse, as Leavis recognized, drove the one poet out of England and into Mussolini's Italy and the other out of the actuality of *The Waste Land* and into the cloud-enfolded spirituality of "Ash Wednesday"; and yet, at the very same time, he is heralding a poetic revival in England as though a desperateness just like that of "Hugh Selwyn Mauberley" were not the underpinning of the whole of *New Bearings*. Leavis' notion that even the composing of poetry was heavily influenced by the single, given social and cultural situation in which it took place proved debilitating in its contradictoriness to any serious notion of creativity. Not until the fifties, when both F. W. Bateson and Raymond Williams were, in quite different ways, attacking Leavis' position in the light of theoretical systems based on the conspicuous collapsing of creativity into just plain construction according to rules provided by the given social and cultural situation, did Leavis undertake to think through the relation between community and creativity so seriously and sharply as to arrive at an integral sense of the nature of communal creativity.

In the thirties, the tension that proved too much for Pound and Eliot led Leavis to split his criticism in two, into criticism emphasizing imitation and moral judgment and criticism emphasizing creative shaping. The imitative half is emphasized in his treatment of fiction and the creative half in his studies of poetry, but each half suffers because not unsettled by the other. In *The Great Tradition*, for example, Henry James's *The Portrait of a Lady* is held to be inferior to the better part of George Eliot's *Daniel Deronda* for such reasons as that a girl like Isabel Archer could not be as free of flaws as James makes her and that English country houses are not as James presents them. James, that is, was a faulty imitator or recorder. Leavis, moreover, has little use for the Marlow of *Lord Jim* and *Chance*, finding him not to be the superbly created and creatively perceptive person he is, but only a rhetorical device that gets in the way of things as they are. When Lawrence, moreover, in Leavis' first book on his work, is praised as a "social historian," the phrase is not intended as a figure of speech. The world, society with its individuals, are there as givens and knowables; critical judgment is based on a comparison between them and the novelist's imitation of them. Even Leavis' poetry criticism is at times marred by a similar notion that the quality of a poet's work depends on whether he keeps his language close to the given single living speech of his time, though in the *Scrutiny* essays, " 'Thought' and Emotional Quality," "Imagery and Movement," and "Reality and Sincerity," all three of which are reprinted in his recent *The Living Principle*, Leavis does emphasize the life of the poems rather than the life they reflect or fail to reflect.[3] Each half of Leavis' criticism during this period seems to contain more, potentially, than it actually articulates, so that it is more vital than the work of his collaborators on *Scrutiny*; even so, it comes across as work broken in half. Leavis is willing, during this period, to use the word "creative" as synonymous with "constructive."[4]

Before sketching the transition from Leavis' partial criticism of the *Scrutiny* period to his maturest criticism, his work during the past twenty years, I would like to focus in some detail on the "Memories of Wittgenstein" of 1973 as an example of what a truly integrated piece of writing by Leavis can be. "Memories" is not, of course, a piece of literary criticism, but the human drama it enacts between Leavis and Wittgenstein closely resembles the drama in most of Leavis' maturest criticism between Leavis as critic and the poet or novelist about whose work he is writing. A critical intelligence is in charge of "Memories" just as in Leavis' literary criticism, but, in addition, Leavis enacts imaginatively, by his style, the dramatic relation he has with his subject. Leavis' dramas, moreover, very much like those of Geoffrey Hill's poems, are basically double. The subject or antagonist who is the focus in the world of Leavis' essay is evoked as himself self-originative, so that he is felt to be present not just as an individual or a self, but as a self-world which includes the author-protagonist of the essay, Leavis, and which, by that inclusion, qualifies, limits, and judges Leavis just as he, as author, qualifies, limits, and judges his subject.

Very much as Lawrence does in his introduction to the *Memoirs of the Foreign Legion* by Maurice Magnus, Leavis simply sets forth a series of encounters between himself and a man for whom he feels strong antipathy, but by whose genius and full humanity he is deeply impressed.[5] But Leavis is not just presenting things the way they were in 1929–30 Cambridge, when Wittgenstein returned there after a long absence and he and Leavis became active acquaintances. Knowing, as Lawrence did, the illusoriness of that sort of objectivity, instead of trying to establish a single ground, place, or field on which he could then meet another individual in memory, Leavis works to evoke encounters which exceed any framework, even his own, encounters between two original and self-originative persons, each both himself and his world, including Cambridge as he lived it and the other person as he saw and thought and spoke him to be. Even more important, Leavis is aiming primarily to evoke those moments in which life is most rich and intense, those moments in which each person, each self-world, senses that he is being impinged upon by a person who is radically other than himself.

In the second paragraph, for example, Wittgenstein seems frighteningly superior and in command of his world and of all who enter it, and the Leavis to whom he speaks seems very small, merely an auditor. But, having just read the masterfully subtle and strong first paragraph, one is prepared to recognize that, in his memory and as the author of this essay, Leavis is exposing and delimiting Wittgenstein as sharply and fiercely as Wittgenstein delimits the occupants of his world. It should be noted, moreover, that after that second paragraph (quoted below), Leavis then mulls over the incident, which clearly wedged itself permanently in his memory, and insists that the trait manifested by Wittgenstein's behavior is not "arrogance" or "singlemindedness," but "the quality of genius: an intensity of a concentration that impressed itself on one as disinterestedness." The adverseness of Leavis' judgment remains intact, though his self-world has opened up with an attitude akin to awe.

> I was walking once with Wittgenstein when I was moved, by something he said, to remark, with a suggestion of innocent inquiry in my tone: "You don't think much of most other philosophers, Wittgenstein?"—"No. Those I have my use for you could divide into two classes. Suppose I was directing someone of the first to Emmanuel,"—it was then my college—"I should say: 'You see that steeple over there? Emmanuel is three hundred and fifty yards to the west-south-west of it.' That man, the first class, would get there. Hm! very rare—in fact I've never met him. To the second I should say: 'You go a hundred yards straight ahead, turn half-left and go forty' . . . and so on. That man would ultimately get there. Very rare too; in fact I don't know that I've met *him*." Thereupon I asked, referring to the well-known young Cambridge genius (who was to die while still young): "What about Frank Ramsey?"—"Ramsey? *He* can see the next step if you point it out." I will give my reason later for assuming that he had a relatively high opinion of Ramsey. I associate with this memory so that I have the impression of his having said it to me too—though I am not sure—what I clearly remember having been told by someone else: "Moore?—he shows you how far a man can go who has absolutely no intelligence whatever."[6]

The condition of genius, as Leavis now understands it, the intensity of concentration "that impressed itself on one as disinterestedness," is not the capacity to see things as they are, as Matthew Arnold would have said, but the capacity to live out one's innermost force and feeling and thought, so that one is not just self, but also world, so that there is a continuousness between one's inwardness, one's acts, and the situations in which one acts. Obviously, when such a capacity is fully lived, as it was by Wittgenstein, it could easily be mistaken for arrogance or singlemindedness. Perhaps, in fact, only another such person, another self-world, could recognize the essential quality of Wittgenstein for what it is. For only after one understands that Leavis is living out his inwardness by acting, speaking, and thinking in a situation, a Cambridge, which is fundamentally at odds with Wittgenstein's Cambridge, is one apt to recognize that, even by the end of the second paragraph of the essay, Wittgenstein's world has been set forth as constituted by measurable directions and distances which are occupied by abstract classes like useful philosophers and by existent creatures who prove to be pathetically wanting.

The limited nature of Wittgenstein's world is brought home to one as Leavis establishes the nature of his own world, his Cambridge, in the paragraph concluding the second incident he recounts, his first meeting with Wittgenstein. They were both present at a Sunday afternoon tea given by the logician, W. E. Johnson, and his sister, "Miss Fanny," and a young viscount who had been asked to sing something of Schubert's nervously said: "Er Wittgenstein will correct my German." Wittgenstein replied: "How can I? How can I possibly?"

> It was essentially meant to be routing. It had its effect, and when the unfortunate singer had finished, Wittgenstein triumphantly—so I thought—got up and left. The front door had hardly shut behind him when I, who had followed him out of the packed drawing-room as fast as I could make my way, opened it again. I caught him up on the Barton Road, which, the Johnson house standing at the corner of Millington Road, flanked one side of it, and, with my hands on my lapels as if (I later realized) I were about to take my coat off, said: "You behaved in a disgraceful way to that young man." He looked at me in surprise: "I thought he was a foolish young man." To which I returned, emphatically containing myself: "You may have done, you may have done, but you had no right to treat him like that. You've no right to treat anyone like that." It was my turn to be surprised. Putting his hand on my shoulder, he said: "We must know one another." Since he, we being at the bottom of the road, turned left towards the Backs and Cambridge, I, muttering "I don't see the necessity," turned right, towards the Grantchester footpath.[7]

Instead of the compass points and measurable distances of Wittgenstein's Cambridge, streets, houses, even areas ("the Backs") have names in Leavis' world. A house, moreover, "flanks" one street, two streets meet at a "corner," and one street even has a "bottom."

In addition, whereas the interchange between the two men as presented within Wittgenstein's world was limited to thinking and speaking (there was no suggestion that Wittgenstein even pointed at the steeple to which he was referring), there is a strong physical, though humanized, sense to the interchange which occurs in Leavis' Cambridge. Leavis registers the manner of a man's leaving, triumphantly, the feel of a room, packed, a door is heard to be closed dismissively, but then opened again, and the two men confront one another not just mentally and verbally, but also with their bodies ("my hands on my lapels," "putting his hand on my shoulder"). Even the men's parting, Wittgenstein "left towards the Backs and Cambridge" and Leavis, in emotional reaction, "right, towards the Grantchester footpath," involves not just compass directions or even bodily-originated directions, left and right, but also moral feelings. This is a world where more than foolishness or intelligence qualifies a man. The spontaneity of Leavis' action as a young man suggests that he must have felt that his world was *the* world as given, an illusion much like that which cripples so much of his fiction criticism, at least through his first book on Lawrence, which was published in 1955. But as the author of the essay, shortly before 1973, he is clearly working over his language with a sense that his world is not *the* world, but his world, and that it is his obligation to make it continuous with his acts and his innermost thoughts and feelings. To have the integrity of genius requires that one struggle constantly to sustain such continuousness.

Though dependent upon it, full humanity, however, calls for more than the integrity of genius. It requires that a man who lives out his genius with integrity also live out the experience of his own self-world's being impinged upon by another actualized and active self-world. Moments of full humanity are moments of surprise, of wonder, of awe. Wittgenstein may often have put his hand on another man's shoulder, it may even have been a characteristic gesture, though Leavis' essay suggests that it was not. In the paragraph just quoted, however, that gesture is utterly spontaneous and exhibits the wondrous delicacy of one person acknowledging the impressiveness of another; it exhibits, that is, Wittgenstein living out his full humanity, even if the limits of his self-world are at once suggested by the "know" of his "We must know one another," as if "knowing" were an adequate word for the relation of two persons. Leavis, in turn, even though so immersed in righteous indignation, was truly impinged upon, struck by surprise, though there is no grace in his parting gesture, only a muttering and a turning away.

The richness and variety in the eleven incidents that make up "Memories of Wittgenstein" depend on the integrity of the essay as a whole. The parts of the essay, that is, are interdependent, each being enlivened and deepened and clarified by the others. Moreover, much of the force of the essay comes from the order in which Leavis develops it. As a result, the last incident, to which I wish now to turn, may seem quite incomplete, taken by itself, even though it is in truth brilliantly conclusive in relation to the rest of the essay.

He said to me once (it must have been soon after his return to Cambridge): "Do you know a man called Empson?" I replied: "No, but I've just come on him in *Cambridge Poetry 1929*, which I've reviewed for *The Cambridge Review*." "Is he any good?" "It's surprising," I said, "but there are six poems of his in the book, and they are all poems and very distinctive." "What are they like?" asked Wittgenstein. I replied that there was little point in my describing them, since he didn't know enough about English poetry. "If you like them," he said, "you can describe them." So I started: "You know Donne?" No, he didn't know Donne. I had been going to say that Empson, I had heard, had come up from Winchester with an award in mathematics and for his Second Part had gone over to English and, working for the Tripos, had read closely Donne's *Songs and Sonnets*, which was a set text. Baulked, I made a few lame observations about the nature of the conceit, and gave up. "I should like to see his poems," said Wittgenstein. "You can," I answered; "I'll bring you the book." "I'll come round to yours," he said. He did soon after, and went to the point at once: "Where's that anthology? Read me his best poem." The book was handy; opening it, I said, with "Legal Fictions" before my eyes: "I don't know whether this is his best poem, but it will do." When I had read it, Wittgenstein said, "Explain it!" So I began to do so, taking the first line first. "Oh! I understand that," he interrupted, and looking over my arm at the text, "But what does this mean?" He pointed two or three lines on. At the third or fourth interruption of the same kind I shut the book, and said, "I'm not playing." "It's perfectly plain that you don't understand the poem in the least," he said. "Give me the book." I complied, and sure enough, without any difficulty, he went through the poem, explaining the analogical structure that I should have explained myself, if he had allowed me.[8]

Taken straight or literally, this last incident suggests that, with no training at all, Wittgenstein proved to be an infinitely superior literary critic to Leavis, whose life was dedicated to the practice of such criticism. It might even seem that, finally, in his old age, Leavis found a way to be humble, for a moment, and in print! But the careful reader is prepared to take this, like the other incidents, doubly or even triply, as lived out of the self-world of each man and, as a dramatic encounter, as exceeding the explanatory framework provided by either of those self-worlds. From the essay as a whole, it is quite clear that Wittgenstein senses the limits of his way of thinking and that he knows that life, the self, God, value, exceed what his notions of explanation and understanding can touch. Leavis has shown him to be not just a genius, but also "a troubled soul," unable to sleep at night until a fair copy of the thoughts of the day has been made out of a fear that he might die during the night, careless about trespassing on the secluded property of others, and suffering from agoraphobia, an unwillingness to be in an open place for fear that without his knowing it he could be observed by someone else. The aggressiveness of his mind, that is, is related to his fear of what it cannot touch. He is, undoubtedly, trespassing on the poem, "Legal Fiction," and he is trespassing on Leavis, whose sense that language used poetically can express that which exceeds Wittgenstein's notions of explanation and understanding has been conveyed repeatedly.

Wittgenstein says, in reference to Empson's poems, "If you like them, you can describe them." One does not need to recall the following passage from *The Living Principle* to know that, for Leavis, describing the analogical structure of a poem as Wittgenstein describes that of Empson's poem is a very small and relatively unimportant part of what can and should be said about a genuine poem:

The argument enforcing the concern that preoccupies me makes me remark here on the contrast between the analogical life in mature Shakespearian verse and the nature of the essential part played by analogy in expositions of Wittgenstein . . . The analogies . . . are all, or nearly all, of the same kind—I should

Wittgenstein was so brilliantly treating as "real estate of mind," for the poem is a terrifying trap, enticing one to do just that, to zip through it analogically while the "you" 's and "your" 's of the poem are being hammered like nails into no other forehead than one's own. With "your dark central cone," if one does not feel the chill of his mortality and the nothingness of that magnificently agile mind of his, then he undoubtedly lacks the "full humanity" which Leavis attributes to Wittgenstein. In other words, Leavis within the incident allows himself to be routed because he senses the dreadful malady which is the fissure splitting Wittgenstein's nature apart, his almighty mind split apart from everything that goes with his mortality, including the living English language; but also, because he senses that Wittgenstein is capable of moments of full human freedom, of being impinged upon by alien, antagonistic, opaque, resistant, living forces, even by the poem, even by Leavis, even by Leavis' silence, his refusal to play, his denial of Wittgenstein's right to suck him up into another one of his little "language games." In this instance, however, Leavis claims no knowledge as to whether Wittgenstein did experience the dramatic aspect of this encounter.

Though it does not say so discursively, the essay expresses more precisely than anything else Leavis wrote the nature and value of the poetry, the literary studies, and the key words like "life" and "creativity" to which he committed his life as a critic, and also the reason he was such a resolute opponent of the main movements of culture in England during the past fifty years. It is the totalitarian tyranny of "the mind," the mind as the single observer that can never be observed because it is unlocatable and supra-individual, the major legacy of Kant, Hegel, and Marx, against which Leavis' intellectual, moral, and emotional enmity, at its deepest, is resolutely directed.[11] Or, perhaps more accurately, it is against that blank unawareness, on the part of so many recent English scholars, critics, and educators, that there is a highly individual, personal aspect to the observing, thinking, speaking, and writing of each of them, against that complacent self-assurance that they are utterly objective because they are indistinguishable from "the mind," or from that totality of individuals and society known or "seen" by the all-mind. Life, as Leavis never tires of saying, can be lived only by individuals. But to be alive as an individual human being is to be developing as a person, to be struggling constantly to attain integrity, a continuousness between one's inward thoughts and feelings, one's outward acts and speech, and the natural and social situations in which one feels, thinks, acts, and speaks. Even more important, human creativity depends upon one's developing as a self-world, a person, in such a way that he is openly expectant that he will be impinged upon by other persons. The wonder of such an encounter is the very heart of great poetry and of the experience of reading it; in a derivative way, it is also the very heart of literary studies, as Leavis conceives of them and practices them.

Before Leavis could attain a clear sense of the nature of that creativity from which authentic poetry emanates, he had to transform his earlier notion of the communal nature of literary studies so as to free it, and also his own practice as a critic, from the tyrannous, even if only latent, model of experience as a single field with its single, right and true thinker-listener-observer. For during the *Scrutiny* period, even in his style, in that subtlest aspect of his life as a critic, Leavis was a victim of what he was most opposed to.

The most striking thing about Leavis' style, from *New Bearings* on, is the sense it conveys of there being a special reader in relation to whom Leavis works out his thoughts before he ever turns them into a form appropriate for a larger audience. Whereas in Leavis' maturest criticism that reader is felt to be an actual, living person with whom Leavis thinks through his thoughts in a collaborative way and with whom his larger audience has a casual, relaxed relationship, in most of his criticism prior to the sixties that reader comes across as representative, as a right reader, as one who hears Leavis exactly as he would wish to be heard and who agrees with his readings and opposes what he opposes. The larger audience of Leavis' earlier criticism is made to feel that, unless it is foolish, ignorant, perhaps even vicious, it will also hear Leavis, not as it would if left on its own, but exactly as his special reader does. This larger audience, in consquence, is made to feel put upon, as though Leavis is badgering it to be better than it is according to Leavis' own exacting notions of goodness and badness. An American reader, because entirely omitted from Leavis' concerns, can recognize the pressure Leavis puts upon his English audience without himself feeling subjected to it. From the many references by English scholars, critics, and students to Leavis' criticism of the *Scrutiny* period, it seems fair to infer an almost uniform undercurrent of disgruntlement, evidence, as I take it, of the unknowingly coercive way in which he was writing.

The latent model of experience as a single field with a single observer is the source not only of Leavis' coercive style and his sovereign assurance concerning the singleness of English society and its great literary tradition as givens, but also of the particular notion of literary studies which he set forth in *Education and the University*. Leavis argues, in that series of essays, the most important of which were first published in *Scrutiny* in 1940 and 1941, that the English School should be central to the University on the grounds that its main form of activity, literary studies, brings together thought and sensibility in relation to the finest possible use of language. In *Culture and Society: 1780–1950*, Raymond Williams condemned this notion as an elitism based on exalting one form of activity over all others. Though related closely to Williams' criticism, my sense of the main flaw in Leavis' presentation is that it conceives of literary studies as attaining their proper value only to the extent that they become identical with what he refers to as the "literary mind": "It is an intelligence so trained that is best fitted to develop into the central kind of mind, the co-ordinating consciousness, capable of performing the function assigned to the class of the educated." [12] "The central kind of mind," "the co-ordinating consciousness," the identity in all essentials of all minds which approximate "true judgment" dominates the following passage in which Leavis elaborates on how the "literary mind" works:

> Analysis is not a dissection of something that is already and passively there. What we call analysis is, of course, a constructive or creative process. It is a more deliberate following-through of that process of creation in response to the poet's words which reading is. It is a re-creation in which, by a considering attentiveness, we ensure a more than ordinary faithfulness and completeness.
>
> As addressed to other readers it is an appeal for corroboration: 'the poem builds up in this way, doesn't it? this bears such-and-such a relation to that, don't you agree?' In the work

of an English School this aspect of mutual check—positively, of collaboration 'in the common pursuit of true judgment'—would assert itself as a matter of course.[13]

"Collaboration," as referred to here, sounds like no more than "corroboration." A single act of thinking, that of the "literary mind," is embodied in the presentation of a master teacher. His "collaborators" corroborate his findings by such responses as "Yes sir" and "Do you mean, sir . . . ?" As a result of this "common pursuit," poems and novels become the special possession of the English School which, aside from flaws caused by eccentricities that keep certain persons from becoming identical with it, reads correctly and judges truly because it has a single head, the "literary mind," that mind which "is best fitted to develop into the central kind of mind."

My guess as to the occasion on which Leavis began to work his way free of the model of experience tyrannizing over his thought and language dates it in 1952–53, when *Scrutiny* died and *Essays in Criticism* was born, accompanied by a manifesto in which F. W. Bateson attributed the originality of criticism like Leavis' to an irresponsible neglect of the verbal, intellectual, and social contexts of poems and novels.[14] Bateson found Leavis' insistence that the poem is *there* only in the reading of a thoughtful, sensitive reader to be, at bottom, the advocacy of readings which are groundless and subjectivistic. He makes his case by "improving" on readings Leavis made, in *Revaluation*, of several lines by Marvell and by Pope. Bateson offers his own readings as "correct" on the grounds that they bring the lines into harmony with their appropriate contexts, contexts which only the scholar, in contrast to the freewheeling critic, can reconstruct as the result of all he knows about matters other than the lines and the poems in which they occur. For Bateson, the correct meaning of a literary work inheres in its basic identity with its contexts; even the value of the work is entirely determined by its contexts. The notion of a single given field, the literary, to be known possessively by the single right mind, the scholarly, could hardly be put in a more unpalatably coercive form than that which Bateson gives it.

As Leavis argues, in his response, to the effect that Bateson's contexts are irrelevant to the understanding of literature, one cannot but feel that he is also shedding that latent verbal context of "living speech" on the basis of which he criticized Milton and that latent social context which he used to "demonstrate" James's inferiority to George Eliot.[15] Even more important, Leavis' quite general readings in *Revaluation* of the lines by Marvell and Pope are replaced, in his response to Bateson, by readings which are compellingly convincing because they are realized in a highly personal, imaginative way. The new readings show that Marvell and Pope are incomparably superior to any context, verbal, intellectual, or social, in which they happened to be writing. The readings, moreover, are not set forth as the assured possessive knowledge of that one and only "literary mind," but are presented evocatively, as if calling for comparably personal, imaginative readings from anyone who recognizes the inertness and flatulence of Bateson's "correct" readings.

Whether the change actually originated in this encounter with Bateson cannot be known with any certainty, but that it did occur is incontrovertible. For literary studies as Leavis describes them in the sixties are very different from that single-headed model of *Education and the University*. Here, for example, is what he said of them in one of the Clark Lectures which he gave in 1967:

> What, of its very nature, the critical activity aims at, in fact, is an exchange, a collaborative exchange, a corrective and creative interplay of judgments. For though my judgment asks to be confirmed and appeals for agreement that the thing is *so;* the response I expect at best will be of the form, 'Yes, but—', the 'but' standing for qualifications, corrections, shifts of emphasis, additions, refinements. The process of personal judgment from its very outset, of course, is in subtle ways essentially collaborative, as my thinking is—as any use of the language in which one thinks and expresses one's thoughts *must* be. But the functioning of criticism demands a fully overt kind of collaboration. Without a many-sided real exchange—the implicitly and essentially collaborative interplay by which the object, the poem (for example) in which the individual minds meet, and, at the same time, the judgments concerning it, are established, the object, which we think of as 'there' in a public world for common contemplation, isn't really 'there'. . . . . [The poem] is 'there' only when it's realized in separate minds, and yet it's not merely private. It's something in which minds can meet, and our business is to establish the poem and meet in it. Merely

private, on the one hand, and, on the other, public in the sense that it can be produced in the laboratory, or tripped over—the poem is neither: the alternatives are not exhaustive. There is a third realm, and the poem belongs to that.[16]

With his emphasis on a "many-sided real exchange," Leavis has clearly broken free of any and every form of that single observer/ field model of experience. His description of critical activity sounds, indeed, very much like Pound's notion that criticism begins only when two mature men who know get together and disagree. Even more precisely, it sounds like the encounters Leavis and Wittgenstein had, moments of meeting between two persons, two self-worlds, each of whom breaks beyond his limits as a person, so that the meeting exceeds any and all explanatory frameworks. There is nothing elitist in such a meeting. Manifestations of such "full humanity" occur whenever and wherever they will. As a literary critic, of course, Leavis' main concern is with their occurrence in relation to poems and novels. Critical activity, as he now conceives it, excludes possessive knowing. As creative, no genuine poem could be rightly treated even as so vast a limited object as a "knowable community," for no reader-critic could be in possession of that totality, whether it be Hegelian, Marxist, Husserlian, Heideggerian, or Derridean, that explanatory framework or methodology, in the light of which he could truly "know" the poem. Critical activity for Leavis involves joint, conflicting, often divisive efforts to define articulately this individual dramatic poem or that one; the human value of the activity, however, is in its evoking, for those involved, for those who are reading and meditating on the poem, the poem as a personal act in words, evoking it, moreover, in such a way that poem and readers exceed their own limits and share that awesome moment of full humanity, the capacity for which is denied to no human being.

The kind of poem that can jar and unsettle a reader to the point where he will strive, out of a sense of deprivation, to develop himself as a person, as a self-world, so that he is ready to respond fully to the impingement on him by another person, whether in poetry or art or discussion or action, this is the poetry focussed upon in this study, a prime example of which is Leavis' own "Memories of Wittgenstein." The creativity at the heart of this poetry is at one with that which impels all great poetry and art, but the special form it has taken in recent English poetry is what I have called the double lyric, a poem with two self-originative centers. Without using such phrases, or even conceiving of creativity in this way with theoretical clarity, Leavis was, in my estimation, living it out critically in his finest recent work. Of course, I have meant that "Memories of Wittgenstein" should be taken in just this way. Read rightly, moreover, his recent literary criticism comes out of a sense of this very special, divisively communal sense of creativity.[17]

The divisively communal encounter which provoked Leavis to the point of sensing in an active way this new, special form of creativity was almost certainly with and against Raymond Williams, especially the Williams of *The Long Revolution* and more recent books like *Modern Tragedy, The English Novel*, and *The Country and the City*. For in these books Williams is developing a very different notion of creativity as communal. It is based upon the reduction of Blakean creative perception, insight that creates as it discovers, to the notion that every act of perception is creative, is as fully creative as it is possible to be, just because it is not passive reception but includes an element of construction according to rules that have to be learned. Williams, in fact, flattens all creation into construction, a flattening which includes the collapse of poetic expressiveness into communication in the form of descriptive statement. All the arts, for that matter, are merely "learned human skills," of use, like everything else in Williams' totalitarian scheme of things, in the Long Revolution, the only intrinsic value of which inheres in a future society which is free of alienation, a society in which all *classes* (not individuals, not persons, not self-worlds) have acquired full membership, which, in his words, is "the capacity to direct a particular society, by active mutual responsibility and cooperation, on a basis of full social equality."[18] With such notions of perception, creation, poetic expressiveness, and art in general, Williams cannot but be blind to any serious creativity in poetry and fiction. Nonetheless, though he shies away from poetry, he has written at length on drama and fiction, but with a heavy emphasis on content, on narrative actions and on characters, and with a devastating blankness concerning the presence of the creating, shaping author. Once, however, he does seem to rise above such Lukács-like limitations, claiming that, in *Ulysses*, Joyce discovered "an ordinary language, heard more clearly than anywhere in the realist novel before it."

> The greatness of *Ulysses* is this community of speech. That is its difference from *Finnegans Wake* in which a single voice—a voice offering to speak for everyone and everything, 'Here Comes Everybody'—carries the dissolution to a change of quality in which the strains already evident in the later sections of *Ulysses* (before the last monologue) have increased so greatly that the interchange of voices—public and private, the voices of a city heard and overheard—has given way to a surrogate, a universal isolated language. [19]

As Williams' evidence inadvertently indicates, however—he quotes the passage in which Bloom, while approaching Larry O'Rourke's, imagines having a meaningful exchange with O'Rourke, and then the subsequent, actual exchange, which consists of no more than flat, empty words of greeting—the characters themselves are not allowed to be critically attentive to their own voices or to those of others, so that they are in truth no more than voices or "forms of consciousness" and in no way persons or self-worlds. It is not Bloom, that is, who listens to and broods over and meditates upon the contrast between the imaginary exchange and the actual one; Joyce reserves such attentive, critical listening for himself as the silent author. It is he alone who makes, by way of organization, of construction, the connections which change mere voices streaming on the wind into what Williams calls "the interchange of voices." Williams, however, is oblivious to Joyce's solitary creativity, which is one more, and perhaps the subtlest, outgrowth of that model of experience in which there is always only one final observer—in this case, the silent, sovereign listener—with everything else being included in the single field which is possessed knowingly by that observer, the author and all proper readers, those, that is, who collapse themselves into an identity with his tyrannous position. Williams fails to recognize the limited nature of the creative source of *Ulysses*, because, even when making so special a claim about the greatness of the novel, he is oblivious to the creative source itself.

He is oblivious to it, moreover, because *Ulysses,* like every other novel, must take its place, in his way of thinking, in that single field of historical evolvement to which he gives the name of the Long Revolution. He can be content with his own tyrannous domination over all fiction, all art, all life for that matter, because he is unaware that as author he too, like Joyce, is occupying the privileged position of the single observer. His authorial power is not, it is true, so subtle as Joyce's, who reserves for himself only the critical listening of the novel, allowing as Williams notes, for many voices. Both the voice and the listening of Williams' writing are single and tyrannous; Williams writes as though he is unaware of this largely, I believe, because he feels that he is identical with totality, that, like the Lukácsian dictatorship of the proletariat, he is the subject that is identical with society as its object. His recurrent use of "we" and "us" and "our" suggests that his voice and ear and mind are taken by him as belonging to the multitude or even to totality, that classless society of the future towards which the Long Revolution moves. Such obliviousness is typical of that inertial drag of English culture and language, against which every serious poet and critic, everyone striving to live personally and creatively, ought, in my opinion, to be struggling with something like Leavis' fierce resolution.

What Williams helped Leavis discover is that a communal freedom and creativity of language depends as much on diversity in the way persons listen to speech as on diversity in the speech itself. If all speech, however diverse it may be, is finally listened to by a single, social, elephantine ear, there can be no free, creative community of language. To treat a speaker as a person, moreover, requires that one be sensitive not just to what he says and to the way he says it, but also to the way he attends critically to his speech at the very time he is speaking. Being sensitive in that way is essential if one would hope to be developing into a person himself, a self-world open and expectant in a free, creative community of language. Analogously, to read a genuine dramatic poem sensitively, one must treat it communally, one must work to reach the moment when he senses how the poet, as distinct from oneself, is listening critically to the expressive language. In the poetry which has been the focus of this study, moreover, one must reach the point of recognizing that it is not just a dramatic interplay between expression and critical listening to which one is attending, but that the poem has become, in effect, two persons, two ways of expressing and attending critically in dramatic, divisive conflict. Leavis' own "Memories of Wittgenstein" is evidence for what I mean by such a free, creative community of language.

That Leavis sharpened his sense of communal creativity in the way I have just sketched, and probably in response to Williams' attack on creativity in language, is evident not just from the vividly evoked dramatic encounters between Wittgenstein and Leavis, each of whom is felt to be a highly developed person, but, even more important, from the very sharp sense the essay conveys of a third highly developed person who hovers about it as the special reader for whom the essay was composed. One has the sense, throughout the essay, of things being shared in such a way as to elude the grasp of one's most alert attention. The last incident of the essay, for example, conveys to me Leavis' unsureness of how Wittgenstein attended to his own aggressive speech and of what he made of Leavis' response to it. But I also sense the presence of a reader who got there before me, whose relationship to the essay is more intimate than mine could ever be, a reader whose way of listening is sufficiently evoked as to provide an atmosphere of intimacy, an imagined affectionateness, for the essay as a whole. That reader hears suggestions that I could hear only as my own fancifulness. She (or he, for it needn't be Q. D. Leavis) would, perhaps, hear Leavis suggesting that the encounter over Empson's poem in 1929, may have been what kept drawing Wittgenstein back to Leavis' presence over the next few years. Perhaps, she might sense, it was Leavis' own reticence in the face of aggressiveness like Wittgenstein's, his refusal to strike back with the force of immediacy, a quietness necessary if he could hope to hear the echoes of implication circling away from the encounter, that exacted as its price Leavis' anguished sense of always being under attack from one center of power or another. Perhaps, even, the psychic pain inherent in such reticent attentiveness is what led Leavis, during the *Scrutiny* period, to live and write under the sway of a tyrannous model of experience that made his criticism, even against his deepest wishes, come across in an aggressive and alienating way. If so, then the pain, the paranoia, and the aggressiveness were caused by the very same strength, that reticent attentiveness, by way of which Leavis was enabled, in recent years, to rise above them. The sense that suggestions something like these are being meditated upon as part of the essay cannot be attributed to Leavis' intentions or to the reader's fancifulness; its source is the hovering presence of the special reader, Leavis' first and main collaborator.

That special reader, not a representative or ideal reader who would make one feel that his own way of listening is flawed, but a person who hears in her own way as Leavis hears in his and as one himself hears in his, this special reader can also be felt as vividly present in much of Leavis' recent criticism. Even though this criticism is criticism and not poetry, because of its evocative power and especially because of its evocation of this highly individualized special reader, it seems to well up from a communally creative source like the source of those double lyrics by Hill, Silkin, Gunn, and Tomlinson which are the finest poetic achievements of recent times.

NOTES

1. DIVISIVENESS IN RECENT ENGLISH POETRY

1. Donald Davie, "Transatlantic Exacerbations," *New Statesman*, June 7, 1974, p. 803.

2. William Empson, *Seven Types of Ambiguity* (Cleveland: Meridian Books, 1955), p. 217. In the sixties, Empson, in a conversation with Christopher Ricks, said of his own poems: "But I think my few good ones are all on the basis of expressing an unresolved conflict. It does seem to me a very good formula which applies to a lot of kinds of poetry. I think it's completely out of fashion, isn't it? Nobody says that now." *The Modern Poet: Essays from The Review*, Ian Hamilton, ed. (London: MacDonald, 1968), p. 186.

3. Jon Silkin, *Nature with Man* (London: Chatto & Windus, 1965), pp. 18–19.

4. Jon Silkin, *Flash Point*, Robert Shaw, ed. (Leeds: Arnold, 1964), p. 19.

5. Charles Tomlinson, *The Way of a World* (London: Oxford University Press, 1969), pp. 4–5.

6. Donald Davie, *Thomas Hardy and British Poetry* (London: Routledge & Kegan Paul, 1973), p. 79.

7. Anthony Thwaite, *Poetry Today: 1960–1973* (Harlow, Essex: Published for the British Council by Longman Group, 1973), p. 58.

8. Geoffrey Hill, *Somewhere Is Such a Kingdom* (Boston: Houghton Mifflin, 1975), p. 46.

2. FLESH OF ABNEGATION: THE POEMS OF GEOFFREY HILL

1. C. H. Sisson, *Agenda* (Autumn 1975), p. 27.

2. *Inferno*, XXXII:124–XXXIII:90.

3. T. S. Eliot, "The Function of Criticism," *Selected Essays* (London: Faber & Faber, 1972), p. 30.

4. T. S. Eliot, "The Dry Salvages II," *The Complete Poems and Plays: 1909–1950* (New York: Harcourt, Brace & World, 1971), p. 133.

5. Geoffrey Hill, *Somewhere Is Such A Kingdom* (Boston: Houghton Mifflin, 1975), p. 74. All quotations from Hill in this chapter are from the *King Log* section of the volume.

6. Hill, *Agenda* (Autumn–Winter 1972/1973), pp. 87–111.

3. GEOFFREY HILL'S "FUNERAL MUSIC"

1. Geoffrey Hill, " 'Perplexed Persistence': The Exemplary Failure of T. H. Green," *Poetry Nation* (1975), no. 4, p. 139.

2. C. H. Sisson, "Geoffrey Hill," *Agenda* (Autumn 1975), p. 26.

3. Jon Silkin, "The Poetry of Geoffrey Hill," *British Poetry Since 1960*, M. Schmidt and G. Lindop, eds. (South Hinksey, Oxford: Carcanet Press, 1972), p. 153.

4. *Ibid.*, p. 152.

5. Geoffrey Hill, *Somewhere Is Such A Kingdom*, (Boston: Houghton Mifflin, 1975), p. 60.

6. T. S. Eliot, *The Complete Poems and Plays: 1909–1950*, pp. 211–12.

7. T. S. Eliot, "Poetry and Drama," *On Poetry and Poets* (New York: Noonday Press, 1961), p. 86.

8. Hill, *Somewhere Is Such A Kingdom*, p. 61.

9. Eliot, *The Complete Poems and Plays: 1909–1950*, p. 140.

10. See *The Complete Poems and Selected Letters and Prose of Hart Crane* (New York: Liveright, 1966), pp. 89, 90. See Eliot, "Baudelaire" (1930), *Selected Essays* (London: Faber & Faber, 1972), p. 428.

11. Hill, *Somewhere Is Such A Kingdom*, p. 66.

12. *Ibid.*, p. 67.

13. *Poetry and Criticism of Matthew Arnold* (Boston: Houghton Mifflin, 1961), p. 162.

4. POETIC OMISSIONS IN GEOFFREY HILL'S MOST RECENT SEQUENCES

1. Richard Kuhns, *Structures of Experience* (New York: Basic Books, 1970), pp. 263–64.

2. Hill, *Somewhere Is Such A Kingdom*, (Boston: Houghton Mifflin, 1975), p. 82.

3. Hill, " 'Perplexed Persistence': The Exemplary Failure of T. H. Green," *Poetry Nation* (1975), no. 4, p. 133.

4. Hill, *Somewhere Is Such A Kingdom*, p. 90.

5. *Ibid.*, p. 91.

6. Donald Davie, *Ezra Pound: Poet as Sculptor* (New York: Oxford University Press, 1964), p. 244.

7. Simone Weil, *The Need for Roots* (New York: Putnam, 1952), p. 219.

8. *Ibid.*, pp. 227–28.

9. Hill, *Somewhere Is Such A Kingdom*, p. 118.

10. See Gabriele Pepe, *Il Medio Evo barbarico d'Italia* (Torino: Einaudi, 1959), p. 155.

11. Hill, *Somewhere Is Such A Kingdom*, p. 119.

12. Eliot, *The Complete Poems and Plays: 1909–1950* (New York: Harcourt, Brace & World, 1971), p. 117.

13. Hill, *Somewhere Is Such A Kingdom*, p. 108.

14. Davie, *Ezra Pound: Poet as Sculptor*, p. 173.

15. See C. H. Sisson, *English Poetry: 1900–1950* (London: Rupert Hart-Davis, 1971), pp. 141–42.

16. Sisson, *In the Trojan Ditch* (Cheadle Hulme, Cheadle, Cheshire: Carcanet Press, 1974), p. 33.

17. Hill, *Tenebrae* (London: André Deutsch, 1978), p. 15.

18. Hill, " 'The Conscious Mind's Intelligible Structure': A Debate," *Agenda* (Autumn–Winter 1971/2), p. 18.

19. Weil, *The Need for Roots*, p. 249.

20. Hill, *Tenebrae*, p. 20.

21. D. M. MacKinnon, *The Problem of Metaphysics* (Cambridge: Cambridge University Press, 1974), p. 129.

22. *Ibid.*, p. 129.

23. Weil, *The Need for Roots*, p. 233.

5. LARKIN AND HIS AUDIENCE

1. Philip Larkin, "Absences," *The Less Deceived* (London: Marvell Press, 1955), p. 40.

2. John Press, "The Poetry of Philip Larkin," *Southern Review* (January 1977), p. 143.

3. Donald Davie, *Thomas Hardy and British Poetry* (London: Routledge & Kegan Paul, 1973), p. 68.

4. Larkin, *Poet's Choice*, P. Engle and J. Langland, eds. (New York: Dial Press, 1962), pp. 202–3.

5. "Four Conversations" by Ian Hamilton, *The London Magazine*, November 1964, p. 76.

6. Larkin, *High Windows* (London: Faber & Faber, 1974), p. 33.

7. Thom Gunn, *Moly* (London: Faber & Faber, 1971), pp. 53–54.

8. A. Alvarez, "The New Poetry, or Beyond the Gentility Principle," *The New Poetry*, (London: Penguin Books, 1962), p. 24.

9. Davie, *Thomas Hardy*, p. 72.

10. Larkin, *All What Jazz* (New York: St. Martin's Press, 1970), p. 8.

11. Larkin, *The North Ship* (London: Faber & Faber, 1973), p. 10.

12. W. B. Yeats, *Collected Poems* (New York: Macmillan, 1956), p. 293.

13. Alvarez, "The New Poetry," p. 26.

14. Larkin, *The Less Deceived*, p. 45.

15. James Wright, *Collected Poems* (Middletown, Conn.: Wesleyan University Press, 1971), p. 135.

16. Larkin, *All What Jazz*, p. 11.

17. *Ibid.*, p. 12.

18. Larkin, *The Less Deceived*, p. 22.

19. "Four Conversations," p. 76.

20. Calvin Bedient, *Eight Contemporary Poets* (London: Oxford University Press, 1974), p. 91.

21. Larkin, *The Whitsun Weddings* (London: Faber & Faber, 1964), p. 9.

22. John Wain, "Engagement or Withdrawal? Some Notes on the Work of Philip Larkin," *Critical Quarterly* (1964), 6:174.

23. Davie, *Thomas Hardy*, p. 81.

24. *Ibid.*

25. Larkin, *The Whitsun Weddings*, pp. 21–22.

26. *Ibid.*, pp. 22–23.

27. John Wain, "Engagement or Withdrawal?" 175.

28. T. S. Eliot, "East Coker I," *The Complete Poems and Plays: 1909–1950* (New York: Harcourt, Brace & World, 1971), p. 124.

6. STRESS IN SILKIN'S POETRY AND THE HEALING EMPTINESS OF AMERICA

1. Jon Silkin, ed., *Poetry of the Committed Individual* (Harmondsworth: Penguin Books, 1973).

2. Silkin, "Concerning strength. . . ," *The Principle of Water* (Cheadle Hulme, Cheadle, Cheshire: Carcanet Press, 1974), p. 16.

3. Silkin, *The Peaceable Kingdom* (1954; rpt. Deerfield, Mass.: Heron Press, 1975), p. 41.

4. Anthony Thwaite, *Poetry Today: 1960–1973* (Harlow, Essex: Published for the British Council by Longman Group, 1973), pp. 62–63.

5. Silkin, "The Poetry of Geoffrey Hill," *British Poetry Since 1960*, M. Schmidt and G. Lindop, eds. (Oxford: Carcanet Press, 1972), p. 154.

6. D. H. Lawrence, "Europe v. America," *Phoenix: The Posthumous Papers of D. H. Lawrence* (New York: Viking Press, 1936), p. 117.

7. Ramon Fernandez, *De la personnalité*, Conciliabule des Trente, vol. 5 (Paris: Au sans pareil, 1928).

8. Originally printed in *The Contemporary Poet as Artist and Critic*, A. Ostroff, ed. (Boston: Little, Brown, 1964), rpt. in *Issues in Contemporary Literary Criticism*, Gregory T. Polletta, ed. (Boston: Little, Brown, 1973), pp. 292–93.

9. *Andrew Marvell: Complete Poems*, George de F. Cord, ed. (New York: Random House, 1968), p. 17.

10. *Stand: Issues 1–12 (1952–57)* (Johnson Reprint Corporation, 1968), no. 5, p. 2.

11. *Ibid.*, no. 1, p. 1.

12. *Ibid.*, p. 2.

13. *Stand*, no. 5, p. 2.

14. Silkin, "Nature with Man," *Nature with Man* (London: Chatto & Windus, 1965), p. 9.

15. F. R. Leavis, *English Literature in Our Time and the University* (London: Chatto & Windus, 1969), p. 146.

16. T. S. Eliot, "Ben Jonson," in *Selected Essays* (London: Faber & Faber, 1972), p. 155.

17. Silkin, "The Poetry of Geoffrey Hill," p. 144.

18. Silkin, *Amana Grass* (London: Chatto & Windus, 1971), p. 15.

19. T. S. Eliot, "Difficulties of a Statesman," Part 2 of "Coriolan," *The Complete Poems and Plays: 1909–1950* (New York: Harcourt, Brace & World, 1971), p. 87.

20. Stephen Spender, *Love-Hate Relations: A Study of Anglo-American Sensibilities* (London: Hamish Hamilton, 1974), p. 140.

21. Silkin, "Worm," *Amana Grass*, p. 38.

22. Spender, p. 40.

23. *Ibid.*, p. 39.

24. Silkin, *Amana Grass*, p. 10.

25. Silkin, *The Little Time-Keeper* (Manchester: Carcanet Press, 1976), p. 72.

26. Merle Brown, "On Jon Silkin's 'Amana Grass,'" *Iowa Review* (Winter 1970), pp. 115–25.

27. "Silkin's Purse," *The Guardian*, March, 26, 1971, p. 12.

28. Silkin, *Amana Grass*, p. 18.

29. Silkin, *The Principle of Water*, p. 16.

7. INNER COMMUNITY IN THOM GUNN'S "MISANTHROPOS"

1. See chapter 14 of R. G. Collingwood's *The Principles of Art* (London: Oxford University Press, 1938) and Richard Poirier's *The Performing Self* (London: Oxford University Press, 1971).

2. René Wellek, "Kenneth Burke and Literary Criticism," *Sewanee Review* (Spring 1971), pp. 187–88.

3. Charles Tomlinson, "Poetry Today," *The Modern Age*, vol. 7 of *The Pelican Guide to English Literature* (London: Penguin Books, 1963), p. 473.

4. In the three editions of Thom Gunn's *Fighting Terms* (1954, 1959, 1962) "Carnal Knowledge" has been much revised.

5. Thomas Whitaker, "Voices in the Open: Wordsworth, Eliot, & Stevens," *Iowa Review* (Summer 1971), pp. 96–112.

6. Yvor Winters, *Forms of Discovery* (Chicago: Alan Swallow, 1967), p. 345.

7. Quentin Anderson, *The Imperial Self* (New York: Knopf, 1971), p. 203.

8. See Poirier's superb analysis of "St. Mawr" in *A World Elsewhere* (London: Oxford University Press, 1966), pp. 40–49.

9. Harold Bloom, *Yeats* (London: Oxford University Press, 1970), pp. 344–49.

10. See chapter 3 of Roger Sessions, *Questions about Music* (Cambridge, Mass.: Harvard University Press, 1970).

11. The antagonism of Hindemith toward performers, expressed in chapter 7 of his *A Composer's World* (Cambridge, Mass.: Harvard University Press, 1952), stems from his feeling that they try to impose themselves dramatically to the neglect of the composer's creation. A similar danger can be seen in the kind of criticism which Walter Slatoff advocates in his otherwise impressive *With Respect to Readers* (Ithaca, N.Y.: Cornell University Press, 1970).

8. INTUITION VS. PERCEPTION: CHARLES TOMLINSON'S "UNDER THE MOON'S REIGN"

1. See my article on Intuition in the enlarged edition of the *Princeton Encyclopedia of Poetry and Poetics*, Alex Preminger, ed. (Princeton, N.J.: Princeton University Press, 1975), pp. 947–50.

2. *I. A. Richards: Essays in his Honor*, Reuben A. Brower, Helen H. Vendler, and John Hollander, eds. (New York: Oxford University Press, 1973), p. 26.

3. Charles Tomlinson, "How Still the Hawk," *Seeing Is Believing* (London: Oxford University Press, 1960), p. 11.

4. Ted Hughes, "Hawk Roosting," *Lupercal* (London: Faber & Faber, 1960), p. 26.

5. This distinction is elaborated in chapter 4 of Gösta Svenaeus's *Methodologie et spéculation esthétique* (Lund: Boktryckeri, 1961).

6. Tomlinson, *The Way In* (London: Oxford University Press, 1974), p. 17.

7. J. Hillis Miller, *Poets of Reality* (New York: Atheneum, 1969), p. 287.

8. *The Selected Letters of William Carlos Williams*, John C. Thirlwall, ed. (New York: McDowell-Obolensky, 1957), p. 147.

9. Miller, *Poets of Reality*, pp. 7–8.

10. *Ibid.*, p. 288.

11. R. G. Collingwood, *The Principles of Art* (London: Oxford University Press, 1938), pp. 144–45.

12. Miller, *Poets of Reality*, p. 291.

13. In a review of *Written on Water*, *The New York Times Sunday Book Review* (April 29, 1973), p. 7.

14. *William Carlos Williams*, Tomlinson, ed. (London: Penguin Books, 1972), pp. 150, 211.

15. Pier Paolo Pasolini, in "Cinema di poesia," *Empirismo eretico* (Milano: Garzanti, 1972).

16. Leopardi, *Zibaldone* (November 30, 1828), p. 4418. My translation.

17. "Ma poétique," *Ungaretti* (Paris: Editions de l'Herne, 1968), p. 123. My translation.

18. See my "Art and the Intellect," *Neo-Idealistic Aesthetics* (Detroit, Mich.: Wayne State University Press, 1966), pp. 230–37.

19. Eugenio Montale, "Portami il girasole," *Ossi di seppia* (Verona: Mondadori, 1948), p. 61.

20. *The Review* (April/May 1962), p. 17.

21. Tomlinson, *Written on Water* (London: Oxford University Press, 1972), pp. 37–38.

22. *Ibid.*, pp. 51–52.

23. *The Review* (Spring–Summer 1972), p. 50.

24. *La Semaison: carnets 1954–1967* (Paris: Gallimard, 1971), p. 136.

25. Anthony Thwaite, *Poetry Today: 1960–1973* (Harlow, Essex: Published for the British Council by Longman Group, 1973), p. 63.

26. "Four Conversations" by Ian Hamilton, *The London Magazine*, November 1964, p. 84.

27. Tomlinson makes the connection himself in *Marianne Moore*, Tomlinson, ed. (Englewood Cliffs, N.J.: Prentice-Hall, 1969), p. 3.

28. See Tomlinson's conversation with Creeley in his "Black Mountain Poets" anthology, *The Review* (January 1964), pp. 24–35.

29. Tomlinson, *Written on Water*, p. 9.

30. "Four Conversations," p. 83.

31. W. S. Merwin, *Writings to an Unfinished Accompaniment* (New York: Atheneum, 1973), p. 4.

32. Philippe Jaccottet, *Breathings*, Cid Corman, trans. (Tokyo: Grossman, 1974), p. vi.

33. "Four Conversations," p. 74.

9. THE AUTHENTIC DUPLICITY OF THOM GUNN'S RECENT POETRY

1. Richard Howard "Ecstasies and Decorum (Gunn, Stafford)," *Parnassus* (Spring/Summer 1974), p. 216.

2. John Bayley, *The Times Literary Supplement*, September 24, 1976, pp. 1,194.

3. Thom Gunn, *Jack Straw's Castle and Other Poems* (New York: Farrar, Straus & Giroux, 1974), p. 61.

4. *Ibid.*, p. 23.

5. Gunn, *To The Air* (Boston: David R. Godine, 1974), pp. 17–18.

6. "Owl's Clover" originally appeared in Wallace Stevens, *The Man with the Blue Guitar and Other Poems* (New York: Knopf, 1937), rpt. in *Opus Posthumous* (New York: Knopf, 1957).

7. Gunn, "Interpenetrating Things," *Agenda* (Summer 1966), p. 40.

8. *Ibid.*, p. 44.

9. William Meredith, "The Luck of It," in *American Poets in 1976*, William Heyen, ed. (Indianapolis, Ind.: Bobbs-Merrill, 1976), pp. 195–96.

10. Gunn, *Moly & My Sad Captains* (New York: Farrar, Straus & Giroux, 1973), p. 17.

11. Gunn, *Jack Straw's Castle*, pp. 38–39.

12. See the ending of "Esthétique du Mal," in Wallace Stevens, *The Collected Poems* (New York: Knopf, 1955), p. 326.

13. See my *Wallace Stevens: The Poem as Act* (Detroit, Mich.: Wayne State University Press, 1970), pp. 65–69.

14. Gunn, *Moly & My Sad Captains*, pp. 40–41.

15. Gunn, *Jack Straw's Castle*, p. 21.

16. Catharine R. Stimpson, "Thom Gunn: The Redefinition of Place," *Contemporary Literature* (Summer 1977), p. 404.

17. John Bayley, *The Times Literary Supplement*, September 24, 1976, pp. 1,194.

18. Yvor Winters, "The Significance of The Bridge, or What Are We To Think Of Professor X?" *In Defense of Reason* (New York: Swallow, 1947), p. 598.

19. *Iowa Review* (Winter 1973), pp. 88, 89.

10. THE IDEA OF COMMUNAL CREATIVITY IN F. R. LEAVIS' RECENT CRITICISM

1. *Thought, Words, and Creativity: Art and Thought in Lawrence* (New York: Oxford University Press, 1976), p. 144.

2. Leavis, *New Bearings in English Poetry* (Ann Arbor: University of Michigan Press, 1960; first publ. 1932). "T. S. Eliot as Critic," first publ. in *Commentary*, 1958, and rpt. in *Anna Karenina and Other Essays* (New York: Pantheon, 1967).

3. These essays are reprinted in *A Selection from Scrutiny*, compiled by Leavis (Cambridge: Cambridge University Press, 1968), 1:211–57, and again in *The Living Principle* (London: Chatto & Windus, 1975), pp. 71–133.

4. See *Scrutiny* (March 1941), p. 309.

5. Lawrence's "Introduction to *Memoirs of the Foreign Legion*," is reprinted in *Phoenix II*, Warren Roberts and Harry T. Moore, eds., (New York: Viking Press, 1970), pp. 303–61.

6. Leavis, "Memories of Wittgenstein," *The Human World* (February 1973), no. 10, p. 66.

7. *Ibid.*, p. 68.

8. *Ibid.*, pp. 78–79.

9. Leavis, *The Living Principle*, pp. 103–04.

10. William Empson, *Collected Poems* (New York: Harvest, 1949), p. 25.

11. Leavis' introductory essays of a general nature in *Nor Shall My Sword* (London: Chatto & Windus, 1972), *The Living Principle*, and *Thought, Words, and Creativity* are not at odds with this contention.

12. Leavis, "Education and the University: Sketch for an English School," *Scrutiny* (Spring 1940), p. 112.

13. Leavis, "Education and the University: (III) Literary Studies," *Scrutiny* (March 1941), p. 309.

14. F. W. Bateson, "The Function of Criticism at the Present Time," *Essays in Criticism* (January 1953), p. 3.

15. Leavis' response, "The Responsible Critic: or the Function of Criticism at any Time," along with a retort by Bateson and a rejoinder by Leavis are printed in *Scrutiny* (Spring 1953), pp. 162–83 and (October 1953), pp. 317–28. In 1966 when the exchange was to be reprinted in *A Selection from Scrutiny* (Cambridge: Cambridge University Press, 1968), Bateson added a postcript. Bateson's final "retrospect," written after Leavis' death and shortly before his own, appears in *Essays in Criticism* (1978), 28:353–61.

16. Leavis, *English Literature in Our Time and the University* (London: Chatto & Windus, 1969), pp. 47–48.

17. See Leavis, "Montale's *Xenia* and 'Impersonality'," rpt. in *Ploughshares* (1975), 2(4):116–24; "Justifying One's Valuation of Blake," *William Blake: Essays in Honour of Sir Geoffrey Keynes*, Morton D. Paley & Michael Phillips, eds. (Oxford: Clarendon Press, 1973), pp. 66–85; "Four Quartets," *The Living Principle*, pp. 155–264; and *Thought, Words, and Creativity*, Leavis' rethinking, as I read it, of his first book on Lawrence in the light of critical attacks like those of Raymond Williams on Lawrence's major novels.

18. For the pertinent passages, see Raymond Williams, *The Long Revolution* (London: Pelican, 1961), pp. 14, 49, 54–55, and *Modern Tragedy* (Stanford, Calif.: Stanford University Press, 1966), pp. 76–77.

19. Raymond Williams, *The Country and the City* (London: Chatto & Windus, 1973), p. 245.

Index

234   INDEX